Foundations of Managerial Mathematics
Using the Graphing Calculator

2nd Edition   Arunas Dagys

PEARSON

Custom
Publishing

Cover prepared by Laura Dagys

Printed in the United States of America

10   9   8   7

ISBN 0-536-35099-X

2006361065

RG

Please visit our web site at *www.pearsoncustom.com*

PEARSON CUSTOM PUBLISHING
75 Arlington Street, Suite 300, Boston, MA 02116
A Pearson Education Company

Contents

Preface

The purpose of this text is to give students an opportunity to strengthen, improve, and update their quantitative skills. This is crucial for the successful pursuit of a graduate degree in business, project management, information systems, or in other fields.

This textbook is significantly different from other mathematics texts. We cover a diverse set of topics (basic computation, algebra, linear functions, finance, statistics, and probability) with a modern perspective in terms of content and pedagogy. We take full advantage of current graphing calculator technology (TI-83/84) in order to make some topics simple that have been an obstacle to learning mathematics, and make other more important topics more interesting, more accessible while providing richer examples of applications of mathematics.

The text is set up as an interactive workbook, with room for notes in the margin. I present material and examples and typically follow up with examples for students to do in the text itself. The answers to these are found at the bottom of the page. The homework exercises are at the end of each chapter.

The entire package of content, pedagogy, and technology presents students with a strong set of "survival skills" as they move ahead. I urge students to take advantage of this opportunity and program themselves to succeed. As students revisit some of the mathematics from days gone by, they need to have an open mind as to the different approaches I present and, in particular, the implementation of the TI-83/84. I know that sometimes it is comfortable to depend on methods and techniques of the past, even when these techniques might have led to weak performance in mathematics. It is time to think "out of the box." The purpose of this book is not to reteach and remind students of their past mathematics but rather to define the mathematics that is important and to prioritize the topics and choose the approaches that will give adult students the best chance to acquire understanding, knowledge and confidence in mathematics. It is really about building a new foundation of quantitative skills to prepare students for future coursework.

Acknowledgments

First and foremost, I thank Patrick Mayers for his ongoing support, encouragement, and engagement. We have had many interesting, challenging, and useful conversations about mathematics instruction and learning over the years. Moreover we have had significant impact on how each of us approaches the task of teaching those who are not prepared to go on because of their poor mathematics background.

I thank Abour Cherif for his continuing support for this project, in particular the piloting of courses.

I thank Michael Hamlet, Larry Reich, Randy Zamin, and Mike Anzollin who classroom tested this text and provided invaluable corrections, comments, and suggestions.

I thank Frank Burrows and Rich Gomes of Pearson Publishing for all of their help and support on this project and getting this textbook to print. Frank always had a creative solution for any difficulties that we ran into. Rich provided us with invaluable technical assistance.

I thank my daughter, Laura, for a wonderful cover for the text. She is a talented graphic designer, and she was generous in giving of her time and talent to this project. It's a thrill to have her collaborate on this text.

And finally, last, but certainly not least, I thank my wife Ramune and my son Paul. Ramune's patience with the author, as well as always taking care of the family first, gave me the time to do this text. My activities with Paul (golf, pool, or other competitions) always gave me quality time off so that I could come back to the task refreshed and ready for work. Ramune and I are both blessed to have such great children.

The Basics

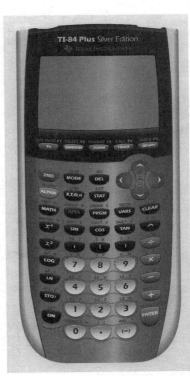

1.1   TI-83 Introduction

Throughout the text, I assume that you have either a TI-83 or TI-84 calculator. Both have similar functionality. I will highlight steps and screens on the TI-83 (TI-83 or TI-83 Plus, or TI-83 Silver Edition). The TI-84 (TI-84 or TI-84 Special Edition) works in almost an identical manner.

First some housekeeping details. To turn the calculator on press the **ON** key (bottom left corner). To turn the calculator off press **2nd** (yellow key) and **ON** (this is the OFF key). The calculator will automatically shut down after several minutes of inactivity.

Press the **MODE** key (right of the yellow 2nd key). Your display should look as follows.

There may be some occurrences where changes in these options will be needed. When that is the case, use the arrow pad to move up, down, right or left and press enter to make a change.

To control the lightness/darkness of the display press **2nd** and the up arrow key to darken, or 2nd and the down arrow key to lighten. The settings appear in the upper right hand corner with each number from 0 to 9 representing 4 settings.

Pressing **2nd** and **MODE** (which represents the **QUIT** key) returns you to the Home Screen where most calculation and evaluation occurs.

Pressing the **CLEAR** (rightmost key just below the arrow pad) clears the line you working in if you are in the middle of a line, or the entire page if you've completed a line.

Pressing **2nd** and **ZOOM** (which represents the **FORMAT** key) gives

For most of our applications we will keep these formats.

We can perform simple calculations using the **+** **−** **×** **÷** and **ENTER** keys (far right in Blue). For example:

To compute 25 + 2 press **2** then **5** then **+** then **2** then **ENTER.**

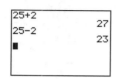

To compute 25 − 2 press **2** then **5** then **−** then **2** then **ENTER.**

Note the difference between the subtraction key **−** and the negative sign key (**−**). If we had incorrectly used the (**−**) we would have gotten an error.

To correct this error we select 2:Goto which gets us to the point of difficulty.

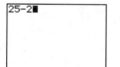 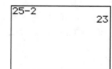

We press **−** and then **ENTER** to get the correct result.

To compute 25 × 2 press **2** then **5** then **×** then **2** then **ENTER.**

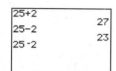

To compute 25 ÷ 2 press **2** then **5** then **÷** then **2** then **ENTER**.

Press **CLEAR** to clear the home screen. Now let's compute $38 + 2 - 7 - 16$. Here is what the screen looks like.

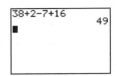

Note that a mistake was made. I erroneously added 16 instead of subtracting 16. To correct this I can edit the previous input line by pressing **2nd** and **ENTER** (this is the ENTRY key).

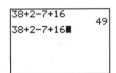

Using the arrow keys move the cursor to the $+$ and type $-$. Then press **ENTER**.

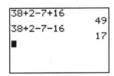

If we then wish to add 7 to the result we simply press $+$ and **7** and **ENTER**.

```
38+2-7+16
              49
38+2-7-16
              17
Ans+7
              24
```

Note that when pressing a function key (like $+$ $-$ $\times$ $\div$) at the beginning of line in the home screen, the calculator operates on the result from the previous line.

Pressing the green **ALPHA** key changes the flashing cursor to a flashing A. Pressing another key at that point causes the green letter or symbol above that key to be displayed. **2nd** and **ALPHA** continues this behavior.

Letters provide a useful means of storing values or results of calculations. Using the **STO** key (far left 2nd row from the bottom) this can be achieved.

Pressing **5** followed by $\times$ followed by **36** followed by **STO** followed by **ALPHA 8** (which is the **P** key) and then **ENTER** generates the first line on the Home Screen. The calculator responds with 180 which is now stored in **P**. Pressing **15** followed by $-$ followed by **7** followed by **STO** followed by **ALPHA 9** (which is the **Q** key) and then **ENTER**. The calculator responds with 8 which is now stored in Q. Pressing **ALPHA 8**

(**P**) then **+** then **ALPHA 9** (**Q**) then **ENTER** gives the last line. The calculator responds with the value of 188.

```
5*36→P
            180
15-7→Q
              8
P+Q
            188
```

The values in P and Q will stay as is until you store another value in those locations, which replaces the previous value.

Notes

Fractions and the TI-83

For some, if not many students, fractions create a large obstacle and are troublesome. Although I describe the rules for operations with fractions and demonstrate these rules, I strongly encourage you to do your fraction operations with the TI-83. If you have struggled with fractions, then struggle no more!

Reducing Fractions

EXAMPLE 1

$$\frac{24}{36} = \frac{2 \cdot 12}{2 \cdot 18} = \frac{12}{18} = \frac{2 \cdot 6}{2 \cdot 9} = \frac{6}{9} = \frac{3 \cdot 2}{3 \cdot 3} = \frac{2}{3}$$

More simply if we can find the Greatest Common Divisor (gcd) of 24 and 36, then we could reduce the fraction more quickly.

$$\frac{24}{36} = \frac{12 \cdot 2}{12 \cdot 3} = \frac{2}{3}$$

However, ex. 1 was a relatively easy example. What if we wanted to reduce the following:

EXAMPLE 2

$$\frac{1058}{3151}$$

This presents some greater challenges. The TI-83 can help here.

We can reduce fractions using the **Frac** feature in the **MATH** menu. For ex.1, press **24** then ÷ then **36** then **MATH** then select **1:Frac** and press **ENTER**. Once your back at the home screen press **ENTER**.

Try this approach on the TI-83 with the following fractions. Note that doing easy problems or complicated problems takes the same amount of effort and knowledge using the TI-83.

EXAMPLE 2

$$\frac{1058}{3151}$$

EXAMPLE 3

$$\frac{1248}{3600}$$

EXAMPLE 4

$$\frac{37}{125}$$

Multiplying Fractions

To multiply two fractions you need to multiply the numerators, multiply the denominators and then reduce the resulting fraction.

EXAMPLE 5

$$\frac{2}{3} \cdot \frac{5}{8} = \frac{2 \cdot 5}{3 \cdot 8} = \frac{10}{24} = \frac{2 \cdot 5}{2 \cdot 12} = \frac{5}{12}$$

Using the TI-83 we press **2 ÷ 3 × 5 ÷ 8** and then **ENTER**. The result given is the decimal equivalent to 5/12. By pressing **MATH** and selecting **1:Frac** and pressing **ENTER** (twice) we get the answer in reduced fraction form.

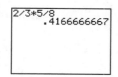

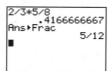

Answers:

Example 2: $\dfrac{46}{137}$

Example 3: $\dfrac{26}{75}$

Example 4: $\dfrac{37}{125}$

Notes

Try the following two examples using the TI-83, with the final answers in reduced fraction form.

EXAMPLE 6

$$\frac{14}{50} \cdot \frac{25}{49} =$$

EXAMPLE 7

$$\frac{15}{28} \cdot \frac{3}{100} =$$

Answers:

Example 6: $\frac{1}{7}$

Example 7: $\frac{9}{560}$

Dividing Fractions

To divide a fraction by another fraction you invert (flip) the 2nd fraction and then multiply and reduce.

EXAMPLE 8

$$\frac{2}{3} \div \frac{8}{5} = \frac{2}{3} \cdot \frac{5}{8} = \frac{10}{24} = \frac{2 \cdot 5}{2 \cdot 12} = \frac{5}{12}$$

On the TI-83 we press $(2 \div 3) \div (8 \div 5)$ and then **ENTER**. Now press MATH and selecting **1:Frac** and pressing **ENTER** (twice) we get the answer in reduced fraction form.

```
(2/3)/(8/5)
          .4166666667
Ans▶Frac
              5/12
```

Notice the use of parentheses in this calculation. We could have used parentheses in examples 5, 6, and 7, resulting in the same answers as were obtained without the parentheses. Let's see what happens with the example above without using parentheses.

```
2/3/8/5
          .0166666667
Ans▶Frac
              1/60
■
```

The problem here has to do with the **Order of Operations.** More precisely, in doing a sequence of divisions, which is what we told the calculator to do, the calculator does the following

$$\frac{2}{3} \div 8 = \frac{2}{3} \times \frac{1}{8} = \frac{2}{24} = \frac{1}{12}$$

$$\frac{1}{12} \div 5 = \frac{1}{12} \times \frac{1}{5} = \frac{1}{60}$$

We will see more on the Order of Operations later in this chapter, but for now, we need to be careful in doing division problems on the calculator and we need to make sure to use parentheses to separate the fractions in these calculations. Some people feel more comfortable using parentheses with any fraction calculation (multiplication, division, addition and subtraction) and that is perfectly fine.

Notes

Try the following two examples using the TI-83, with the final answers in reduced fraction form.

EXAMPLE 9

$$\frac{7}{12} \div \frac{49}{36} =$$

EXAMPLE 10

$$\frac{9}{22} \div \frac{18}{35} =$$

Adding and Subtracting Fractions

To add (or subtract) fractions with like denominators, add (or subtract) the numerators and leave the denominator as is and then reduce. If the fractions have unlike denominators then you first need to rewrite the fractions with like denominators. Note that these problems, done by hand, can range from very easy to somewhat complicated. On the TI-83 they are all about the same degree of difficulty and in fact are no more complicated than multiplication or division problems.

EXAMPLE 11

$$\frac{1}{8} + \frac{5}{8} = \frac{1+5}{8} = \frac{6}{8} = \frac{2 \cdot 3}{2 \cdot 4} = \frac{3}{4}$$

```
1/8+5/8
             .75
Ans▶Frac
             3/4
■
```

EXAMPLE 12

$$\frac{1}{4} + \frac{3}{8} = \frac{1 \cdot 2}{4 \cdot 2} + \frac{3}{8} = \frac{2}{8} + \frac{3}{8} = \frac{5}{8}$$

```
1/4+3/8
            .625
Ans▶Frac
             5/8
■
```

Answer:

Example 9: $\frac{3}{7}$

Example 10: $\frac{35}{44}$

EXAMPLE 13

$$\frac{2}{3} + \frac{1}{8} = \frac{2 \cdot 8}{3 \cdot 8} + \frac{1 \cdot 3}{8 \cdot 3} = \frac{16}{24} + \frac{3}{24} = \frac{19}{24}$$

```
2/3+1/8
         .7916666667
Ans▶Frac
            19/24
```

EXAMPLE 14

$$\frac{2}{5} - \frac{1}{6} = \frac{2 \cdot 6}{5 \cdot 6} - \frac{1 \cdot 5}{6 \cdot 5} = \frac{12}{30} - \frac{5}{30} = \frac{7}{30}$$

```
2/5-1/6
         .2333333333
Ans▶Frac
             7/30
■
```

Try the following problems on the TI-83

EXAMPLE 15

$$\frac{11}{45} + \frac{7}{16}$$

EXAMPLE 16

$$\frac{23}{40} - \frac{9}{25}$$

Answers:

Example 15: $\frac{491}{720}$

Example 16: $\frac{43}{200}$

Common and Decimal Fractions

Convert Fractions to Decimals

EXAMPLE 17

$$\frac{25}{36} = .69444444444 = .69\overline{4}$$

```
25/36
       .6944444444
```

Convert Decimals to Fractions

EXAMPLE 18

$$.4582 = \frac{4582}{10000} = \frac{2291}{5000}$$

```
.4582▶Frac
         2291/5000
```

1.3   **Ratios and Percents**

Ratios can be denoted in several ways:

$$a:b \qquad a \text{ to } b \qquad \frac{a}{b}$$

EXAMPLE 1

$$40 \text{ to } 10 \Rightarrow 40:10 \Rightarrow \frac{40}{10} \Rightarrow \frac{4}{1} \Rightarrow 4:1 \Rightarrow 4 \text{ to } 1$$

EXAMPLE 2

$$40 \text{ to } 25 \Rightarrow 40:25 \Rightarrow \frac{40}{25} \Rightarrow \frac{8}{5} \Rightarrow 8:5 \Rightarrow 8 \text{ to } 5$$

This could also be expressed as 1.6:1 or 1.6 to 1

Notes

Consider the following example of an application of ratios.

EXAMPLE 3

The proceeds of a business deal are $100,000 to be allocated in three parts in a ratio of 8:7:5. How much should each partner receive?

It would help to visualize the "equal parts" of this relationship:

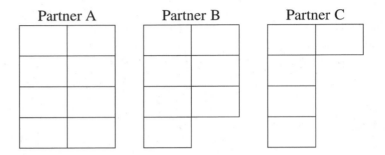

So we can express this 8:7:5 ratio as the ratio of three fractions:

$$\frac{8}{20} : \frac{7}{20} : \frac{5}{20}$$

since Partner A has 8 parts out of the total of 20 parts, Partner B has 7 parts out of the total of 20 parts and Partner C has 5 parts out of the total of 20 parts. We can determine amounts for each:

Partner A : $\dfrac{8}{20} \cdot 100,000 = \$40,000$

Partner B : $\dfrac{7}{20} \cdot 100,000 = \$35,000$

Partner C : $\dfrac{5}{20} \cdot 100,000 = \$25,000$

Try the next example:

EXAMPLE 4

A $10,000,000 inheritance is to be divided among five recipients according to the ratio: 10:7:4:3:1. How much money does each recipient receive.

Percent

% "per cent" or "per one hundred"

The following examples illustrate various forms of percents.

EXAMPLE 5

Express 63% as a ratio

$$63\% = \frac{63}{100} = .63 = 63{:}100 = .63{:}1$$

EXAMPLE 6

Express $98\frac{3}{8}\%$ as a decimal

$$98\frac{3}{8}\% = 98.375\% = \frac{98.375}{100} = .98375$$

EXAMPLE 7

Express 18.75% as a fraction

$$18.75\% = \frac{18.75}{100} = .1875 = \frac{1875}{10,000} = \frac{3}{16}$$

```
18.75/100
              .1875
Ans▶Frac
               3/16
```

Answers:

Example 4:   4,000,000
              2,800,000
              1,600,000
              1,200,000
                400,000

Notes

EXAMPLE 8

Express .325 as a percent.

$$.325 = \frac{325}{1000} = \frac{325/10}{1000/10} = \frac{32.5}{100} = 32.5\%$$

EXAMPLE 9

Express 1.32 as a percent.

$$1.32 = 1^{32}/_{100} = \frac{132}{100} = 132\%$$

EXAMPLE 10

Express 2/5 as a percent.

$$\frac{2}{5} = .4 = \frac{4}{10} = \frac{4 \times 10}{10 \times 10} = \frac{40}{100} = 40\%$$

The last 6 examples are summarized below. Note the relationship between decimal and percent.

Fraction	Decimal	Percent
63/100	0.63	63%
787/800	0.98375	98.375%
3/16	0.1875	18.75%
13/40	0.325	32.5%
33/25	1.32	132%
2/5	0.4	40%

Operations with Real Numbers

This section reviews the basic facts and operations on real numbers, focusing on signed numbers, exponents, order of operations, scientific notation, and evaluating expressions.

Signed Numbers

We can think of the real numbers as residing on a number line as shown below. Real numbers are either positive (greater than 0), negative (less than 0) or 0. Each positive number has an opposite (-2 is the opposite of 2, -7 is the opposite of 7). Each negative number has an opposite (2 is the opposite of -2, 7 is the opposite of -7). Zero is the only number that is the opposite of itself.

It is useful to think of a model situation to represent signed numbers. For example:

a) Temperature (above or below zero)

b) Temperature (went up 10 degrees, went down 12 degrees)

c) Deposit and Withdraw

d) Miles North/South

e) Weight gained and weight lost

Absolute Value

The Absolute Value concept can be described in one of several ways. One definition states:

$$|a| = \begin{cases} a & \text{if } a > 0 \\ -a & \text{if } a < 0 \end{cases}$$

Another more conceptual definition states that

"The Absolute Value of a real number is the distance between that number and zero."

Thus

$$|15| = 15$$
$$|-7| = 7$$
$$|0| = 0$$

since 15 is 15 units away from 0, -7 is 7 units from 0, and 0 is 0 units away from 0. Note that distance can never be a negative number. If we were 6 units away from 0, we might be 6 units to the right (at +6) or 6 units to the left (at −6), yet we are still a distance of 6 units from 0.

Adding Signed Numbers

One approach here is to use a model. For instance consider the mail today.

If you get a check for $10 and a bill for $6, then you have a net of $4. This example models $10 + (-6) = 4$.

If you get a bill for $10 and a bill for $6, then you have a net of −$16. This example models $-10 + (-6) = -16$

Perform the following four additions without the use of a calculator

$$4 + 2 =$$
$$4 + (-2) =$$
$$-4 + 2 =$$
$$-4 + (-2) =$$

Subtraction of Signed Numbers

Subtraction can be thought of as "adding the opposite." That is:

$$a - b = a + (-b)$$

So for example

$$10 - 6 = 10 + (-6) = 4$$

since subtracting 6 is like adding the opposite of 6, which would be −6, giving the end result of 4.

Similarly,

$$10 - (-6) = 10 + (6) = 16$$

since subtracting −6 is like adding the opposite of −6, which would be 6, giving the end result of 16.

Perform the following four subtractions without the use of a calculator

$$4 - 2 =$$
$$4 - (-2) =$$
$$-4 - 2 =$$
$$-4 - (-2) =$$

Answers:
6, 2, -2, -6
2, 6, -6, -2

Multiplication or Division of Signed Numbers

When multiplying or dividing two numbers:

$\qquad$ Like Signs $\Rightarrow$ Positive Product

$\qquad$ Unlike Signs $\Rightarrow$ Negative Product

$(+2) \cdot (+2) =$

$(+2) \cdot (-2) =$

$(-2) \cdot (+2) =$

$(-2) \cdot (-2) =$

$$\frac{12}{3} =$$

$$\frac{-12}{3} =$$

$$\frac{12}{-3} =$$

$$\frac{-12}{-3} =$$

Division by 0

One of few operations that we cannot do with real numbers is to divide by 0. When you attempt to do this on the TI-83 you get the following:

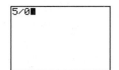 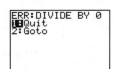

Answers:

4, -4, -4, 4

4, −4, −4, 4

Often times when students are asked what 5 divided by 0 will equal, they respond 0. That's incorrect but understandable, in that 0 divided by 5 would be 0. If you think about it a bit more deeply you will see that 0 is a bad guess.

$$\frac{5}{0} = ?$$

$$\frac{5}{1} = 5$$

$$\frac{5}{.1} = 50$$

$$\frac{5}{.01} = 500$$

$$\frac{5}{.001} = 5,000$$

$$\frac{5}{.0001} = 50,000$$

Note the closer the denominator was to 0, the larger the result was. So certainly 0 would not be a reasonable guess after seeing this information. But why can't we divide by 0?

One of the reasons division works is that we can check:

$$\frac{12}{4} = 3 \Leftrightarrow 12 = 4 \cdot 3 \quad \textit{checks}$$

So if $\frac{5}{0}$ can be computed then it must check once we do the multiplication by the divisor. So lets say that

$$\frac{5}{0} = \boxed{}$$

Multiplying both sides by 0 we get

$$5 = \boxed{} \cdot 0$$

There is no number we can place in the box that will make the above statement true. So there is no real number that is the result of dividing 5 by 0.

Exponents

Exponents provide us a shortcut for writing repeated multiplication of factors.

$$2^{3 \Leftrightarrow \text{exponent}}$$
$$\Downarrow$$
$$\text{base}$$

EXAMPLE 1

$$2^3 = 2 \cdot 2 \cdot 2 = 8$$

We can compute this on the calculator as follows: press 2 then ^ (the key below the CLEAR key) then 3 then ENTER.

```
2^3
                8
```

EXAMPLE 2

$$(-2)^3 = (-2) \cdot (-2) \cdot (-2) = -8$$

```
(-2)^3
               -8
■
```

Notice the following pattern

$$(-2) \cdot (-2) = (-2)^2 = 4$$
$$(-2) \cdot (-2) \cdot (-2) = (-2)^3 = -8$$
$$(-2) \cdot (-2) \cdot (-2) \cdot (-2) = (-2)^4 = 16$$
$$(-2) \cdot (-2) \cdot (-2) \cdot (-2) \cdot (-2) = (-2)^5 = -32$$

Summarizing the pattern for exponents:

$(+)^{\text{any}}$ is positive $3^5 = +243$
$(-)^{\text{odd}}$ is negative $(-2)^7 = -128$
$(-)^{\text{even}}$ is positive $(-2)^6 = +64$

On the TI-83

```
3^5
               243
(-2)^7
              -128
(-2)^6
                64
```

Notes

Try the next two examples without a calculator.

EXAMPLE 3

$$(-1)^{40} =$$
$$(-1)^{1,453} =$$
$$(1)^{589} =$$

EXAMPLE 4

$$-2^3 =$$
$$(-2)^3 =$$
$$-2^4 =$$
$$(-2)^4 =$$

Consider ex.4 on the TI-83

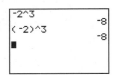 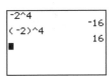

So what's going on here? It almost seems inconsistent, but it isn't. It's all about the order of operations again.

$$-2^3 = -(2 \cdot 2 \cdot 2) = -8$$
$$(-2)^3 = (-2) \cdot (-2) \cdot (-2) = -8$$
$$-2^4 = -(2 \cdot 2 \cdot 2 \cdot 2) = -16$$
$$(-2)^4 = (-2) \cdot (-2) \cdot (-2) \cdot (-2) = 16$$

Notice that in the first and third examples we apply the exponent before we apply the sign. In the second and fourth examples the parentheses causes the base to be negative and then the exponent is applied.

So what are rules here? That's next.

Order of Operations

How do we handle:

$$8 + 12/4$$

Do we add the 8 and 12 and then divide the result by 4?

Do we divide 12 by 4 and add that result to 8?

Answers:
Example 3: 1, −1, 1
Example 4: −8, −8, −16, 16

Using parenthesis the order of operations are clarified.

Note: $(8 + 12)/4 = 20/4 = 5$

Note: $8 + (12/4) = 8 + 3 = 11$

How do we handle:
$$2 \cdot 3^2$$

Do we multiply 2 by 3 and raise the result to the 2nd power?

Do we raise 3 to the 2nd power and then multiply the result by 2?

Using parenthesis the order of operations are clarified.

Note: $2 \cdot (3)^2 = 2 \cdot 9 = 18$

Note: $(2 \cdot 3)^2 = 6^2 = 36$

Order of Operations

1. **Parentheses**
2. **Exponents**
3. **Multiplication & Division (Left to Right)**
4. **Addition and Subtraction (Left to Right)**

Calculators are programmed to follow the Order of Operations. Since we rely on calculators to do many computations we need to understand the Order of Operations completely.

EXAMPLE 5
$$8 + 12/4 = 8 + 3 = 11$$

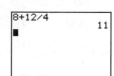

EXAMPLE 6
$$2 \cdot 3^2 = 2 \cdot 9 = 18$$

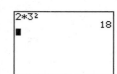

Notes

EXAMPLE 7

$$5 \cdot 3 - 2 \cdot 4^2 = 5 \cdot 3 - 2 \cdot 16$$
$$= 15 - 32$$
$$= -17$$

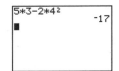

EXAMPLE 8

$$800\left(1 + .06 \cdot \left(\tfrac{150}{360}\right)\right)^2 - 320 \cdot 2 = 800(1 + .025)^2 - 320 \cdot 2$$
$$= 800 \cdot 1.025^2 - 320 \cdot 2$$
$$= 800 \cdot 1.050625 - 320 \cdot 2$$
$$= 840.5 - 640$$
$$= 200.5$$

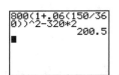

Note that when using multiple parentheses you do need to use parentheses. The symbols {, }, [,], have other meanings on the TI-83.

Scientific Notation

Consider the following table of powers of 10.

$$10^0 = 1 \qquad\qquad 10^0 = 1$$
$$10^1 = 10 \qquad\qquad 10^{-1} = .1$$
$$10^2 = 100 \qquad\qquad 10^{-2} = .01$$
$$10^3 = 1000 \qquad\qquad 10^{-3} = .001$$
$$10^4 = 10000 \qquad\qquad 10^{-4} = .0001$$

We can use these powers of 10 to represent (or approximate) numbers that are too large or too small to display in the calculator.

Consider the following examples

EXAMPLE 9

Computing 2^{40} on the TI-83 we find the following.

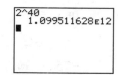

Since 2^{40} results in a very large number, the calculator approximates the result using scientific notation.

$$2^{40} = 1.099511628E12$$
$$= 1.099511628 \times 10^{12}$$
$$= 1,099,511,628,000$$

EXAMPLE 10

Computing 2^{-10} on the TI-83 we find the following.

This time the result is a very small number, close to 0.

$$2^{-10} = 9.765625E - 4$$
$$= 9.765625 \times 10^{-4}$$
$$= 0.0009765625$$

Evaluating Expressions

Consider the expression: $-3x^2 + 6x + 5$

EXAMPLE 11

Evaluate the above expression for $x = 5$

$$-3(5)^2 + 6(5) + 5 = -3 \cdot 25 + 6 \cdot 5 + 5$$
$$= -75 + 30 + 5$$
$$= -40$$

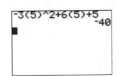

We can compute this result another way on the TI-83 by doing the following. First press **5** then **STO** (right above the **ON** key) then **X** (just to the right of the green key), then **ENTER**.

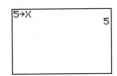

Next press (**−**) then **3** then **X** then **x²** then **+** then **6** then **X** then **+** then **5** then **ENTER**.

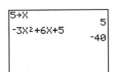

EXAMPLE 12

Evaluate the above expression for $x = -2$

$$-3(-2)^2 + 6(-2) + 5 = -3 \cdot 4 + 6 \cdot (-2) + 5$$
$$= -12 - 12 + 5$$
$$= -19$$

The TI-83 works as follows:

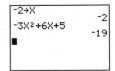

Try this one:

EXAMPLE 13
Evaluate $5x^4 - 3x^3 - x^2 + 7x - 1$ for x = -3.

Answer:
Example 13: 455

Notes

Chapter 1 Exercise Set

Simplify.

1. $\dfrac{10}{14}$ **2.** $\dfrac{16}{56}$ **3.** $\dfrac{19}{76}$ **4.** $\dfrac{75}{80}$

Perform the indicated operation and, if possible, simplify using a calculator.

5. $\dfrac{1}{2} \cdot \dfrac{3}{7}$ **6.** $\dfrac{9}{2} \cdot \dfrac{3}{4}$ **7.** $\dfrac{4}{9} + \dfrac{13}{18}$ **8.** $\dfrac{3}{10} + \dfrac{8}{15}$

9. $\dfrac{13}{18} - \dfrac{4}{9}$ **10.** $\dfrac{7}{6} \div \dfrac{3}{5}$ **11.** $\dfrac{8}{9} \div \dfrac{4}{15}$

12. $4 + (-7)$ **13.** $-5 + 9$

14. $8 + (-8)$ **15.** $-3 + (-5)$

16. $-15 + 0$ **17.** $12 + (-12)$

18. $18 + (-11)$ **19.** $-3 + 14$

20. $-14 + (-19)$

21. $6 - 8$ **22.** $-9 - (-3)$

23. $-8 - (-8)$ **24.** $14 - 19$

25. $5 - (-6)$ **26.** $12 - (-5)$

27. $-4 \cdot 9$ **28.** $8 \cdot (-3)$ **29.** $-5 \cdot (-9)$

30. $\dfrac{36}{-9}$ **31.** $\dfrac{-16}{8}$ **32.** $\dfrac{-48}{-12}$

33. 2^4 **34.** $(-3)^2$

35. -3^2 **36.** $(-5)^4$

37. $8 \cdot 7 + 6 \cdot 5$ **38.** $9 \div 3 + 16 \div 8$

39. $4 - 8 \div 2 + 3^2$ **40.** $(8 - 2 \cdot 3) - 9$

41. $\dfrac{7 + 2}{5^2 - 4^2}$ **42.** $\dfrac{(-2)^3 + 4^2}{3 - 5^2 + 3 \cdot 6}$

Evaluate.

43. $-x^2 - 5x$, for $x = -3$

44. $\dfrac{3a - 4a^2}{a^2 - 20}$, for $a = 5$

45. $13 - (y - 4)^3 + 10$, for $y = 6$

Find decimal notation.

46. 82% **47.** 9% **48.** 43.7% **49.** 0.46%

Find percent notation.

50. 0.29 **51.** 0.998 **52.** 1.92 **53.** $\frac{7}{25}$

Solving Equations and Inequalities

2

2.1 Solving Equations of One Variable

Solving equations is one of the more important skills in elementary algebra. Much of what we do in the rest of this text depends on being able to consistently and efficiently solve equations.

What do we mean by solving an equation of one variable?

Solving an equation of one variable means finding the value of the variable that makes the equation a true statement. This value is called the **solution** to the equation.

For example, if we consider the equation $x - 2 = 0$. The value $x = 2$ makes the equation true since $2 - 2 = 0$. Thus $x = 2$ is a solution to $x - 2 = 0$. Note that $x = 3$ is not a solution since $3 - 2 \neq 0$.

But how do we go about finding solutions to equations? One approach is to guess the answer or use trial and error. That would work well with $x - 2 = 0$. In fact, I suspect most students could solve this equation by guessing. But I also suspect that few students could solve $3(x + 2) - 4(3 - x) = 2x - 5$ by guessing.

So generally, guessing is not a good strategy. The approach that you may have seen involved "moving" things around in equations. Unfortunately that process leads to all kinds of mistakes. The technique that I will demonstrate will be based on two main principles. If you follow these principles correctly, you will solve equations correctly and more efficiently that in the past.

Main Principles for Equation Solving
"Opposites Principle"
"Golden Rule"

The "Opposites Principle" recognizes that solving equations is a process of undoing or getting rid of certain operations, and doing so by using the opposite operation.

The "Golden Rule" states that whatever operation you perform to one side of the equation, you must perform the same operation to the other side of the equation.

Using these two principles together, along with some strategic tips, gives you a new way of thinking about equation solving. I will demonstrate this approach in four very easy problems. These equations could be solved by guessing.

EXAMPLE 1
Solve: $x + 12 = 42$

To solve for x, we want to isolate x on one side of the equation. To do this we need to "get rid" of the addition of 12 on the left hand side of the equation. We get rid of the addition of 12 by doing the opposite operation, namely subtract 12. Because of the "Golden Rule" we must do the same to the right hand side of the equation.

$$\begin{aligned} x + 12 &= 42 \\ -12 &= -12 \\ x &= 30 \end{aligned}$$

EXAMPLE 2
Solve: $x - 40 = 72$

To get rid of the subtraction of 40, we add 40 to both sides.

$$\begin{aligned} x - 40 &= 72 \\ +40 &= +40 \\ x &= 112 \end{aligned}$$

EXAMPLE 3

Solve: $3x = 24$

To get rid of the multiplication by 3, we divide both sides by 3.

$$3x = 24$$

$$\frac{3x}{3} = \frac{24}{3}$$

$$x = 8$$

EXAMPLE 4

Solve: $\frac{x}{6} = 20$

To get rid of the division by 6 we multiply both sides by 6.

$$\frac{x}{6} = 20$$

$$6 \cdot \frac{x}{6} = 6 \cdot 20$$

$$x = 120$$

Note that addition and subtraction are opposite operations, and multiplication and division are opposite operations.

EXAMPLE 5

Solve: $3x - 12 = 27$

Consider the following alternative approaches.

$$3x - 12 = 27 \qquad\qquad 3x - 12 = 27$$

$$ +12 = +12 \qquad\qquad \frac{3x}{3} - \frac{12}{3} = \frac{27}{3}$$

$$3x = 39 \qquad\qquad\qquad x - 4 = 9$$

$$\frac{3x}{3} = \frac{39}{3} \qquad\qquad\qquad +4 = +4$$

$$x = 13 \qquad\qquad\qquad\quad x = 13$$

Both are correct – which is better? We got lucky with the approach on the right, in that we did not create any fractions.

Notes

_____
_____
_____
_____
_____
_____
_____
_____
_____
_____
_____
_____
_____
_____
_____
_____
_____
_____
_____
_____
_____
_____
_____
_____
_____
_____
_____
_____
_____
_____
_____
_____

Notes

Equation Solving Tip #1: Don't create fractions before the last step. This means you do not want to use division until the very last step of the problem.

One nice feature of solving equations is that you can check your solution for correctness, by simply substituting the solution back into the original equation.

$$
\begin{aligned}
\text{Check:} \quad 3(13) - 12 &= 27 \\
39 - 12 &= 27 \\
27 &= 27 \qquad \textbf{Check!}
\end{aligned}
$$

EXAMPLE 6

Solve: $\dfrac{4x - 10}{3} = 30$

There is a lot going on in this problem; multiplication, subtraction, division. What do we get rid of first?

Equation Solving Tip #2: Get rid of fractions as soon as you can. Since fractions are caused by division, we can get rid of fractions by multiplication. Once we do that in this example the equation looks very much like ex. 5.

$$
\begin{aligned}
\frac{4x - 10}{3} &= 30 \\
3 \cdot \frac{4x - 10}{3} &= 3 \cdot 30 \\
4x - 10 &= 90 \\
+10 &= +10 \\
4x &= 100 \\
\frac{4x}{4} &= \frac{100}{4} \\
x &= 25
\end{aligned}
$$

Try the following two examples:

EXAMPLE 7

Solve: $12x + 47 = 23$

EXAMPLE 8

Solve: $\dfrac{5x + 10}{4} = -15$

_____

Answers:
Example 7: -2
Example 8: -14

Notes

EXAMPLE 9

Solve: $13x - 8 = -17x + 22$

Our goal is to isolate x on one side of the equation. There are several ways to begin that process. One way is to add 17x to both sides. After that step the equation looks like example 5.

$$13x - 8 = -17x + 22$$
$$+17x = +17x$$
$$30x - 8 = 22$$
$$+8 = +8$$
$$30x = 30$$
$$\frac{30x}{30} = \frac{30}{30}$$
$$x = 1$$

We could have started this problem by adding 8 both sides, or subtracting 13x from both sides, or subtracting 22 from both sides. It really makes no difference which of these four ways you start this problem. So don't spend too much time deciding which first step is best here!

The following rule is helpful in dealing with equations that have parentheses:

Distributive Law

$$a(b + c) = ab + ac$$

The following three examples illustrate the distributive law:

$$3(x - 5) = 3x - 15$$
$$-2(x - 5) = -2x + 10$$
$$-(x - 5) = -x + 5$$

Notes

Equation Solving Tip #3: When solving equations having parentheses, use the distributive law to get rid of the parentheses early in the process. After applying the distributive law combine like terms if possible.

EXAMPLE 10

Solve: $3(2x - 5) = 5$

As tempting as it might be, you do not want to divide both sides by 3, since that creates a fraction. Use the distributive law first and then proceed as in example 5.

$$3(2x - 5) = 5$$
$$6x - 15 = 5$$
$$+15 = +15$$
$$6x = 20$$
$$\frac{6x}{6} = \frac{20}{6}$$
$$x = \frac{10}{3}$$
$$x = 3.3\overline{3}$$

EXAMPLE 11

Solve: $3(x + 2) - 4(3 - x) = 2x - 5$

Use the distributive law to get rid of the parentheses and collect like terms and and proceed as in example 9.

$$3(x + 2) - 4(3 - x) = 2x - 5$$
$$3x + 6 - 12 + 4x = 2x - 5$$
$$7x - 6 = 2x - 5$$
$$+6 = +6$$
$$7x = 2x + 1$$
$$-2x = -2x$$
$$5x = 1$$
$$\frac{5x}{5} = \frac{1}{5}$$
$$x = \frac{1}{5}$$

EXAMPLE 12

Solve: $\dfrac{x}{5} - \dfrac{x}{3} = 6$

We first need to get rid of the fractions. Since one fraction has a 5 in the denominator and the other fraction has a 3 in the denominator, we multiply both sides of the equation by 15. We then use the distributive law, simplify and collect like terms, and solve for x.

$$\frac{x}{5} - \frac{x}{3} = 6$$

$$15\left(\frac{x}{5} - \frac{x}{3}\right) = 15 \cdot 6$$

$$\frac{15x}{5} - \frac{15x}{3} = 90$$

$$3x - 5x = 90$$

$$-2x = 90$$

$$\frac{-2x}{-2} = \frac{90}{-2}$$

$$x = -45$$

Don't rush through these kind of problems. Take your time working through the step which eliminates the fractions.

Try the following examples

EXAMPLE 13

Solve: $5(x - 1) - 2(x + 4) = -7x - 3$

EXAMPLE 14

Solve: $\dfrac{5x}{9} + \dfrac{x}{2} = 38$

Answers:
Example 13: 1
Example 14: 36

Proportions

When two ratios are equal we say they form a ***proportion.***

EXAMPLE 15

Solve: $x:3 = 75:4$

Rewrite the proportion as an equation with two fractions Solve for x by multiplying both sides by 3.

$$x:3 = 75:4$$

$$\Updownarrow$$

$$\frac{x}{3} = \frac{75}{4}$$

$$3 \cdot \frac{x}{3} = 3 \cdot \frac{75}{4}$$

$$x = \frac{225}{4}$$

$$x = 56.25$$

EXAMPLE 16

The country of Oz has a base currency called goldbricks. If 1200 goldbricks is equivalent to \$500, then find the dollar equivalent of 44,400 goldbricks.

To solve this problem we first need to set up the proportion that describes the relationship between goldbricks and dollars. That would be

$$\frac{1200 \text{ goldbricks}}{\$500} = \frac{44{,}400 \text{ goldbricks}}{\$x}$$

Note that the units of each ratio must be consistent with the other. In this case it was goldbricks to dollars (we could have used dollars to goldbricks for both ratios as well). Then we proceed to solve the equation by first getting rid of the fractions.

$$\frac{1200 \text{ goldbricks}}{\$500} = \frac{44{,}400 \text{ goldbricks}}{\$x}$$

$$\frac{1200}{500} = \frac{44400}{x}$$

$$500x \cdot \frac{1200}{500} = \frac{44400}{x} \cdot 500x$$

$$1200x = 22{,}200{,}000$$

$$1200x = \frac{22{,}200{,}000}{1200}$$

$$x = \$18{,}500$$

EXAMPLE 17

Bob owns a home that is valued at $250,000, while his neighbor Bill owns a home that is valued at $300,000. If Bob's property taxes are $8000 per year then find Bill's property taxes (assuming property taxes and value are proportional).

$$\frac{\$8,000 \text{ taxes}}{\$250,000 \text{ value}} = \frac{\$x \text{ taxes}}{\$300,000 \text{ value}}$$

To solve for x simply multiply both sides of the equation by 300,000, thereby giving you the solution.

$$\frac{\$8,000 \text{ taxes}}{\$250,000 \text{ value}} = \frac{\$x \text{ taxes}}{\$300,000 \text{ value}}$$

$$\frac{8,000}{250,000} = \frac{x}{300,000}$$

$$300,000 \cdot \frac{8,000}{250,000} = 300,000 \cdot \frac{x}{300,000}$$

$$\$9,600 = x$$

Try the following examples

EXAMPLE 18

Solve: $x:8 = 35:10$

EXAMPLE 19

If 5 kilometers is equivalent to 3 miles, then find the the number of miles in 12 kilometers.

Answers:
Example 18: 28
Example 19: 7.2 miles

Basic Formulas with Percent

The following formulas traditionally describe the relationship between Percentage, Rate (Percent), and Base

$$\text{Percentage} = \text{Rate} \times \text{Base}$$

$$\text{Rate} = \frac{\text{Percentage}}{\text{Base}}$$

$$\text{Base} = \frac{\text{Percentage}}{\text{Rate}}$$

Given two of these three quantities (or unknowns), we should be able to solve for the third. However, instead of memorizing these formulas and identifying individual variables, we will approach these kind of problems by identifying key words. More precisely, consider the following translations: "OF" means multiplication and "IS" means equals.

$$\text{OF means} \times$$
$$\text{IS means} =$$

In addition when doing calculations with percents you must first convert the percent to a decimal equivalent and then proceed.

EXAMPLE 20

42% of 90 is what number

Translate this sentence as follows:

$$42\% \times 90 = .42 \times 90 = 37.8$$

EXAMPLE 21

45 is what percent of 900

Translate this sentence as follows:

$$45 = \text{Rate} \times 900$$

Solving

$$\text{Rate} = \frac{45}{900} = .05 = 5\%$$

EXAMPLE 22

120% of what amount is 78

Translate this sentence as follows:

$$120\% \times \text{Base} = 78$$

Solving

$$\text{Base} = \frac{78}{120\%} = \frac{78}{1.2} = 65$$

Try the following three examples:

EXAMPLE 23

85% of what amount is 10,625

EXAMPLE 24

45.6% of 100,000 is what number

EXAMPLE 25

1800 is what percent of 24,000

Answers:
Example 23: 12,500
Example 24: 45,600
Example 25: 7.5%

Percentage Increase, Percentage Decrease

Original Quantity + Increase = New Quantity
Original Quantity − Decrease = New Quantity

EXAMPLE 26

What number increased by 25% of itself equals 90

$$N + 25\% \cdot N = 90$$
$$N + .25 \cdot N = 90$$
$$1.25 \cdot N = 90$$
$$N = \frac{90}{1.25}$$
$$N = 72$$

Another approach to this problem is to translate the problem as follows. Since you increase the number by 25% of itself that means that you have 125% of the number. Thus

$$125\% \cdot N = 90$$
$$1.25 \cdot N = 90$$
$$N = \frac{90}{1.25}$$
$$N = 72$$

EXAMPLE 27

What amount decreased by 37.5% gives 120

$$N - 37.5\% \cdot N = 120$$
$$N - .375 \cdot N = 120$$
$$.625 \cdot N = 120$$
$$N = \frac{120}{.625}$$
$$N = 192$$

Another approach to this problem is to translate the problem as follows. Since you decrease the number by 37.5% of itself that means that you have 62.5% of the number. Thus

$$62.5\% \cdot N = 120$$
$$.625 \cdot N = 120$$
$$N = \frac{120}{.625}$$
$$N = 192$$

EXAMPLE 28

Your annual salary is increased to $60,320, which represents a 4% increase over your previous salary. What was your previous salary?

EXAMPLE 29

Your car is now valued at 17,000. Your car's value has decreased by 32% of the original value. What was the original value?

Notes

Answers:
Example 28: 58,000
Example 29: 25,000

Notes

2.2 Literal Equations and Formulas

Literal equations and formulas typically include two or more variables. In order to solve literal equations or formulas for a particular variable we once again use the "Opposites Principle" and the "Golden Rule."

The following formula arises in Finance:

$$\mathbf{I = PRT}$$

where

      I = Principle
      R = Interest Rate (as a decimal)
      T = Time in Years

EXAMPLE 1

Find **I** if **P** = 10,000, **R** = .08, and **T** = 5.

Substituting the values of P, R, and T into the formula we obtain

$$\mathbf{I} = (10{,}000)(.08)(5) = 4{,}000$$

Note that this problem was very easy and in fact just required some arithmetic to solve.

EXAMPLE 2
Find **R** if **I** = 500, **P** = 800, and **T** = 10.

Substituting the values of I, P, and T we then solve for the remaining unknown R.

$$500 = (800)R(10)$$
$$500 = 8000R$$
$$\frac{500}{8000} = \frac{8000R}{8000}$$
$$.0625 = R$$

An alternative approach here would be to solve the equation I = PRT for R and then substitute the values of I, P, T, and do the arithmetic.

$$I = PRT$$
$$\frac{I}{PT} = \frac{PRT}{PT}$$
$$\frac{I}{PT} = R$$
$$\frac{500}{800 \cdot 10} = R$$
$$.0625 = R$$

Which approach is better? It's really up to you. It's whether you want to do the algebra earlier or later in the problem.

Try the following two examples

EXAMPLE 3
Find **P** if **I** = 1,000 **R** = .0725 and **T** = 8

EXAMPLE 4
Find **T** if **I** = 2,000 **P** = 4,000 and **R** = .05

Answers:
Example 3: 1,724.14
Example 4: 10

Notes

2.3 Solving Inequalities

Four Basic Kinds of Simple Inequalities

"X is less than 2" or X < 2 or $(-\infty, 2)$

"X is less than or equal to 2" or X ≤ 2 or $(-\infty, 2]$

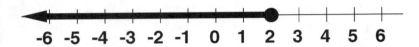

"X is greater than 2" or X > 2 or $(2, \infty)$

"X is greater than or equal to 2" or X ≥ 2 or $[2, \infty)$

Notice when the endpoint is excluded, as in the first and third example, we use a parenthesis for that endpoint of the interval. When the endpoint is included as in the second and fourth example we use a bracket for that endpoint of the interval.

By solving inequalities we mean to find values of the variable that make the inequality a true statement. Solving inequalities is similar to solving equations, by using the **GOLDEN RULE** and the **OPPOSITES PRINCIPLE.** When we proceed to our solution, we will represent our final answers using simple inequalities, interval notation, and with a graph on the number line.

EXAMPLE 1

Solve: $x + 7 \geq 8$

$$x + 7 \geq 8$$
$$-7 \quad -7$$
$$x \geq 1$$

Interval Notation: $[1, \infty)$

In words, our solution is the set of all numbers x that are at least 1, or equivalently, all numbers x that are greater than or equal to 1 or all numbers x that are to the right of 1 and including 1.

EXAMPLE 2

Solve: $-3 + 2x \leq 5$

$$-3 + 2x \leq 5$$
$$+3 +3$$
$$2x \leq 8$$
$$\frac{2x}{2} \leq \frac{8}{2}$$
$$x \leq 4$$

Interval Notation: $(-\infty, 4]$

In words, our solution is the set of all numbers x that are at most 4, or equivalently, all numbers x that are less than or equal to 4 or all numbers x that are to the left of 4 and including 4.

So far it seems fairly straightforward. However, there are two special cases that we have to consider when solving inequalities. Namely:

when **multiplying** or **dividing** both sides of an inequality by a **negative** number then the **direction of the inequality sign switches.**

Notes

EXAMPLE 3

Solve: $12 - 3x < 24$

$$12 - 3x < 24$$
$$\underline{-12 \qquad\quad -12}$$
$$-3x < 12$$
$$\frac{-3x}{-3} > \frac{12}{-3}$$
$$x > -4$$

Note that when we divided both sides of the inequality by -3 in the last step, we had to switch the inequality from $<$ to $>$.

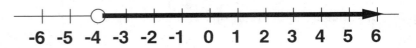

Interval Notation: $(-4, \infty)$

In words, our solution is the set of all numbers x that are at greater than -4, or equivalently, all numbers x that are to the right of -4 (but not including -4).

EXAMPLE 4

Solve: $\dfrac{x}{-6} > \dfrac{1}{3}$

$$\frac{x}{-6} > \frac{1}{3}$$
$$-6 \cdot \frac{x}{-6} < \frac{1}{3} \cdot -6$$
$$x < -2$$

Again, note the sign switch from $>$ to $<$, when we multiplied both sides by -6.

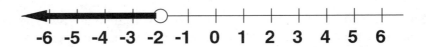

Interval Notation: $(-\infty, -2)$

In words, our solution is the set of all numbers x that are less than -2, or equivalently, all numbers x that are to the left of -2.

One final note here. The inequality sign switch only occurs when we divide or multiply both sides by a **negative number.** If you divide or multiply both sides by a **positive number,** then the inequality sign stays the same.

Try the following examples. In each case write your final answer as a simple inequality, graph on the number line, show the interval notation, and describe your solution in words.

EXAMPLE 5
Solve: $3x - 15 < -9$

EXAMPLE 6
Solve: $-5x + 25 \geq 35$

Answers:
Example 5: $x < 2$ $(-\infty, 2)$ x is less than 2

-6 -5 -4 -3 -2 -1 0 1 2 3 4 5 6

Example 6: $x \leq -2$ $(-\infty, -2]$ x is less than or equal to -2

-6 -5 -4 -3 -2 -1 0 1 2 3 4 5 6

Chapter 2 Exercise Set

Solve.

1. $x + 8 = 23$

2. $y + 7 = -3$

3. $x - 9 = 6$

4. $12 = -7 + y$

5. $5x = 80$

6. $-x = 23$

7. $\dfrac{a}{4} = 13$

8. $\dfrac{3}{4}x = 27$

9. $\dfrac{2}{7} = \dfrac{x}{3}$

10. $\dfrac{-3r}{2} = -\dfrac{27}{4}$

11. $5x + 3 = 38$

12. $7t - 8 = 27$

13. $8z + 2 = -54$

14. $9 - 4x = 37$

15. $-39 = 1 + 8x$

16. $-91 = 9t + 8$

17. $x + \frac{1}{3}x = 8$

18. $9y - 35 = 4y$

19. $6x - 5 = 7 + 2x$

20. $7 + 3x - 6 = 3x + 5 - x$

21. $\frac{2}{3} + \frac{1}{4}t = 6$

22. $2(3 + 4m) - 6 = 48$

23. $7r - (2r + 8) = 32$

24. $7(5x - 2) = 6(6x - 1)$

25. $\frac{1}{4}(3t - 4) = 5$

Solve each formula for the indicated letter.

26. $Q = \dfrac{c + d}{2}$, for d

27. $M = \dfrac{A}{s}$, for A

Solve. Graph and write interval notation for the answers.

28. $y + 2 > 9$

29. $5x - 6 \geq 4x - 1$

30. $-9x + 17 > 17 - 8x$

31. $9y \leq 81$

32. $-7x < 13$

33. $7 + 3x < 34$

34. $4t - 5 \leq 23$

35. $\dfrac{x}{3} - 4 \leq 1$

36. On a recent 7 day vacation you spent $300 for meals. If you stayed for 10 days and spent proportionally the same amount for meals, how much would you spend on meals?

37. If it takes 3 gallons of paint to cover 4 rooms (each 15 feet by 12 feet). How many gallons would be required to cover 50 such rooms?

38. If 3 miles is approximately 5 kilometers, then find the number of kilometers in 22 miles.

39. If 3 miles is approximately 5 kilometers, then find the number of miles in 12 kilometers

Solve.

40. What percent of 68 is 17?

41. What percent of 125 is 30?

42. 14 is 30% of what number?

43. 0.3 is 12% of what number?

44. What number is 35% of 240?

Solve.

45. *Price of Sneakers.* Amy paid $63.75 for a pair of New Balance 903 running shoes during a 15%-off sale. What was the regular price?

46. *Price of a CD Player.* Doug paid $72 for a shockproof portable CD player during a 20%-off sale. What was the regular price?

47. *Price of a Textbook.* Evelyn paid $89.25, including 5% tax, for her biology textbook. How much did the book itself cost?

48. *Price of a Printer.* Jake paid $100.70, including 6% tax, for a color printer. How much did the printer itself cost?

49. *Stock Prices.* Sarah's investment in America Online stock grew 28% to $448. How much did she invest?

Notes

Sets and Counting

3

3.1 Definitions and Notation

What is a **set?** In many ways this may seem like a vague term.

A **set** is a collection of objects which are called elements of members of the set.

Thus, a set is defined by its contents.

EXAMPLE 1

$$A = \{1, 2, 3, 4\}$$

EXAMPLE 2

$$B = \{\heartsuit, \diamondsuit, \clubsuit, \spadesuit\}$$

EXAMPLE 3

$$C = \{Buy, Sell, Stand Pat\}$$

EXAMPLE 4

$$D = \{1, 2, 4, 6, h, \%, \&, H\}$$

$\in$ (Greek letter **epsilon**)

represents "**is an element of**"

$\notin$ represents "**is not an element of**"

$2 \in A$	$\clubsuit \in B$	$Buy \in C$	$4 \in D$
$6 \notin A$	$9 \notin B$	$Quit \notin C$	$- \notin D$

The sets in ex. 1, 2, 3, 4 were described by the **LISTING** method, which simply gives a list or roster of the set.

We may also describe sets using properties that elements of this set must have.

$A = \{$whole numbers between 1 and 4 inclusive$\}$

$C = \{$decisions made in the stock market$\}$

Set Builder Notation

Another way of describing a set is by specifying the description using some set shorthand.

EXAMPLE 5

$$E = \{x \,|\, x \in A \text{ and } x < 3\}$$

This is read as "the set of all x's such that x is an element of A and x is less than 3.

Note: $E = \{1, 2\}$

EXAMPLE 6

$$F = \{x \,|\, x \text{ is a positive integer and } x > 5\}$$

This is read as "the set of all x's such that x is a positive integer and x is greater than 5.

Note: $F = \{6, 7, 8, \dots\}$

Try these two examples:

EXAMPLE 7

$$\mathbf{G} = \{x \,|\, x \in \mathbf{B} \text{ and } x \text{ is Red}\}$$

EXAMPLE 8

$$\mathbf{H} = \{x \,|\, x \text{ is a positive integer and } x \le 5\}$$

Relationships between Sets

Given two sets **A** and **B** , **A** is a *subset* of **B** if every member of **A** is a member of **B.**

$$\mathbf{A} \subset \mathbf{B}$$
"A is a subset of B"

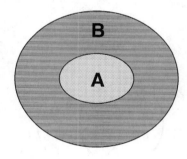

EXAMPLE 9

Given the following sets:

$$\mathbf{A} = \{\text{all Illinois residents}\} \quad \mathbf{B} = \{\text{all US residents}\}$$

Is A a subset of B? Is B a subset of A?

A is a subset of B, denoted by **A ⊂ B,** since every member of A is a member of B. That is, every Illinois resident is a US resident.

B is **not** a subset of A, which we denote by **B ⊄ A,** since there are members of B that are not members of A. That is, there are US residents that are not Illinois residents.

Answers:
Example 7: {♥, ♦}
Example 8: {1, 2, 3, .4, 5}

Notes

EXAMPLE 10

For the following three sets:

$$A = \{1, 2, 3, 4\} \quad B = \{1, 2, 3, 4, 5, 6\} \quad C = \{1, 2, 7\}$$

which of the following statements are true and which are false?

a. $A \subset B$
b. $B \subset A$
c. $C \not\subset A$
d. $C \subset A$
e. $C \not\subset B$
f. $C \subset B$

EXAMPLE 11

What can be said about two sets R and S if $R \subset S$ and $S \subset R$?

Do sets always have a subset or equality relationship? No they do not. Below you see the five different kind of relationships between two sets **A** and **B.** We have seen the first three, and we will encounter the fourth and fifth in our discussion in this chapter.

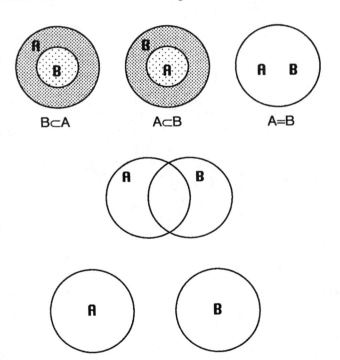

The **EMPTY SET** is the set with no elements, denoted by Φ or **{ }.**

The **UNIVERSAL SET** is the set of all objects under consideration at a particular time, usually denoted by U.

Answers:
Example 10: a. T b. F c. T d. F e. T f. F
Example 11: R = S

3.2 Operations on Sets

In this section we will discuss operations on sets; the **complement,** the **union,** and the **intersection.**

Complementary Sets

The **complement** of a set **A** is the set of all elements that are **not members of A.**

Notation: $\overline{A}$ or A' or A^c
Definition: $A' = \{x \mid x \notin A\}$

Venn Diagram for Complement

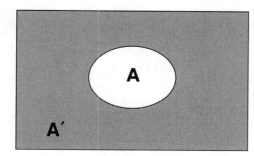

EXAMPLE 1
Find A' if $\mathbf{A} = \{1, 3, 9\}$ and with universal set
$\mathbf{U} = \{1, 2, 3, 4, 5, 6, 7, 8, 9\}$

$$\mathbf{A'} = \{2, 4, 5, 6, 7, 8\}$$

Note that without the universal set **U** as our frame of reference we would have no way to determine the complement of set A.

EXAMPLE 2
The complement of the **Empty Set** is the **Universal Set.**

$$\Phi' = \mathbf{U}$$

EXAMPLE 3
The complement of the **Universal Set** is the **Empty Set.**

$$\mathbf{U'} = \Phi$$

Notes

Try the following example

EXAMPLE 4

Find A′ if A = {1, 2, 3, 4, 5} and
U = {−2, −1, 0, 1, 2, 3, 4, 5, 6, 7}.

Union of Sets

The *union* of two sets **A** and **B** is the set of elements that belongs to **either A *or* B.**

Notation: **A ∪ B**
Definition: **A ∪ B** = {x|x ∈ A   or   x ∈ **B**}

Venn Diagram for Union

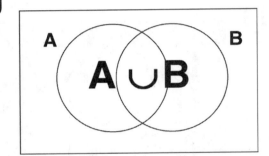

EXAMPLE 5

Find the union of the following two sets:

$$\mathbf{A} = \{1, 3, 9\} \qquad \mathbf{B} = \{1, 9, 25, 30\}.$$

$$\mathbf{A} \cup \mathbf{B} = \{1, 3, 9, 25, 30\}$$

EXAMPLE 6

Find the union of the following two sets:

$$\mathbf{C} = \{Bob, Sally, Jim\} \qquad \mathbf{D} = \{John, Sam, Susan\}$$

$$\mathbf{C} \cup \mathbf{D} = \{Bob, Sally, Jim, John, Sam, Susan\}$$

Answers:
Example 4: A′ = {−2, −1, 0, 6, 7}

Try the following example.

EXAMPLE 7
Find S ∪ T, where S = {5, 10, 15, 20} and T = {0, 10, 20, 30, 40}.

Intersection of Sets

The *intersection* of two sets **A** and **B** is the set of elements that belong to **both A** *and* **B.**

Notation: **A ∩ B**
Definition: **A ∩ B** = {x | x ∈ A **and** x ∈ **B**}

Venn Diagram for Intersection

 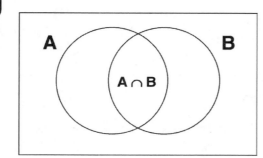

EXAMPLE 8
Find the intersection of the following two sets:

  A = {1, 3, 9}   **B** = {1, 9, 25, 30}

    A ∩ B = {1, 9}

EXAMPLE 9
Find the intersection of the following two sets:

  C = {Bob, Sally, Jim}   **D** = {John, Sam, Susan}

    C ∩ D = Φ   or   **C ∩ D** = { }

Answers:
Example 7: S ∪ T = {0, 5, 10, 15, 20, 30, 40}

Notes

Try the following example.

EXAMPLE 10

Find $S \cap T$, where $S = \{5, 10, 15, 20\}$ and $T = \{0, 10, 20, 30, 40\}$.

If two sets **A** and **B** have no elements in common, that is

$$A \cap B = \Phi$$

then A and B are called ***DISJOINT SETS***.

Venn Diagram for Disjoint Sets

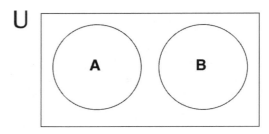

SUMMARIZING

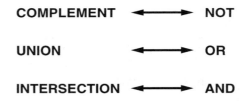

COMPLEMENT	←→	**NOT**
UNION	←→	**OR**
INTERSECTION	←→	**AND**

EXAMPLE 11

Cicero Avenue is a street which goes north and south. 95th Street is a street which goes east and west. 103rd Street is also a street which goes east and west. Both 95th Street and 103rd Street cross Cicero Avenue. 95th Street and 103rd Street do not cross.

Let   **A** = Cicero Avenue

B = 95th Street

C = 103rd Street

Then

A ∩ **B** = intersection of 95th & Cicero

A ∩ **C** = intersection of 103rd & Cicero

B ∩ **C** = Φ

A ∪ **B** = 95th or Cicero

Answers:
Example 10: $S \cap T = \{10, 20\}$

3.3 Counting and Venn Diagrams

We introduce the following notation:

$n(A)$ = number of elements in set A
  "count" of set A

$n(B)$ = number of elements in set B
  "count" of set B

$n(A \cup B)$ = number of elements in set $A \cup B$
  "count" of set $A \cup B$

$n(A \cap B)$ = number of elements in set A
  "count" of set $A \cap B$

$n(A')$ = number of elements in set A'
  "count" of set A'

Note: $n(A)$ reads as the number of elements for set A not n times A.

EXAMPLE 1

A survey of applicants for a position at your company reveals the following:

25 people born in Arizona

15 people with black hair

10 people that were born in Arizona and have black hair

23 people were neither born in Arizona nor had black hair

How many people were interviewed?

Generally the answer to this question is not obvious and requires some work to completely analyze all of the information given. We need to use our critical reading skills and logic and deduction to determine how many of each kind of individual we have in this group of applicants.

Hair Color

Birthplace	Black	Not Black
Arizona		
Not Arizona		

Let A = born in Arizona   B = black hair

$n(A) = 25$ $n(B) = 15$ $n(A \cap B) = 10$ $n(A' \cap B') = 23$

Notes

The four kinds of people in this survey can be described as follows:

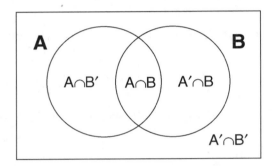

	B	**B′**
A	**A ∩ B**	**A ∩ B′**
A′	**A′ ∩ B**	**A′ ∩ B′**

A ∩ B = Arizona and Black Hair
A ∩ B′ = Arizona and Non-Black Hair
A′ ∩ B = Non-Arizona and Black Hair
A′ ∩ B′ = Non-Arizona and Non-Black Hair

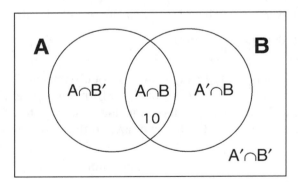

n(A ∩ B) = 10 implies that:

Hair Color

Birthplace	Black	Not Black	Totals
Arizona	10		
Not Arizona			

Totals

n(A) = 25 implies:

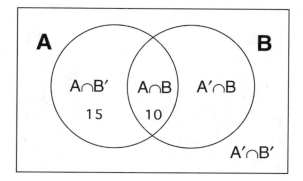

Hair Color

Birthplace	Black	Not Black	Totals
Arizona	10	15	25
Not Arizona			

Totals

n(B) = 15 implies:

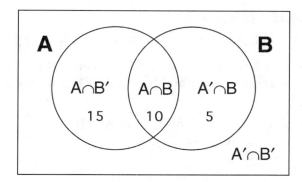

Hair Color

Birthplace	Black	Not Black	Totals
Arizona	10	15	25
Not Arizona	5		

Totals   15

Notes

n(A′ ∩ B′) = 23 implies :

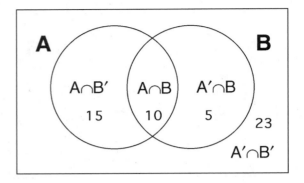

Hair Color

Birthplace	Black	Not Black	Totals
Arizona	10	15	25
Not Arizona	5	23	28
Totals	15	38	53

Thus the total number interviewed was **53.**

How many individuals were born in Arizona or have black hair?

That is, find n(A ∪ B).

Since n(A) = 25 and n(B) = 15 is it true that **n(A ∪ B) = 40?**

NO!!! What we have done here is double count the folks who were both born in Arizona and had black hair. Thus we must adjust for that.

$$n(A \cup B) = n(A) + n(B) - n(A \cap B)$$
$$= 25 + 15 - 10$$
$$= 30$$

or

$$n(A \cup B) = 15 + 10 + 5$$
$$= 30$$

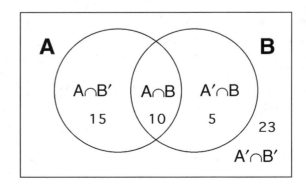

EXAMPLE 2

A survey of **200** people results in **60** born in Arizona, **70** having black hair, **90** people own cars, **30** people born in Arizona and have black hair, **38** people were born in Arizona and have cars, **25** people have black hair and cars, and **10** people were born in Arizona and have black hair, and have a car.

Let   A = born in Arizona   B = black hair   C = owns car

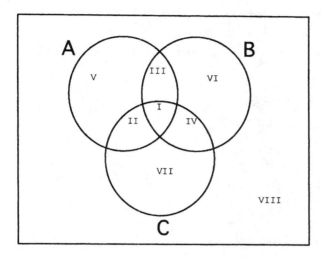

Describe, in words, the eight different kind of people in the survey and match these up to the Roman Numerals I-VIII.

    I. A ∩ B ∩ C
   II. A ∩ B' ∩ C
  III. A ∩ B ∩ C'
   IV. A' ∩ B ∩ C
    V. A ∩ B' ∩ C'
   VI. A' ∩ B ∩ C'
  VII. A' ∩ B' ∩ C
 VIII. A' ∩ B' ∩ C'

Answers:
     I. A ∩ B ∩ C   Arizona and Black Hair and Car
    II. A ∩ B' ∩ C   Arizona and Non-Black Hair and Car
   III. A ∩ B ∩ C'   Arizona and Black Hair and No Car
    IV. A' ∩ B ∩ C   Non-Arizona and Black Hair and Car
     V. A ∩ B' ∩ C'   Arizona and Non-Black Hair and No Car
    VI. A' ∩ B ∩ C'   Non-Arizona and Black Hair and No Car
   VII. A' ∩ B' ∩ C   Non-Arizona and Non-Black Hair and Car
  VIII. A' ∩ B' ∩ C'   Non-Arizona and Non-Black Hair and No Car

Notes

Identify the quantitative information given in Example 2:

A survey of **200** people results in

60 born in Arizona,

70 having black hair,

90 people own cars,

30 people born in Arizona and have black hair,

38 people were born in Arizona and have cars,

25 people have black hair and cars,

10 people were born in Arizona and have black hair and have a car.

We denote the above as follows:

1. $n(U) = 200$
2. $n(A) = 60$
3. $n(B) = 70$
4. $n(C) = 90$
5. $n(A \cap B) = 30$
6. $n(A \cap C) = 38$
7. $n(B \cap C) = 25$
8. $n(A \cap B \cap C) = 10$

We want to fill out the Venn Diagram, labeling the counts of the 8 regions (numbered I-VIII). We can't do anything with statements 1-7 above, at this point. However statement 8, $n(A \cap B \cap C) = 10$ does give a count we can place in the Venn Diagram.

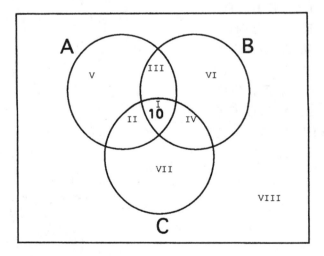

Using statement 7, $n(B \cap C) = 25$ we note that regions I and IV together total to 25. Since I has 10, then we deduce that IV has 15.

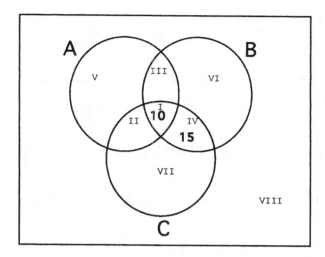

We proceed in a similar manner with statements 5 and 6, $n(A \cap B) = 30$, $n(A \cap C) = 38$, giving us the counts for III and II.

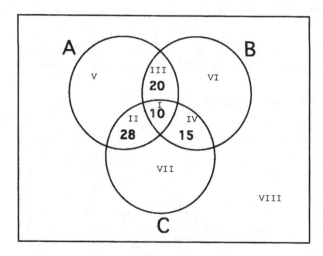

Statement 4, $n(C) = 90$, gives us that 90 people have cars, and we already have accounted for 53 of these from region I, II, and IV. Thus we have 37 people for region VII (90-53).

Using a similar procedure with statements 2 and 3, n(A) = 60 and n(B) = 70, we find that region V has 2 people and region VI has 25 people.

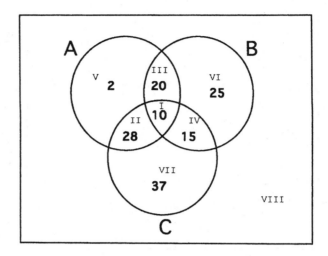

That leaves statement 1, n(U) = 200, and region VIII. How do we determine the count for region VIII? Give it a try.

Here's our final Venn Diagram:

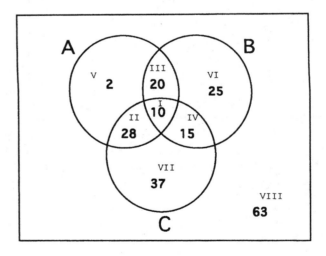

Answer: 63

Questions

1. How many people were not born in Arizona?

    $$n(A') = 25 + 15 + 37 + 63 = 140$$

2. How many people had black hair and did not have a car?

    $$n(B \cap C') = 20 + 25 = 45$$

3. How many people did not have a car?

    $$n(C') = 2 + 20 + 25 + 63 = 110$$

4. How many people were born in Arizona but did not have black hair and did not have a car?

    $$n(A \cap B' \cap C') = 2$$

5. How many people did not have black hair?

6. How many people were born in Arizona and did not have a car?

7. How many people were not born in Arizona?

8. How many people were not born in Arizona, have black hair and have a car?

Answers:
130, 22, 140, 15

Chapter 3 Exercise Set

Let $U = \{2, 3, 4, 5, 7, 9\}$; $X = \{2, 3, 4, 5\}$; $Y = \{3, 5, 7, 9\}$; *and* $Z = \{2, 4, 5, 7, 9\}$. *List the members of each set, using set braces.*

1. $X \cap Y$ **2.** X' **3.** $X' \cap Y'$

Cable Television The following table lists the top five cable television networks in 1999. Use this information for Exercises 4–9.

Network	Subscribers (million)	Major Content
TBS	77.0	Movies, variety, sports
Discovery Channel	76.4	Scientific exploration, variety
ESPN	76.2	Sports, specials, documentaries
USA	75.8	Movies, specials, variety
C-SPAN	75.7	Specials, political broadcasts

List the elements of the following sets.

4. F, the set of networks with more than 76 million subscribers

5. G, the set of networks that feature sports events

6. M, the set of networks that feature movies

7. $F \cap G$ **8.** $M \cup G$ **9.** F'

Draw a Venn diagram and use the given information to fill in the number of elements for each region.

10. $n(U) = 38$, $n(A) = 16$, $n(A \cap B) = 12$, $n(B') = 20$

Use Venn diagrams to answer the following questions.

11. *Harvesting Fruit* Toward the middle of the harvesting season, peaches for canning come in three types, early, late, and extra late, depending on the expected date of ripening. During a certain week, the following data were recorded at a fruit delivery station:

     34 trucks went out carrying early peaches;
     61 carried late peaches;
     50 carried extra late;
     25 carried early and late;
     30 carried late and extra late;
     8 carried early and extra late;
     6 carried all three;
     9 carried only figs (no peaches at all).

a. How many trucks carried only late variety peaches?

b. How many carried only extra late?

c. How many carried only one type of peach?

d. How many trucks (in all) went out during the week?

12. *Investment Survey* Most mathematics professors love to invest their hard-earned money. A recent survey of 150 math professors revealed that

111 invested in stocks;
98 invested in bonds;
100 invested in certificates of deposit;
80 invested in stocks and bonds;
83 invested in bonds and certificates of deposit;
85 invested in stocks and certificates of deposit;
70 invested in stocks, bonds and certificates of deposit.

How many mathematics professors invested in stocks or bonds or certificates of deposit?

13. *Blood Antigens* Human blood can contain the A antigen, the B antigen, both the A and B antigens, or neither antigen. A third antigen, called the Rh antigen, is important in human reproduction, and again may or may not be present in an individual. Blood is called type A-positive if the individual has the A and Rh, but not the B antigen. A person having only the A and B antigens is said to have type AB-negative blood. A person having only the Rh antigen has type O-positive blood. Other blood types are defined in a similar manner. Identify the blood types of the individuals in regions (a)–(h) below.

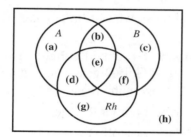

14. *Blood Antigens* (Use the diagram from previous exercise.) In a certain hospital, the following data were recorded.

25 patients had the A antigen;
17 had the A and B antigens;
27 had the B antigen;
22 had the B and Rh antigens;
30 had the Rh antigen;
12 had none of the antigens;
16 had the A and Rh antigens;
15 had all three antigens.

How many patients

a. were represented?

b. had exactly one antigen?

c. had exactly two antigens?

d. had O-positive blood?

e. had AB-positive blood?

f. had B-negative blood?

g. had O-negative blood?

h. had A-positive blood?

15. *Living Arrangements* In 2000, there were 3,842,000 children under the age of 18 living with their grandparents. Of these children, 531,000 had both parents also living with them, 1,732,000 had only their mother living with them, and 220,000 had only their father living with them.[§] How many children lived with their grandparents only?

16. *Chinese New Year* A survey of people attending a Lunar New Year celebration in Chinatown yielded the following results:

> 120 were women;
> 150 spoke Cantonese;
> 170 lit firecrackers;
> 108 of the men spoke Cantonese;
> 100 of the men did not light firecrackers;
> 18 of the non-Cantonese-speaking women lit firecrackers;
> 78 non-Cantonese-speaking men did not light firecrackers;
> 30 of the women who spoke Cantonese lit firecrackers.

a. How many attended?

b. How many of those who attended did not speak Cantonese?

c. How many women did not light firecrackers?

d. How many of those who lit firecrackers were Cantonese-speaking men?

17. You talk to a group of 180 avid golfers. You discover that 80 read Golf World, 125 read Golf Digest, and that 45 read both Golf World and Golf Digest. How many read

a. neither Golf World nor Golf Digest,

b. either Golf World or Golf Digest,

c. only Golf World,

d. only Golf Digest.

18. Your company has 1200 male employees and 1550 employees that are over 50 years of age. Your company also has 550 female employees who are not over age 50 and has 800 male employees that are over age 50. How many employees

a. are at your company,

b. are female,

c. are not over 50,

d. male or over 50 or both.

19. Your company has a fleet of 100 cars. 25 are nonwhite Dodges, 10 are white non-Dodges, and 30 cars are white Dodges. How many cars are

a. nonwhite and non-Dodges

b. are not Dodges

c. are not white

d. Dodges or White or both

Linear Functions

4.1 Functions

The concept of **function** is central to your interaction with and use of mathematics. Fundamentally, functions are about relationships between variables or unknowns. Some examples are listed below.

EXAMPLE 1
Total Revenue depends on **# of units sold.**

EXAMPLE 2
Total Daily Cost depends on **# of units produced.**

EXAMPLE 3
Profit depends on **# of units sold.**

EXAMPLE 4
Value of a car depends on the **age of a car.**

EXAMPLE 5
Amount of Air Pollution depends on the **# of cars on the road.**

EXAMPLE 6
The **# of new housing starts** depends on the **mortgage interest rate.**

Mathematical Definition—*a function relates two sets of numbers in a consistent way*

This is a difficult concept to understand if one relies solely on the above definition. To simplify this, we consider a three component model of function. More specifically, we think of functions as an **input,** a rule, and an output.

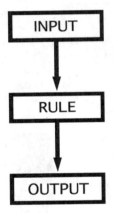

We will discuss the concept of function from four perspectives.

VERBAL—expressing functions using phrases

SYMBOLIC—expressing functions using traditional mathematical symbols and notation

NUMERICAL—expressing functions using tables of numerical values

GRAPHICAL—expressing functions using graphs on a two dimensional coordinate system

Consider the following functions:

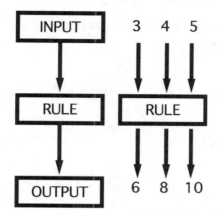

"Multiply by 2 Rule"

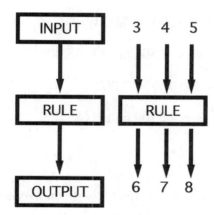

"Add 3 Rule"

How else might we describe these different rules?

"Multiply by 2"	"Add 3"
$x \rightarrow 2x$	$x \rightarrow x + 3$
Output $= 2 \cdot$ Input	Output $=$ Input $+ 3$
$y = 2x$	$y = x + 3$
$f(x) = 2x$	$g(x) = x + 3$

Function Notation

"f of x equals 2x"   "g of x equals x + 3"
$f(5) = 2 \cdot 5 = 10$ $g(10) = 10 + 3 = 13$
means an input of 5   means an input of 10
results in an output of 10   results in an output of 13

EXAMPLE 1

You sell each unit for $10 each. Let

$\mathbf{y}$ = total revenue for $\mathbf{x}$ units sold

$\mathbf{x}$ = # of units sold

Then

$$\mathbf{y = 10x}$$

or

$$\mathbf{R = 10x}$$

or

$$\mathbf{R(x) = 10x}$$

"Total revenue for x units sold" equals 10x.

This could be expressed as the "Multiply by 10 Rule"

$$R(500) = 10 \cdot 500 = 5,000$$

The revenue for sales of 500 units is $5,000.

$$R(700) = 10 \cdot 700 = 7,000$$

The revenue for sales of 700 units is $7,000.

EXAMPLE 2

The cost of producing 1 unit is $5, with an overhead of $100 per day.

$$\text{Total Daily Cost} = 5 \cdot (\text{\# of units produced}) + 100$$
$$C = 5x + 100$$
$$C(x) = 5x + 100$$

"Total Daily Cost of producing x units" equals 5x + 100.

This could be expressed as the "Multiply by 5 and add 100 Rule".

$$C(1000) = 5(1000) + 100 = \$5,100$$

The "total daily cost for producing 1000 units" is $5,100.

$$C(1200) = 5(1200) + 100 = \$6,100$$

The "total daily cost for producing 1200 units" is $6,100.

4.2 Graphing Functions by Hand

In order to graph functions we first must know how to plot points in our two dimensional coordinate system. This system consists of two axes, an x-axis (horizontal number line) and a y-axis (vertical number line).

Every point in our xy coordinate system is referenced by its horizontal and vertical displacement from the center of our system, which is located where the x and y axis cross. This point is called the origin and has coordinates (0,0). All other points are referenced by **ordered pairs** (x,y), where x is the horizontal displacement from (0,0) and y is the vertical displacement from (0,0). Below you will find the point (2,3).

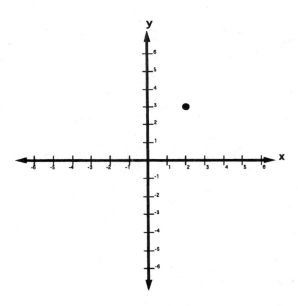

Label the following points with the appropriate (x,y) coordinates.

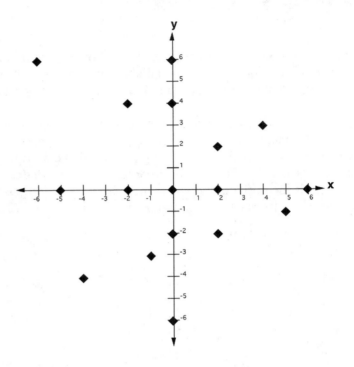

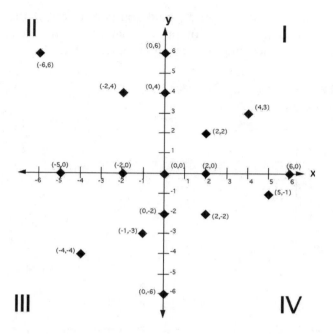

Note:

All points on the x-axis have y coordinate of 0.

All points on the y-axis have x coordinate of 0.

The coordinate system is divided into four quadrants.

In Quadrant I both $x > 0$ and $y > 0$

In Quadrant II $x < 0$ and $y > 0$

In Quadrant III both $x < 0$ and $y < 0$

In Quadrant IV $x > 0$ and $y < 0$

To graph a function, we graph the equation that describes the function. To graph an equation, we plot points that make the equation true. Choose some x-values and use the equation to find y.

EXAMPLE 1

Graph $y = 2x$

x	y
0	0
1	2
2	4
-1	-2
-2	-4

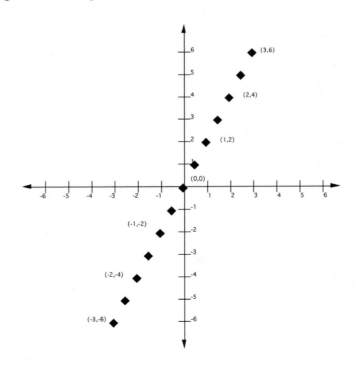

Plotting a few more points:

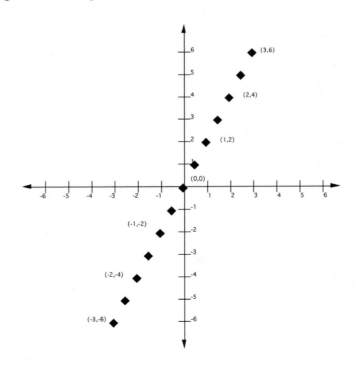

Finally we get a straight line:

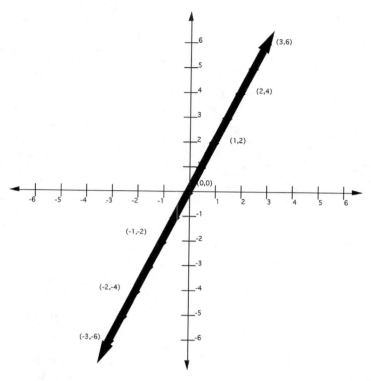

EXAMPLE 2
Graph y = x + 3

We select some x-values and use the equation to find the y-values.

x	y
-3	0
-2	1
-1	2
0	3
1	4
2	5
3	6

Notes

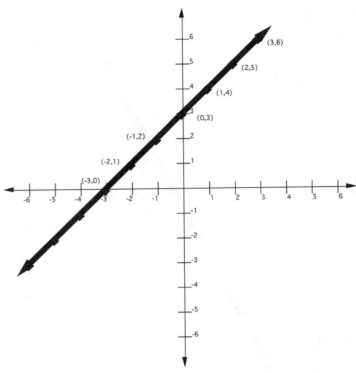

It would be nice if we knew by looking at the equation that the graph was going to be a straight line. It turns out that we can! Stay tuned.

Before we discuss this let's look at the TI-83 and how we can generate tables and graphs of functions.

Tables on the Calculator

We've discussed the following functions from a verbal, symbolic, numerical, and graphical view:

$$Y = 2X$$
$$Y = X + 3$$
$$Y = 10X$$
$$Y = 5X + 100$$

Let's enter these functions into our TI-83 by pressing the **Y=** key (blue key, top row, far left).

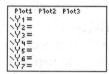

Move the cursor to the right of the = for Y1 and enter in 2X, then move the cursor downward and enter X + 3 for Y2, then move downward and enter 10X for Y3 and finally move downward and enter 5X + 100 for Y4.

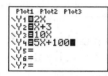

Note the darkened = signs which indicate the these functions are all turned on. Move the cursor onto the second, third, and fourth = and press **ENTER.** This will "turn off" the last three functions.

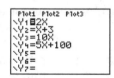

To generate a table of values for our first function, we use the **TBLSET** and **TABLE** features. Press **2nd WINDOW** (this is the **TBLSET** key) and you will see a screen like the one below (don't worry about the numerical values you see). Enter in −2 for **TblStart** and enter **1** for **ΔTbl.**

Now press **2nd** and **GRAPH** (which is the **TABLE** key) and you'll see the following.

Notes

Scroll up and down and you see an extensive table of values of X and Y (actually Y1). If you move the cursor to Y1 you will see the following.

Let's return to the **TBLSET** feature (**2nd** and **WINDOW**) and this time move the cursor to **Indpnt:** and select **ASK**

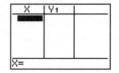

Now press **2nd GRAPH** (**TABLE** key) and select some values for X (for instance let's enter **10** for X then press **ENTER,** then enter −**37** for X and press **ENTER**) and see what happens.

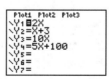 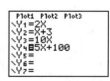

So you can make up your own table with any values you chose or define a starting point (TblStart) and specify the increment (∆Tbl).

To work with another one of our functions return to the Y= editor (press the **Y=** key) and deselect Y1 (move the cursor onto the = sign for Y1 and press **ENTER**) and select whichever other function you want to work with. Let's select Y4 (move the cursor to the = sign for Y4 and press **ENTER**).

Use **TBLSET** and select the **ASK** option for **Indpnt:.** Then use **TABLE** to evaluate the cost of producing 1000 items (that is input 1000 as an X value

Another way of getting this value would be to return to the home screen by pressing **2nd** and **MODE** (the **QUIT** key), and then press **VARS** (next to the **CLEAR** key) and select **Y-VARS**).

Select **1:Function** and then select **4:Y4.**

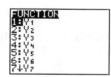 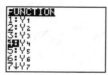

This pastes Y4 to the home screen after which you press (then **1000** then) and **ENTER** to get the result.

 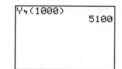

We can evaluate more than one function at a time. Press **Y=** select Y1 (leave Y4 selected as before). Now go to the **TABLE** (**2nd** and **GRAPH**).

Try the following.

Generate a table starting at -10 and increasing by 5 units from one entry to the next, for both Y_2 and Y_3.

4.4 Graphing on the Calculator

Return to the **Y=** editor and deselect all functions with the exception of Y1.

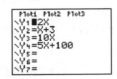

Press **GRAPH** (blue key, top row, far right). Here's what happens.

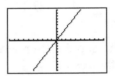

If the graph does not look like this press **ZOOM** (blue key, top row, middle key), and press 6 (this is the Zoom Standard feature).

Pressing the **WINDOW** key (blue key next to **Y=**) shows you the graphing window settings which you can control (change). These are the standard settings below.

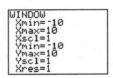

You can also control the window by the ZOOM options. Press **ZOOM** (blue key, top row, middle key).

These options do the following:

1:ZBox	Draws a box to define the viewing window
2:Zoom In	Magnifies the graph around the cursor
3:Zoom Out	Views more of the graph around the cursor
4:ZDecimal	Sets ΔX and ΔY TO .1
5:ZSquare	Sets equal size pixels on the X and Y axes
6:ZStandard	Sets the standard window variables
7:ZTrig	Sets the built in trig window variables
8:ZInteger	Sets integer values on the X and Y axes
9:ZoomStat	Sets the values for the current stat lists
0:ZoomFit	Fits YMin & YMax between XMin & XMax

Let's try one of these. Press ZOOM and select 8:ZInteger.

 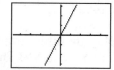

If you now press one of the four arrow keys you will generate a cursor on the screen and the x and y values are given. This is a free floating cursor.

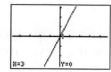 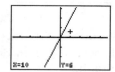

Pressing the **TRACE** key (blue key next to the **GRAPH** key) generates a cursor that resides on the graph. Using the left or right arrow keys you can move along the graph.

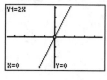 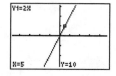

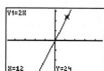 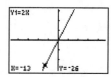

If you press **ENTER** while in the TRACE feature you will get what is called a Quick Zoom, with the graph being centered at the cursor.

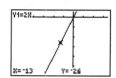

Notes

You can also type in an **X** value and the TRACE feature will find the point on the graph. For example type −**10** and then **ENTER.**

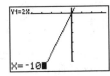 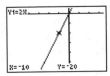

Remember, you can always return to the standard settings by pressing **ZOOM** followed by selecting **6:ZStandard.**

 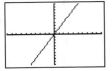

We can also display multiple graphs using the **GRAPH** feature. Press **Y=** and select both Y1 and Y2. Then press **GRAPH.**

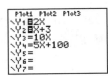 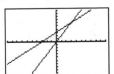

Pressing **TRACE** allows us to trace as before. Pressing the up arrow key allows tracing of the 2nd graph. Pressing the down arrow key gets you back to the first graph.

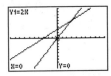 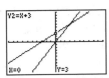

4.5   Linear Functions

Back in section 4.2, we hoped that there was a way to know whether the graph of an equation will be a straight line, without having to do the graph. If we did know that a certain type of equation would graph into a line, we would call that a linear equation (or a linear function) and thus we would only need to plot two points to do the graph. So here's the deal.

Linear Functions

General Form:

$$y = mx + b$$

or

$$f(x) = mx + b$$

where **m** and **b** are constants.

So it's really a matter of recognition. We look at an equation and determine whether it fits the above pattern and if it does, then identify what **m** and **b** are.

Notes

EXAMPLE 1

Determine whether each equation is linear or not and if it is linear then find m and b. I will demonstrate the first three. You try the rest.

Equation	Linear	m	b	$y = m \cdot x + b$
$y = 7x + 10$	YES	7	10	$y = 7 \cdot x + 10$
$y = -5x - 8$	YES	-5	-8	$y = -5 \cdot x + (-8)$
$y = -x + 6$	YES	-1	6	$y = -1 \cdot x + 6$
$y = 3x + 2$				
$y = 3x - 1$				
$y = x + 3$				
$y = 2x$				
$y = 3$				
$y = -\dfrac{3}{2}x + 1$				
$y = 2x + \dfrac{3}{5}$				
$y = 3x^2 + 2$				
$y = \dfrac{3}{x} + 2$				

Let's try to graph the last two nonlinear functions using the TI-83.

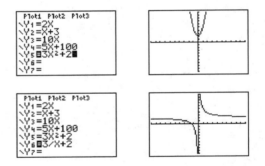

Clearly these two graphs are not straight lines.

Answers:

$y = 3x + 2$	YES	3	2	$y = 3 \cdot x + 2$
$y = 3x - 1$	YES	3	-1	$y = 3 \cdot x + (-1)$
$y = x + 3$	YES	1	3	$y = 1 \cdot x + 3$
$y = 2x$	YES	2	0	$y = 2 \cdot x + 0$
$y = 3$	YES	0	3	$y = 0 \cdot x + 3$
$y = -\dfrac{3}{2}x + 1$	YES	$-\dfrac{3}{2}$	1	$y = \left(-\dfrac{3}{2}\right) \cdot x + 1$
$y = 2x + \dfrac{3}{5}$	YES	2	$\dfrac{3}{5}$	$y = 2 \cdot x + \dfrac{3}{5}$
$y = 3x^2 + 2$	NO			
$y = \dfrac{3}{x} + 2$	NO			

4.6 Slopes and Intercepts

Linear graphs or more simply lines, have several important characteristics. The first to consider is the **slope** which measures the slant or tilt of the line. Consider a line passing through the two points (x_1, y_1) and (x_2, y_2). The slope is the ratio of the change in y to the change in x as we move from (x_1, y_1) to (x_2, y_2) along the line. Sometimes this is referred to as the ratio of rise to run.

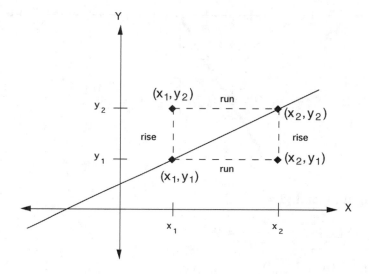

$$\text{SLOPE} = \frac{\text{change in y}}{\text{change in x}} = \frac{\text{vertical change}}{\text{horizontal change}} = \frac{\text{rise}}{\text{run}}$$

$$= \frac{y_2 - y_1}{x_2 - x_1}$$

EXAMPLE 1
Find the slope for the line $y = 2x$

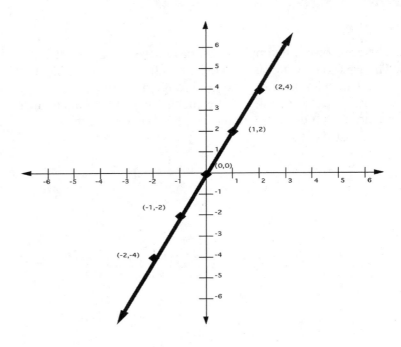

Using (0,0) and (2,4)

$$\text{SLOPE} = \frac{4 - 0}{2 - 0} = 2$$

Using (0,0) and (1,2)

$$\text{SLOPE} = \frac{2 - 0}{1 - 0} = 2$$

Using $(-2, -4)$ and (2,4)

$$\text{SLOPE} = \frac{4 - (-4)}{2 - (-2)} = \frac{8}{4} = 2$$

Note that it makes no difference which two points on the line we choose to compute the slope. This is a fundamental property of lines, that is that they have constant slope.

In the graph below we find the ratio of rise overrun graphically, using a number of different pairs of points.

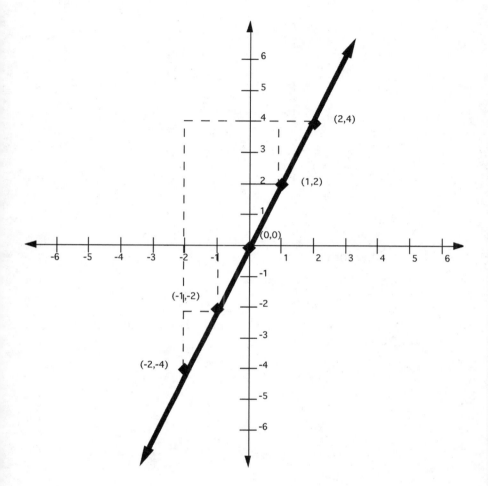

Notes

EXAMPLE 2

Find the slope of the line passing through (1,2) and (4,3)

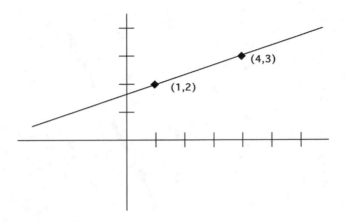

Using the slope formula:

$$\text{SLOPE} = \frac{3-2}{4-1} = \frac{1}{3}$$

Using the rise over run ratio, starting at (1,2) we go up 1 and over 3 to get to (4,3). Thus the slope is 1/3.

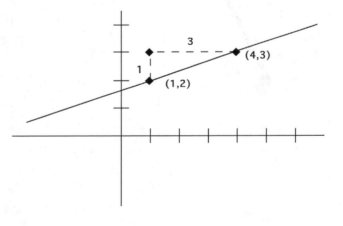

EXAMPLE 3

Find the slope of the line passing through $(-1, 3)$ and $(2, -4)$.

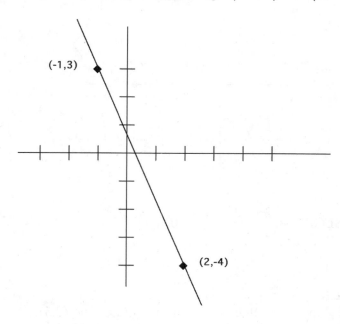

$$\text{SLOPE} = \frac{-4 - 3}{2 - (-1)} = \frac{-7}{3} = -\frac{7}{3}$$

Note that it does not make a difference which is your first point and which is your second point.

$$\text{SLOPE} = \frac{3 - (-4)}{-1 - (2)} = \frac{7}{-3} = -\frac{7}{3}$$

Using the rise over run ratio, starting at $(-1, 3)$ we go down 7 units (rise of -7) and go over 3 (run of 3). Thus the slope is $-7/3$.

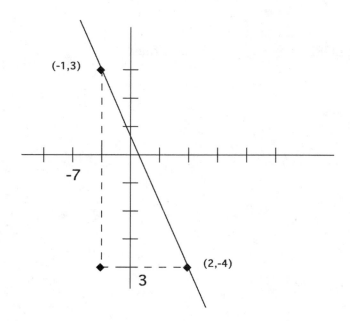

Notes

EXAMPLE 4

Find the slope of the line passing through (1,2) and (3,2).

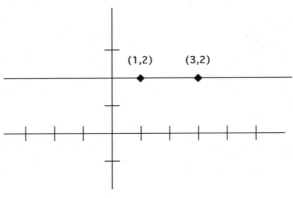

$$\text{SLOPE} = \frac{2-2}{3-1} = \frac{0}{2} = 0$$

EXAMPLE 5

Find the slope of the line passing through (2,0) and (2,3).

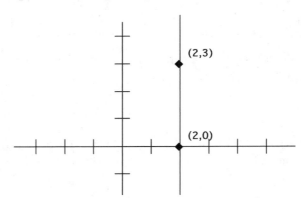

$$\text{SLOPE} = \frac{3-0}{2-2} = \frac{3}{0} = \text{undefined}$$

EXAMPLE 6
Find the slope of the line going through each of the following pairs of points.

a. $(-3, 0)$ and $(2,5)$

b. $(0,10)$ and $(5,10)$

c. $(-1, 4)$ and $(1,1)$

d. $(-2, 1)$ and $(-2, -2)$

Answers:
Example 6: a. 1; b. 0; c. −3/2; d. undefined

Notes

Basically there are four kinds of lines, in terms of slope:

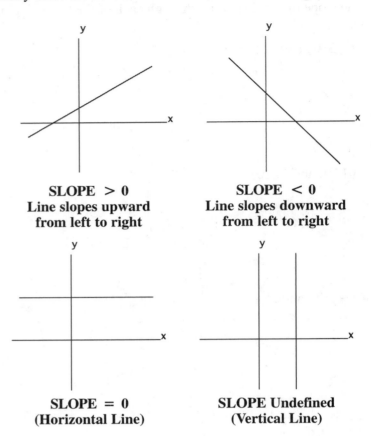

Another important characteristic of lines is their intercepts, as defined below

X-intercept

x coordinate of the point where the line crosses the x-axis.

Y-intercept

y coordinate of the point where the line crosses the y-axis.

EXAMPLE 7

Find the x-intercept, y-intercept and slope for the following line.

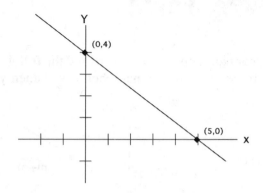

Answers:
Example 7: x-intercept = 5, y-intercept = 4, slope = −4/5

4.7 Slope–Intercept Form

Consider the linear equation $y = mx + b$, and the following table. Note that when $x = 0$ then $y = b$ and that when $x = 1$ then $y = m + b$.

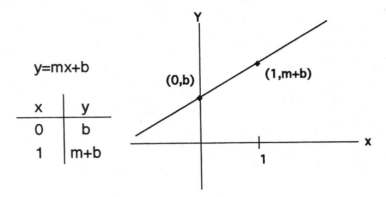

First, note that the the y-intercept is **b.** So a line with equation $y = mx + b$ always has a y-intercept of b.

Second, note that if we use the points (0,b) and (1, m + b) to determine the slope of this line we get **m.**

$$\text{SLOPE} = \frac{m + b - b}{1 - 0} = \frac{m}{1} = m$$

Thus, a line with equation $y = mx + b$ always has slope of m. This generates the Slope Intercept Form for equation of a line.

Since vertical lines have undefined slope and in most cases do not have a y-intercept, the $y = mx + b$ form would not apply. However, for vertical lines all points have the same x coordinate. If $x = a$ is the x-intercept, then every point on the vertical line has the same x-coordinate. Thus, in this case the equation would simply be $x = a$.

Slope–Intercept Form

y = mx + b

m = slope and **b** = y-intercept

This equation describes all non-vertical lines. Vertical lines have equations of the form:

x = a

a = x-intercept.

This now gives us a way of determining the slope and y-intercept of a line directly from the equation of the line. Reconsidering the linear equations that we saw in Section 4.5, we find that we were not just identifying m and b to show that the equations were linear but also to find the slope **m** and the y-intercept **b.**

Equation	Slope	Y-int.
$y = 7x + 10$	7	10
$y = -5x - 8$	-5	-8
$y = -x + 6$	-1	6
$y = 3x + 2$	3	2
$y = 3x - 1$	3	-1
$y = x + 3$	1	3
$y = 2x$	2	0
$y = 3$	0	3
$y = -\dfrac{3}{2}x + 1$	$-\dfrac{3}{2}$	1
$y = 2x + \dfrac{3}{5}$	2	$\dfrac{3}{5}$

With this new information, we have some options for graphing linear functions. Graphs can be done by hand either by plotting points or by using the information about the slope and y-intercept of the line. Graphs can be done with the TI-83 as well. However learning to graph using the slope and the y-intercept will give you a visual connection between the graph and the concepts of slope and y-intercept. The approach used will be to first plot the y-intercept and then use the slope as rise over run as directions to another point. This technique will be demonstrated in the next two examples.

EXAMPLE 1

Graph the line $y = 3x + 2$

Note this line has y-intercept **2** (**b = 2**) and slope **3** (**m = 3**). Plot the y-intercept at (0,2). The slope is 3, and we need to think of the slope as a ratio. In this case that ratio would be 3/1. In fact whenever the slope is an integer we will think of the slope as a ratio to 1. Since the slope is the rise over the run, we have

$$\frac{\text{rise}}{\text{run}} = \frac{3}{1}$$

This gives us directions to another point. Starting at the y-intercept (0,2) we move up three and to the right 1, which gets us to our second point. Sketching the graph of the line through these two points gives us the following graph.

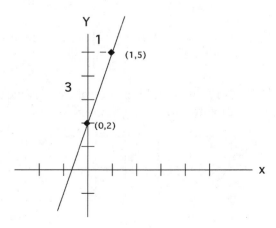

Notes

Notes

EXAMPLE 2

Graph the line

$$y = -\frac{3}{2}x + 1$$

Note this line has y-intercept **1** (**b = 1**) and slope **−3/2** (**m = −3/2**).

Since the slope is the rise over the run, we have

$$\frac{\text{rise}}{\text{run}} = \frac{-3}{2}$$

This gives us directions to another point. Starting at the y-intercept (0,1) we move down three (since the rise is −3) and to the right 2, which gets us to our second point. Sketching the graph of the line through these two points gives us the following graph.

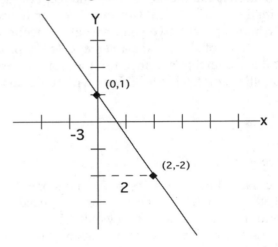

To generate the graph on the TI-83, we enter in the linear function in Y1 and then press **ZOOM** and select **6:ZStandard**.

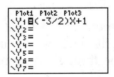 

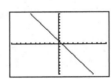

By pressing **WINDOW** and making the following selections we can alter the graph window to look like the graph above.

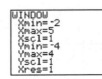 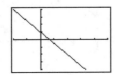

Try the following three examples. In each case do the following:

1. identify the slope and y-intercept,
2. plot the y-intercept,
3. use the slope (rise/run) as directions to another point,
4. draw the line passing through the two points,
5. generate a graph on the TI-83.

EXAMPLE 3
Graph the line $y = -2x + 3$

EXAMPLE 4
Graph the line $y = \dfrac{2}{5}x - 2$

EXAMPLE 5
Graph the line $y = -4$

Answers:
Examples 3–5: Answers on next page

Notes

Notes

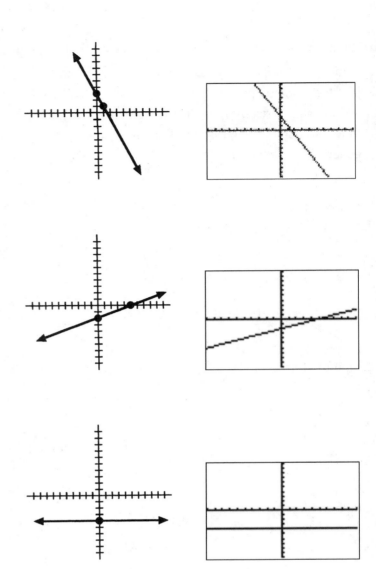

4.8 Equations of Lines

There are three forms for equations of lines. The slope intercept form is the most important, but others arise in certain specific situations.

1. Slope-Intercept:

$$y = mx + b$$

where m = **slope** and b = **y-intercept.**

Vertical Lines: $x = a$ where a = **x-intercept**

2. General or Standard:

$$Ax + By + C = 0 \quad \text{or} \quad Ax + By = C$$

(handles all lines)

3. Point-Slope:

$$y - y_1 = m(x - x_1)$$

where m = **slope** and (x_1, y_1) is a **given point.**

(again, vertical lines are $x = a$ where a = **x-intercept**)

The next two examples show how we can go from slope-intercept form to standard form.

EXAMPLE 1

Convert $y = 3x - 5$ from slope intercept form to standard form.

Our first step is to subtract y from both sides.

$$y = 3x - 5$$
$$y - y = 3x - 5 - y$$
$$0 = 3x - y - 5$$

EXAMPLE 2

Convert $y = -\dfrac{3}{2}x + 2$ into standard form.

Here our first step was to multiply by 2 to eliminate the fractions.

$$y = -\frac{3}{2}x + 2$$

$$2y = 2\left(-\frac{3}{2}x + 2\right)$$

$$2y = 2\left(-\frac{3}{2}x\right) + 2 \cdot 2$$

$$2y = -3x + 4$$

$$2y - 2y = -3x + 4 - 2y$$

$$0 = -3x - 2y + 4$$

$$0 = 3x + 2y - 4$$

The next two examples show how we can go from standard form to slope-intercept form.

EXAMPLE 3

Convert $5x + y - 10 = 0$ into slope intercept form.

Here we need to solve for y.

$$5x + y - 10 = 0$$

$$5x + y - 10 + 10 = 0 + 10$$

$$5x + y = 10$$

$$-5x + 5x + y = -5x + 10$$

$$y = -5x + 10$$

EXAMPLE 4

Convert $2x - 3y = 6$ into slope intercept form.

Again we solve for y.

$$2x - 3y = 6$$

$$-2x + 2x - 3y = -2x + 6$$

$$-3y = -2x + 6$$

$$\frac{-3y}{-3} = \frac{-2x}{-3} + \frac{6}{-3}$$

$$y = \frac{2}{3}x - 2$$

The next set of problems ask to find the equation of the line given certain information about the line.

What is being asked here?

Given information about the line, you need to find the equation $y = mx + b$, which means that you need to be given or to figure out the slope and the y-intercept, and then state the equation of the line.

I always suggest that you graph the line first based on the given information. In fact, if you are given enough information about the line to graph the line, then you have enough information to find the equation of the line.

EXAMPLE 5

Find the equation of the line passing through (0,4) with slope 3.

Graph the line first by plotting the y-intercept (0,4) and using the slope 3 (3/1) as directions to another point (up 3 and right 1).

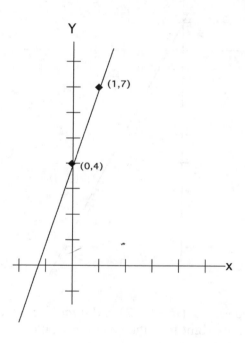

Slope $= 3 \Rightarrow m = 3$ y-intercept $= 4 \Rightarrow b = 4$

So the equation is:

$$y = 3x + 4 \quad \text{or} \quad 3x - y + 4 = 0$$

Note this problem was made easier since we were given exactly the information needed, namely the slope and y-intercept.

EXAMPLE 6

Find the equation of the line passing through $(3, -5)$ and with slope -2.

Again we begin by graphing the line. Plot the given point $(3, -5)$ and then use the slope $(-2/1)$ as directions to another point (down 2 and right 1).

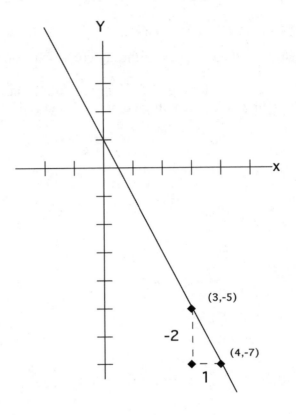

We know the slope is -2 ($m = -2$) and it *looks like* the y-intercept is 1 ($b = 1$). If we are right then the equation would be:

$$y = -2x + 1 \quad \text{or} \quad 2x + y - 1 = 0$$

We need to verify this algebraically. We can not depend on our graphing to be that accurate. We have two techniques we can use.

Technique #1 (Using slope-intercept form)

Slope $= -2 \Rightarrow m = -2$

$$y = -2x + b \qquad \text{We need to solve for b using } (3, -5)$$
$$-5 = -2 \cdot 3 + b$$
$$-5 = -6 + b$$
$$+6 - 5 = +6 - 6 + b$$
$$1 = b$$

Thus the equation of this line is $y = -2x + 1$

Technique #2 (Using the point-slope form)

Use the fact that $m = -2$ and that the given point is $(3, -5)$

$$y - y_1 = m(x - x_1)$$
$$y - (-5) = -2(x - 3)$$
$$y + 5 = -2x + 6$$
$$y + 5 - 5 = -2x + 6 - 5$$
$$y = -2x + 1$$

It is your choice as to which technique to use. You don't need to do both techniques. Just pick the one that seems easier, and stick with it!

EXAMPLE 7

Find the equation of the line passing through the points $(1,7)$ and $(-1, -3)$.

We graph the line by plotting the two points and drawing the line.

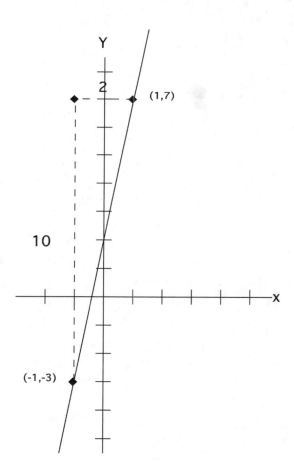

Graphically, it looks like the **slope** is $10/2 = 5$ and the **y-intercept** is **2.** Thus the equation would be:

$$y = 5x + 2 \quad \text{or} \quad 5x - y + 2 = 0$$

Notes

We need to verify this algebraically.

First we find the slope:

$$m = \frac{7 - (-3)}{1 - (-1)} = \frac{10}{2} = 5$$

Technique #1 (Using slope-intercept form)

$$y = 5x + b \qquad \textbf{We need to solve for b using (1,7)}$$
$$7 = 5 \cdot 1 + b$$
$$7 = 5 + b$$
$$7 - 5 = 5 - 5 + b$$
$$2 = b$$

Thus the equation of this line is y $=$ 5x $+$ 2

Technique #2 (Using the point-slope form)

Use the fact that m $=$ 5 and that the given point is (1,7)

$$y - y_1 = m(x - x_1)$$
$$y - 7 = 5(x - 1)$$
$$y - 7 = 5x - 5$$
$$y - 7 + 7 = 5x - 5 + 7$$
$$y = 5x + 2$$

EXAMPLE 8

Find the equation of the line passing through (7,2) and (1,2).

Sketching the graph here is helpful.

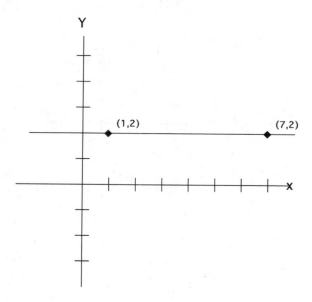

$$m = \frac{2 - 2}{7 - 1} = \frac{0}{6} = 0 \qquad b = 2$$

This is a **horizontal line** with equation:

$$y = 2 \text{ or } y - 2 = 0$$

There is no need to verify this algebraically, since we recognize that this line is horizontal.

Notes

EXAMPLE 9

Find the equation of the line passing through $(1, -2)$ and $(1,2)$. Once again, sketching the graph is helpful.

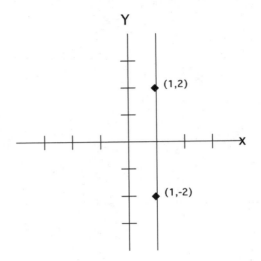

$$m = \frac{2 - (-2)}{1 - 1} = \frac{4}{0} \qquad \text{undefined}$$

There is no y-intercept.

The x-intercept is 1.

This is a **vertical line** with equation:

$$x = 1 \qquad \text{or} \qquad x - 1 = 0$$

Again, there is no need to verify this algebraically, since we recognize that this line is vertical.

Try the following two problems.

EXAMPLE 10

Find the equation of the line passing through the point $(-5, 2)$ with slope -2.

EXAMPLE 11

Find the equation of the line passing through $(3,8)$ and $(-1, -12)$.

Answers:
Example 10: $y = 2x - 8$
Example 11: $y = 5x - 7$

Chapter 4 Exercise Set

Graph each equation by hand.

1. $y = x - 1$ **2.** $y = x$

3. $y = 3x - 2$ **4.** $y = \frac{1}{2}x + 1$

5. $x + y = -5$ **6.** $y = \frac{3}{2}x + 1$

Graph each equation using a graphing calculator. Remember to solve for y first if necessary.

7. $y = -\frac{3}{2}x + 1$ **8.** $4y - 3x = 1$

Graph each equation using both viewing windows indicated. Determine which window best shows the shape of the graph and where the graph crosses the x- and y-axes.

9. $y = x - 15$

     a) $[-10, 10, -10, 10]$, **Xscl = 1, Yscl = 1**
     b) $[-20, 20, -20, 20]$, **Xscl = 5, Yscl = 5**

For Exercises 10–11, find (a) the coordinates of the y-intercept and (b) the coordinates of all x-intercepts.

10.

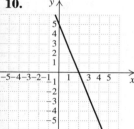

11.

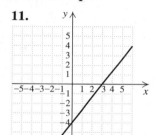

Graph.

12. $y = 5$ **13.** $x = 4$

Write an equation for each graph.

14.

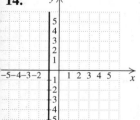

15.

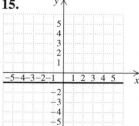

Notes

Find the slope, if it is defined, of each line. If the slope is undefined, state this.

16.

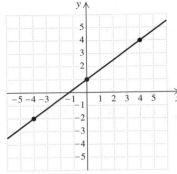

17.

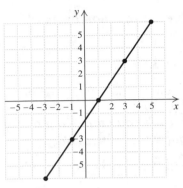

18.

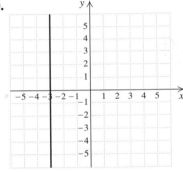

19.

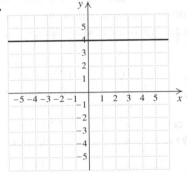

20.

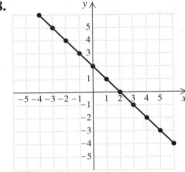

Find the slope of the line containing each given pair of points. If the slope is undefined, state this.

21. $(1, 2)$ and $(5, 8)$

22. $(-2, 4)$ and $(3, 0)$

23. $(-4, 0)$ and $(5, 7)$

24. $(-2, \frac{1}{2})$ and $(-5, \frac{1}{2})$

Find the slope of each line. If the slope is undefined, state this.

25. $x = -3$

26. $y = 4$

Draw a line that has the given slope and y-intercept.

27. Slope $\frac{2}{5}$; y-intercept $(0, 1)$

28. Slope $\frac{5}{3}$; y-intercept $(0, -2)$

29. Slope $-\frac{3}{4}$; y-intercept $(0, 5)$

Notes

Find the slope and the y-intercept of each line.

30. $y = \frac{3}{7}x + 5$ **31.** $y = -\frac{5}{6}x + 2$

32. $y = \frac{9}{4}x - 7$ **33.** $y = -\frac{2}{5}x$

34. $y = 4$

Find the slope–intercept equation for the line with the indicated slope and y-intercept.

35. Slope $\frac{7}{8}$; y-intercept $(0, -1)$

Determine the slope and the y-intercept. Then graph by hand.

36. $y = \frac{3}{5}x + 2$ **37.** $y = -\frac{3}{5}x + 1$

38. $y = \frac{5}{3}x + 3$ **39.** $y = -\frac{3}{2}x - 2$

Write the slope–intercept equation for the line with the given slope that contains the given point.

40. $m = 2; (5, 7)$ **41.** $m = \frac{7}{4}; (4, -2)$

42. $m = -3; (1, -5)$

Write the slope–intercept equation for the line containing the given pair of points.

43. $(1, 5)$ and $(4, 2)$

44. $(-3, 1)$ and $(3, 5)$

45. $(5, 0)$ and $(0, -2)$

46. Graph the line with slope $\frac{4}{3}$ that passes through the point $(1, 2)$.

Find the equation of the lines below:

47.

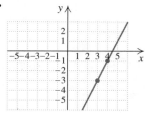

48.

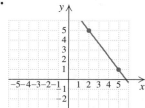

Applications of Linear Equations

In this chapter we show several in depth applications of linear equations and linear functions. We use the skills learned in Chapter 4 to gain insight into these applications. In particular we focus on the meaning of slope and y-intercept in these applications.

 **Linear Models**

Cost Functions

The total daily cost of production for a number of items depends on many things. It depends on the number of items produced and it depends on other costs that are not directly related to the number of items produced. These two kinds of costs are often referred to as **variable costs** and **fixed costs**. Thus

$$\text{Total Daily Cost} = \text{Variable Cost} + \text{Fixed Cost}$$

Notes

Consider the following example.

EXAMPLE 1

Fixed cost of operation of **$100/day**

Each item costs **$2** to produce

x = number of items produced

$C(x)$ = Total Daily Cost of Producing x items

= Variable Cost + Fixed Cost

= 2x + 100

So the cost function is this example is

$$C(x) = 2x + 100$$

Note that:

Slope = 2

Y-int. = 100

The cost of producing 0 items is

$$C(0) = 2 \cdot 0 + 100 = 100$$

The cost of producing 400 items is

$$C(400) = 2 \cdot 400 + 100 = 900$$

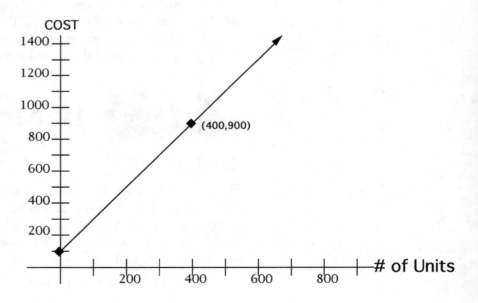

Using the TI-83, we enter this cost function in the **Y=** editor and select the **WINDOW** values to obtain a graph similar to the one above.

Pressing **GRAPH** and then **TRACE** and making selections of X = 0 and X = 400 finds the points (0,200) and (400,900) on the graph.

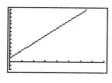 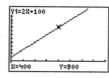

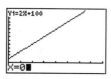 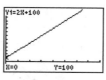

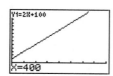 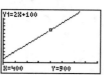

We can also use the **TBLSET** and **TABLE** features to get numerical information about our Cost function.

Notes

EXAMPLE 2

Fixed cost of operation of **$300/day**

Each item costs **$2** to produce

And so the cost function is

$$C(x) = 2x + 300$$

Slope = 2   Y-int. = 300

The cost of producing 0 items is

$$C(0) = 2 \cdot 0 + 300 = 300$$

The cost of producing 400 items is

$$C(400) = 2 \cdot 400 + 300 = 1100$$

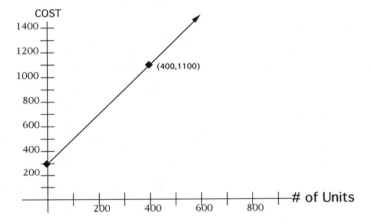

With the TI-83

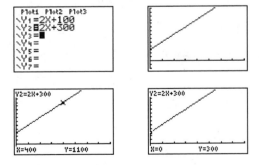

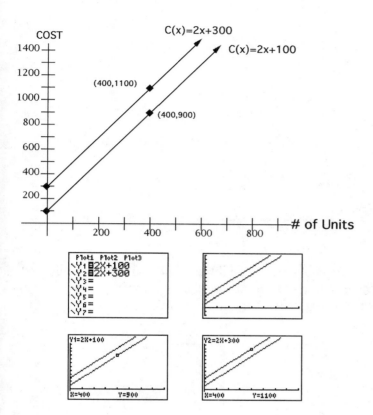

EXAMPLE 3

Fixed cost of operation of **$700/day**

Each item costs **$1** to produce

And so the cost function is

$$C(x) = x + 700$$

Slope = 1   Y-int. = 700

The cost of producing 0 items is

$$C(0) = 0 + 700 = 700$$

The cost of producing 400 items is

$$C(400) = 400 + 700 = 1100$$

Notes

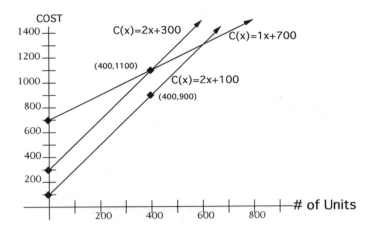

Using the TI-83 we can generate all three graphs on the same window. Pressing **TRACE** and repeatedly using the up arrow (or down arrow) will allow us to trace on any of the three graphs.

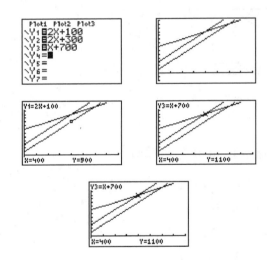

General Linear Cost Function:

$$C(x) = mx + b$$

where

$$m = \text{slope} = \text{per unit cost}$$
$$b = \text{y-int.} = \text{fixed cost}$$

Linear Depreciation

Consider the relationship between the value of a product and the age of the product. If this relationship is linear, and we know the value when the product is purchased and the length of time it takes to depreciate, then we can determine the linear equation relating these variables using the techniques in the previous chapter.

EXAMPLE 4

A \$3000 computer is depreciated linearly over 3 years. Find the equation that describes the value of the computer as a function of the age of the computer.

$$\mathbf{x} = \textbf{age of computer} \qquad \mathbf{V(x)} = \textbf{value at x years of age}$$

The information on the price of the computer and the length of time that it takes to depreciate, gives us two points on the graph of the depreciation line. Specifically, the points (0,3000) and (3,0) are on the depreciation line.

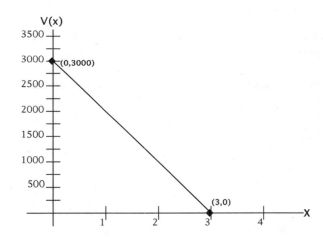

To find the equation of this line, we need to find the equation of the line passing through (0,3000) and (3,0). We compute the slope by formula, and we notice the y-intercept is 3000.

$$m = \frac{0 - 3000}{3 - 0} = \frac{-3000}{3} = -1000 \qquad b = 3000$$

Thus the equation is

$$V(x) = -1000x + 3000$$

Recall that the slope represents the rise/run or the change in y over the change in x. More specifically in this example:

$$m = \frac{-1000}{1} = \frac{\text{decrease of \$1,000 in value}}{\text{increase of 1 year}} = \text{annual depreciation}$$

Notes

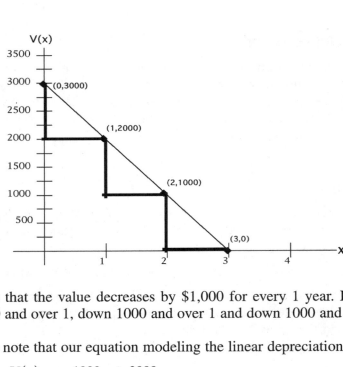

Note that the value decreases by $1,000 for every 1 year. It's down 1000 and over 1, down 1000 and over 1 and down 1000 and over 1.

Also note that our equation modeling the linear depreciation

$$V(x) = -1000x + 3000$$

is only valid for $0 \leq x \leq 3$, since the value does not continue to drop beyond year 3.

Another way to describe this relationship is with two conditional equations.

$$V(x) = \begin{cases} -1000x + 3000 & \text{if } 0 \leq x \leq 3 \\ 0 & \text{if } x \geq 3 \end{cases}$$

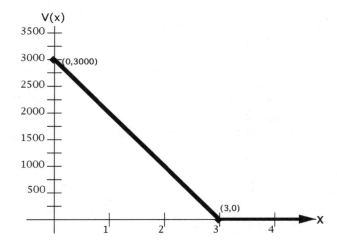

Sometimes the item does not depreciate to 0 but rather to a scrap value, which is maintained forever.

EXAMPLE 5

A $20,000 car depreciates linearly to a scrap value of $500 during a 10 year period. Find the equation (or equations) that describes the relationship between the value of the car and the age of the car. In addition, find the value at 4 years and at 12 years.

First we identify our variables

$$t = \textbf{age of car (yrs.)} \qquad V(t) = \textbf{value of car at t yrs.}$$

Using the information in the problem we plot the points (0,20000) and (10,500). Sketch the line segment between those two points and then sketch a horizontal line representing the scrap value.

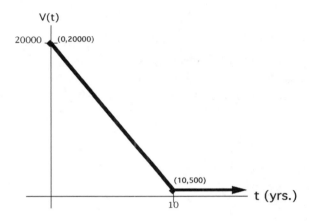

To find the equation of the line segment between (0,20000) and (10,150), we determine the slope and y-intercept.

$$m = \frac{500 - 20000}{10 - 0} = \frac{-19500}{10} = -1950 \qquad b = 20000$$

If $t \geq 10$ then the value is 500. All of these results give us the two conditional equations that model our situation.

$$V(t) = \begin{cases} -1950t + 20000 & \text{if } 0 \leq t \leq 10 \\ 500 & \text{if } t \geq 10 \end{cases}$$

After 4 years $V(4) = -1950(4) + 20000 = 12,200$
After 12 years $V(12) = 500$

Notes

In general, if

t = **age in years**

and

$V(t)$ = **value at t years of age**

then

$V(t) = mt + b$

where

m = **annual depreciation**

and

b = **original value**

Once again, notice the importance of the slope and the y-intercept in these models. In the linear depreciation models, the slope represents the annual depreciation and the y-intercept is the original value.

Try the following two examples

EXAMPLE 6

Your company purchases $900,000 of equipment that depreciates linearly over 5 years (to a value of $0). Find the equation (or equations) that describes the relationship between the value of the equipment and the age of the equipment. Sketch a graph of this function. In addition, find the value at 3 years and at 9 years.

Answers:
Example 6:

$$V(t) = \begin{cases} -180{,}000t + 900{,}000 & \text{if } 0 \le t \le 5 \\ 0 & \text{if } t \ge 5 \end{cases}$$

$$V(3) = 360{,}000 \qquad V(9) = 0$$

EXAMPLE 7

Do Example 6 with the following change. The equipment depreciates linearly to a scrap value of $100,000 over 5 years. Find the equation (or equations) that describes the relationship between the value of the equipment and the age of the equipment. Sketch a graph of this function. In addition, find the value at 3 years and at 9 years.

Answers:
Example 7:

$$V(t) = \begin{cases} -160{,}000t + 900{,}000 & \text{if } 0 \leq t \leq 5 \\ 100{,}000 & \text{if } t \geq 5 \end{cases}$$

$$V(3) = 420{,}000 \qquad V(9) = 100{,}000$$

Tax Rates

Tax law can be complicated. For a variety of reasons some taxation systems apply different tax rates for different income levels. Most taxation systems can be modeled by a linear equation or by a set of conditional linear equations. Consider the following example

EXAMPLE 8

Single filers in the country Z pay taxes following these rules:

15% of the **first $25,000 of** *taxable income*, and

28% of the **next $75,000 of** *taxable income*, and

36% of the **next $100,000 of** *taxable income*, and

40% of the *taxable income* **exceeding $200,000.**

How can we express this tax rule in an equation (or equations)?

Let

$$x = \text{taxable income}$$
$$T(x) = \text{total taxes on taxable income of } \$x$$

Let's consider a few specific calculations. Suppose a person has taxable income of $20,000. Then the total taxes will be

$$T(20,000) = .15 \cdot 20,000 = 3,000$$

Similarly the total taxes for taxable income of $22,000 will be

$$T(22,000) = .15 \cdot 22,000 = 3,300$$

So if the taxable income is x (and $0 \le x \le 25,000$), then

$$T(x) = .15x$$

Suppose a person has taxable income of $50,000. The first $25,000 is taxed at 15% and the remaining $25,000 is taxed at 28%.

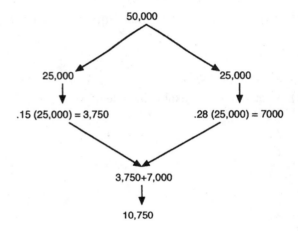

So $T(50,000) = 10,750$.

Using a similar approach we can find that

$$T(52,000) = .15 \cdot 25,000 + .28 \cdot 27,000$$
$$= 3,750 + 7560$$
$$= 11,310$$

Thus, if the taxable income is x (and $25,000 \le x \le 100,000$) then

$$T(x) = .15(25,000) + .28(x - 25,000)$$

Suppose a person has taxable income of \$150,000. The first \$25,000 is taxed at 15% and the next \$75,000 is taxed at 28%, and the remaining \$50,000 is taxed at 36%.

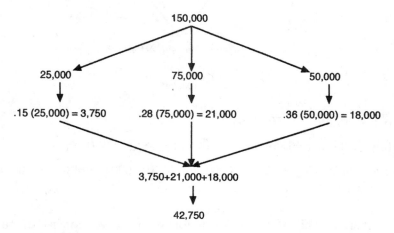

So $T(150,000) = 42,750$.

Using a similar approach we can find that

$$T(180,000) = .15 \cdot 25,000 + .28 \cdot 75,000 + .36 \cdot 80,000$$
$$= 3,750 + 21,000 + 28,800$$
$$= 53,550$$

Thus, if the taxable income is x (and $100,000 \le x \le 200,000$) then

$$T(x) = .15(25,000) + .28(75,000) + .36(x - 100,000)$$

Notes

Suppose a person has taxable income of $300,000. The first $25,000 is taxed at 15%, the next $75,000 is taxed at 28%, the next $100,000 is taxed at 36% and the remaining $100,000 is taxed at 40%.

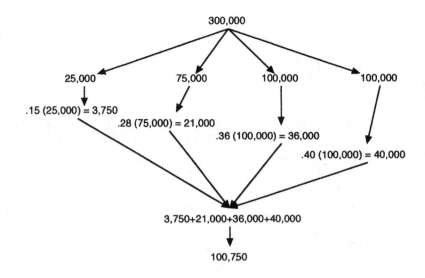

So T(300,000) = 100,750.

Thus, if the taxable income is x (and x ≥ 200,000) then

$$T(x) = .15(25,000) + .28(75,000) + .36(100,000) + .48(x - 200,000)$$

Summarizing all of this information we have version #1 of our tax function

#1

$$T(x) = \begin{cases} .15x & \text{if } 0 \le x \le 25,000 \\ .15(25,000) + .28(x - 25,000) & \text{if } 25,000 \le x \le 100,000 \\ .15(25,000) + .28(75,000) + .36(x - 100,000) & \text{if } 100,000 \le x \le 200,000 \\ .15(25,000) + .28(75,000) + .36(100,000) \\ +.40(x - 200,000) & \text{if } x \ge 200,000 \end{cases}$$

We simplify arithmetically we get version #2

#2

$$T(x) = \begin{cases} .15x & \text{if } x \le 25,000 \\ 3,750 + .28(x - 25,000) & \text{if } 25,000 \le x \le 100,000 \\ 24,750 + .36(x - 100,000) & \text{if } 100,000 \le x \le 200,000 \\ 60,750 + .40(x - 200,000) & \text{if } x \ge 200,000 \end{cases}$$

As an example of how this works, if someone has at least $200,000 of taxable income, then they pay $60,750 plus 40% of taxable income above $200,000.

Using the distributive law we arrive at version #3

#3

$$T(x) = \begin{cases} .15x & \text{if } x \leq 25,000 \\ 3,750 + .28x - 7000 & \text{if } 25,000 \leq x \leq 100,000 \\ 24,750 + .36x - 36,000 & \text{if } 100,000 \leq x \leq 200,000 \\ 60,750 + .40x - 80,000 & \text{if } x \geq 200,000 \end{cases}$$

And finally, if we collect like terms we get the most efficient version of our tax function.

#4

$$T(x) = \begin{cases} .15x & \text{if } x \leq 25,000 \\ .28x - 3250 & \text{if } 25,000 \leq x \leq 100,000 \\ .36x - 11,250 & \text{if } 100,000 \leq x \leq 200,000 \\ .40x - 19,250 & \text{if } x \geq 200,000 \end{cases}$$

Using version #4 of the Tax function, find the tax for someone that has taxable income of

   a. $20,000

   b. $50,000

   c. $150,000

   d. $300,000

Answers:

a. $T(20,000) = .15 \cdot 20,000 = 3,000$

b. $T(50,000) = .28 \cdot 50,000 - 3,250 = 10,750$

c. $T(150,000) = .36 \cdot 150,000 - 11,250 = 42,750$

d. $T(300,000) = .40 \cdot 300,000 - 19,250 = 100,750$

Notice how much simpler this was than doing the calculations using versions #1, #2, or #3, or by our previous approach.

Each of our four conditional equations in our final version of our tax function is of the form $y = mx + b$. When we graph this function it consists of four line segments pieced together.

$$T(x) = \begin{cases} .15x & \text{if } x \le 25{,}000 \\ .28x - 3250 & \text{if } 25{,}000 \le x \le 100{,}000 \\ .36x - 11{,}250 & \text{if } 100{,}000 \le x \le 200{,}000 \\ .40x - 19{,}250 & \text{if } x \ge 200{,}000 \end{cases}$$

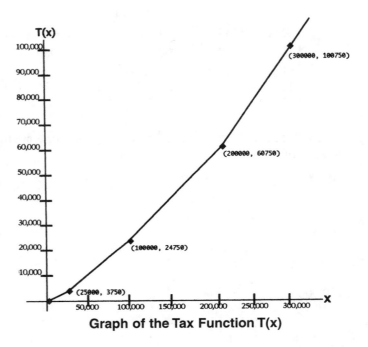

Graph of the Tax Function T(x)

5.2   Intersecting Lines

Intersecting lines lead us to some interesting applications. But first we need to understand the algebra of intersecting lines.

EXAMPLE 1

Find the point of intersection of the lines $y = 2x + 3$ and $y = x - 1$.

Graphically

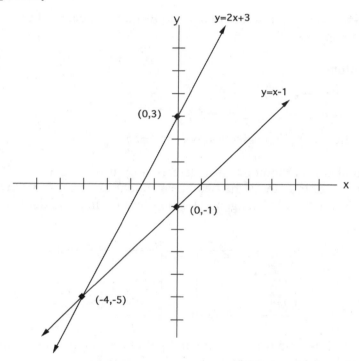

Recall that points on the line make the equation of that line true. Thus, the point of intersection has the unique property that it makes both equations true at the same time. It looks like $(-4, -5)$ is the point of intersection for our two lines. We can verify this by substituting $x = -4$ and $y = -5$ into both equations and showing that both equations are true.

$$y = 2x + 3 \qquad\qquad\qquad y = x - 1$$
$$-5 = 2(-4) + 3 = -8 + 3 = -5 \qquad -5 = -4 - 1 = -5$$
$$\text{TRUE} \qquad\qquad\qquad\qquad \text{TRUE}$$

So one approach to finding the point of intersection is to graph both lines, as we did above. However this approach is limited in several ways. First we have to be very precise in graphing both lines so we can get an accurate point of intersection. Second, if the point of intersection were something like $(-3.87, -4.08)$, it would be virtually impossible to graph the lines accurately enough to see this answer. So we need another approach.

Notes

How can we algebraically find the point of intersection?

We want to find the x value that gives us equal y's in our two equations. To make that happen, we let the y's equal each other and solve for x.

$$\left.\begin{array}{l} y = 2x + 3 \\ y = x - 1 \end{array}\right\} \quad \Rightarrow \quad 2x + 3 = x - 1$$

$$2x + 3 - 3 = x - 1 - 3$$
$$2x = x - 4$$
$$2x - x = x - x - 4$$
$$x = -4$$

So $x = -4$ will cause the two y's to be equal to each other. Let's see if that happens.

Substitute:

$$y = -4 - 1 = -5$$
$$y = 2(-4) + 3 = -5$$

Thus the point of intersection is $(-4, -5)$.

We can also find the point of intersection by using the TI-83. First use the **Y=** editor to enter in the two linear functions. Press **ZOOM** and selecting 6:ZStandard. This generates both graphs in a standard window

 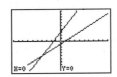

We could use the trace feature and get close to the point of intersection and get an approximation of what it might be.

But this answer is not exact. We can get an exact answer by pressing

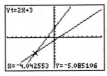

2nd then **TRACE** (this is the **CALC** key) and then selecting **5:intersect**.

The calculator asks if this is the first curve. Simply press **ENTER**. The calculator then asks if this is the second curve. Again simply press **ENTER**.

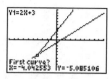
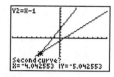

The calculator then asks for a guess. Move the cursor close to where you see the intersection and then press **ENTER**.

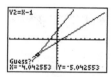
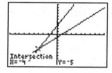

Voila! Your intersection occurs at $(-4, -5)$.

Note that for the calculator to find the point of intersection, the lines must cross in the window being used.

Notes

EXAMPLE 2

Find the point of intersection of the lines:

$$y = 2x + 3$$
$$y = 2x - 1$$

$$\left.\begin{array}{l} y = 2x + 3 \\ y = 2x - 1 \end{array}\right\} \quad \Rightarrow \quad 2x + 3 = 2x - 1$$

$$2x + 3 - 3 = 2x - 1 - 3$$
$$2x = 2x - 4$$
$$2x - 2x = 2x - 2x - 4$$
$$0 = -4 \quad ???$$

This means that there is no point of intersection!

Graphically,

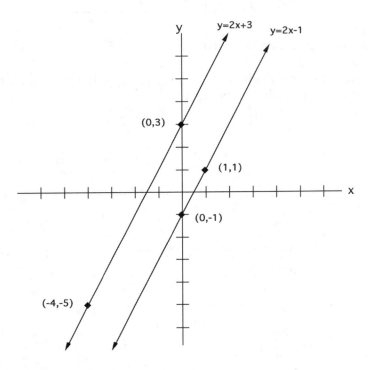

No points of intersection ⇔ lines are parallel

Here's what happens on the TI-83.

 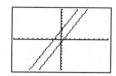

 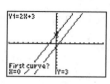

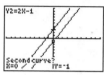 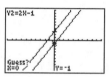

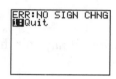

Which is the TI-83's way of saying no point of intersection.

Given two lines there are three possibilities.

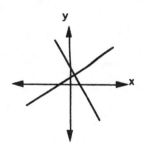

**Intersecting Lines
Slopes Different**

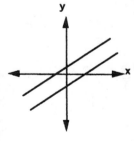

**Parallel Lines
Slopes Same
Y-Intercepts Different**

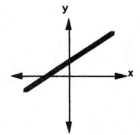

**Coincident Lines
Slopes Same
Y-Intercepts Same**

Notes

Try the following two examples.

EXAMPLE 3

Find the point of intersection (if any) for the following two lines:

$$y = 3x - 7$$
$$y = -2x + 3$$

EXAMPLE 4

Find the point of intersection (if any) for the following two lines:

$$y = 6x$$
$$y = 6x - 5$$

Answers:
Example 3: $(2, -1)$
Example 4: no solution-parallel lines

5.3   **Break-Even Analysis**

Let

  x = number of units produced and sold

  R(x) = total revenue from the sale of x units

  C(x) = total cost for producing x units

We are interested in finding when total revenue equals total cost. The value of x that makes that happen is called the break even value. If R(x) and C(x) are linear functions then we want to find the point of intersection. At the point, for that x value, the total revenue R(x) equals the total cost C(x).

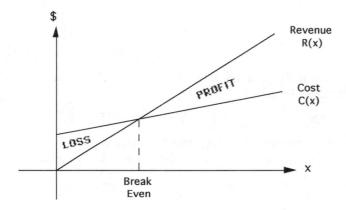

Notes

EXAMPLE 1

Suppose that the fixed cost is $300, the cost for each unit is $1.75 and the selling price is $2.50. How many items need to be sold and produced to break even?

Let

$$x = \text{number of units produced and sold}$$
$$R(x) = 2.50x$$
$$C(x) = 1.75x + 300$$

Set $R(x)$ equal to $C(x)$ and solve for x.

$$R(x) = C(x) \implies 2.50x = 1.75x + 300$$
$$\underline{-1.75x \quad -1.75x}$$
$$.75x = 300$$
$$\frac{.75x}{.75} = \frac{300}{.75}$$
$$x = 400$$

Check to see if the total revenue of 400 items and the total cost for 400 items is indeed equal.

$$R(400) = 2.50(400) = 1000 \quad C(400) = 1.75(400) + 300 = 1000$$

We can present this result by graphing the revenue line and the cost line, showing the point of intersection or break even point.

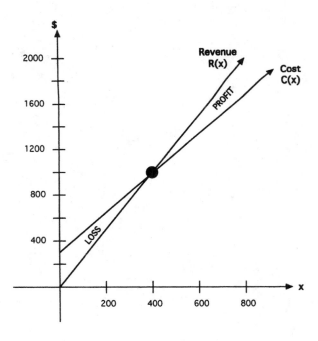

LOSS if x < 400
PROFIT if x > 400
BREAK EVEN if x = 400

Let's try this on the TI-83. First enter the revenue and cost functions in **Y1** and **Y2** in your **Y=** editor. Then press **GRAPH**.

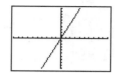

Note that only one graph appeared in the window. Where did the graph of $Y_2 = 1.75X + 300$ go? It's a WINDOW problem! Our standard window provides a snapshot of the graph, but only for

$$-10 \leq X \leq 10 \text{ and } -10 \leq Y \leq 10$$

Our first graph passes through this window but the 2nd graph does not. We can pick a better window by pressing **WINDOW** and selecting the range of values for X and then pressing **ZOOM** and selecting 0:ZoomFit.

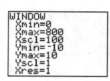

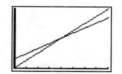

Notes

We may want to change the Yscl so that we can see the scale. Select WINDOW and change the Yscl to 100.

Then press **GRAPH**.

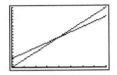

Press **2nd** and **TRACE** (**CALC** key) and select **5:intersect** and proceed as before.

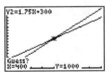

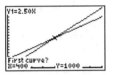

 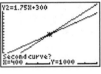

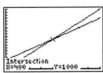

Thus our point of intersection is (400,1000). Our Break-Even point is X = 400 units with a Cost and Revenue equal to $1000.

Try the following example.

EXAMPLE 2A

The item you produce costs $12 for each additional item plus a fixed overhead of $24,000. The item is sold for $72. Find the break even value.

EXAMPLE 2B

If you were to change the price to $37, then find the break even value.

Profit Function P(x)

Let

$$x = \text{number of units produced and sold}$$
$$R(x) = \text{total revenue from the sale of x units}$$
$$C(x) = \text{total cost for producing x units}$$
$$P(x) = \text{profit from sale and production of x units}$$

The profit function $P(x)$ is obtained as follows:

$$P(x) = R(x) - C(x)$$

and can be described graphically below:

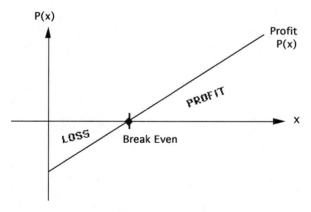

Break Even occurs when $P(x) = 0$

Answer:
Example 2a: 400
Example 2b: 960

Notes

This gives us another way to approach break even analysis. We want to find x so that the profit $P(x) = 0$. The way we proceed is to let $P(x) = 0$ and then solve the equation for x.

Returning to example 1 we determine the profit function

$$P(x) = R(x) - C(x)$$
$$= 2.50x - (1.75x + 300)$$
$$= 2.50x - 1.75x - 300$$
$$= .75x - 300$$
$$P(x) = .75x - 300$$

To find the break even point you set $P(x) = 0$ and solve for x.

$$P(x) = 0 \Rightarrow \quad .75x - 300 = 0$$
$$+300 \quad +300$$
$$.75x = 300$$
$$\frac{.75x}{.75} = \frac{300}{.75}$$
$$x = 400$$

Try this approach with Example 2 (both parts).

One of the advantages of the profit function approach is that it allows us to solve some additional, interesting problems in the same way as the break even problem.

EXAMPLE 3

Consider the information from Example 1. How many units would need to be produced and sold in order to have a profit of $1200.

The approach here is to set $P(x) = 1200$ and solve for x. In other words you are finding the value of x (number of items) that generates a profit of $1200.

$$P(x) = 1200 \implies .75x - 300 = 1200$$
$$+300 \quad +300$$
$$.75x = 1500$$
$$\frac{.75x}{.75} = \frac{1500}{.75}$$
$$x = 2000$$

Thus, 2000 units would need to be produced and sold for a profit of $1200.

EXAMPLE 4

Look back at Example 2 and find the number of units needed to generate a profit of $100,000 in both cases of this example.

Answers:
Example 4: approx. 2067, 4960

Notes

We can also solve this problem with the aid of the TI-83. First turn off **Y1** and **Y2**. Then enter in $Y_1 - Y_2$ for **Y3**. Here's how that's done. Once you're in the **Y=** editor move the cursor to **Y3**. Press **VARS** select **Y-VARS** and select **1:Function** and then **1:Y1**.

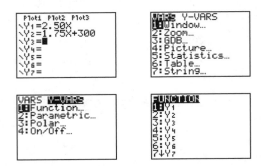

Thus, we have pasted **Y1** into the **Y=** editor. Now press − and go thru the **VARS**, **Y-VARS**, **1:Function**, but now select **2:Y2**.

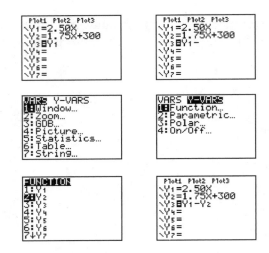

Now enter 1200 for Y4. If we try graphing at this point we will have an improper window to see the intersection of these graphs

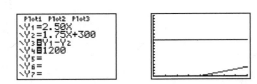

Notes

To get a better idea of what the window might be we use **TABLE**.

Scroll down the table until we see how large **X** has to be so that **Y3** and **Y4** are the same (or close to it).

Note: WE LUCKED OUT! The two lines cross at (2000,1200). We can adjust our window appropriately and then follow up with pressing **CALC** and selecting intersect and proceeding as before.

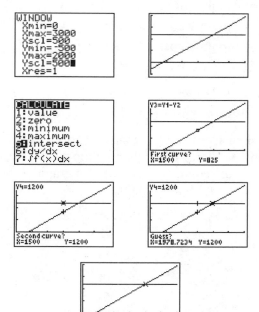

There's the graphical solution at (2000, 1200). Thus, 2000 units would need to be produced and sold for a profit of $1200.

Notes

5.4   Other Linear Models

We can apply the techniques of break even analysis to a wider range of problems. In particular when comparing cost functions to find the better deal, one considers finding when the cost functions are equal and proceed from there. Let's take a look an example of this.

EXAMPLE 1
Phone Service

Phone Company A charges $20 per month plus $.25 per long distance call, while Phone Company B charges $30 per month plus $.20 per long distance call. **Which one is the better deal?**

The correct answer here is that **it depends!** It depends on how many long distance calls you make each month.

Let

$$x = \text{number of long distance calls}$$
$$C_A(x) = \text{monthly cost for Company A}$$
$$C_B(x) = \text{monthly cost for Company B}$$

Note:

$$C_A(x) = 20 + .25x$$
$$C_B(x) = 30 + .20x$$

To find out when Company A charges more than Company B and when Company A charges less than Company B, we first determine when the charges are equal. We then draw a graph of the two cost lines and give the answer to this problem.

$$
\begin{aligned}
C_A(x) = C_B(x) \Rightarrow \quad 20 + .25x &= 30 + .20x \\
-20 \quad &\quad -20 \\
.25x &= 10 + .20x \\
-.20x \quad &\quad -.20x \\
.05x &= 10 \\
\frac{.05x}{.05} &= \frac{10}{.05} \\
x &= 200 \text{ calls}
\end{aligned}
$$

Check: $C_A(200) = 20 + .25(200) = \$70$ $C_B(200) = 30 + .20(200) = \$70$

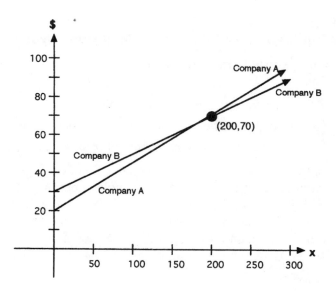

If x > 200 calls then choose Company B

If x < 200 calls then choose Company A

X = 200 is the decision point

Using the TI-83, we define **Y1** and **Y2**, select the **WINDOW** as shown below.

Press **GRAPH** and then go thru the procedure for finding the intersection.

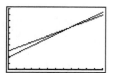 

Thus the intersection is (200,70). This means at 200 calls both Company A and Company B cost $70 per month.

Notes

EXAMPLE 2
Market Equilibrium and the Law of Supply and Demand

In economics we study the relationship between supply and demand. If we define

p = market price of the commodity

$S(p)$ = supply of the commodity at price p

$D(p)$ = demand of the commodity at price p

If the supply function $S(p)$ and the demand function $D(p)$ are linear, then we would expect the graph of the supply function to have a positive slope (higher price, higher supply, and lower price, lower supply) and the graph of the demand function to have a negative slope (higher price, lower demand, and lower price, higher demand).

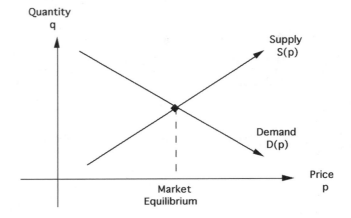

If pure competition is present, then a commodity will tend to be sold at the equilibrium price. Market equilibrium occurs at the intersection of the demand line with the supply line.

EXAMPLE 3
Theater Problem

Adults are charged $4 for admission to a discount movie theater, while children are charged $2.50. Over the past weekend, this theater collected $29,000 from 11,000 patrons. **How many patrons were adults? How many were children?**

We note that there are two unknowns:

x = number of adults

y = number of children

and there are two conditions, one for the total number of people attending, and one for the total amount of money collected.

Clearly $x + y = 11,000$ since the number of adults plus the number of children equals the the total number of patrons.

Since the amount of money due to the adults attending would be $4x$ and the amount of money due to the children attending would be $2.50y$, then the total would be $4x + 2.5y = 29,000$.

Thus we have the following two equations that must be true simultaneously

$$x + y = 11,000$$
$$4x + 2.5y = 29,000$$

These are two linear equations and will have a solution if there is a point of intersection. Let's find this point algebraically, by first writing each equation in slope-intercept form.

$$x + y = 11,000 \qquad 4x + 2.5y = 29,000$$
$$\Downarrow \qquad\qquad\qquad \Downarrow$$
$$y = -x + 11,000 \qquad y = -1.6x + 11,600$$

We set the y's equal to each other and solve for x, and substitute to find y.

$$\left. \begin{array}{l} y = -x + 11,000 \\ y = -1.6x + 11,600 \end{array} \right\} \implies -x + 11,000 = -1.6x + 11,600$$

$$-x + 11,000 = -1.6x + 11,600$$
$$-11,000 = -11,000$$
$$-x = -1.6x + 600$$
$$+1.6x = +1.6x$$
$$.6x = 600$$
$$\frac{.6x}{.6} = \frac{600}{.6}$$
$$x = 1000$$
$$y = -1000 + 11,000 = 10,000$$

Notes

Thus $(1,000 , 10,000)$ is the point of intersection.

$$x = \textbf{1000 adults}$$

and

$$y = \textbf{10,000 children}$$

make both equations true simultaneously.

5.5 The Elimination Method

Let's consider another approach to solving this system of equations from the Theater Problem. This technique is called **Multiplication and Elimination** or just **Elimination** (for short). In doing the Theater Problem, we were fortunate that when putting both equations in slope intercept form that things went nicely (exact numerical values and no fractions). Let's try Elimination.

EXAMPLE 1

$$x + y = 11{,}000$$
$$4x + 2.5y = 29{,}000$$

Multiply both sides of the first equation by -4. This gives:

$$-4x - 4y = -44{,}000$$
$$4x + 2.5y = 29{,}000$$

Adding the left hand side (LHS) of each equation and the right hand side (RHS) of each equation we obtain

$$-1.5y = -15{,}000$$

and then solve for y

$$y = \frac{-15{,}000}{-1.5} = 10{,}000$$

Substituting this value of y back into the first equation and solving for x we obtain

$$x + 10{,}000 = 11{,}000$$
$$x = 1{,}000$$

Notes

EXAMPLE 2

Solve

$$-5x + 4y = 29$$
$$3x - y = -9$$

Multiplying both sides of the second equation by 4 we will then add the equations and eliminate y, and solve for x.

$$-5x + 4y = 29$$
$$12x - 4y = -36$$
$$7x = -7$$
$$x = -1$$

Substituting this value of x back into the second of our original equations we then solve for y

$$3x - y = -9$$
$$3(-1) - y = -9$$
$$-3 - y = -9$$
$$-y = -6$$
$$y = 6$$

Thus our solution is

$$x = -1 \text{ and } y = 6$$

EXAMPLE 3

Solve

$$3x - 5y = 6$$
$$2x + 7y = 4$$

In this case multiply the first equation by 2 and the second equation by -3. This will allow us to eliminate the x's. What would we have done to eliminate the y's if that had been our choice?

$$6x - 10y = 12$$
$$-6x - 21y = -12$$

Adding the equations we obtain

$$-31y = 0$$

and thus

$$y = 0$$

Substituting this y value back into the original first equation and solving for x we obtain

$$3x - 5y = 6$$
$$3x - 5 \cdot 0 = 6$$
$$3x = 6$$
$$x = 2$$

Thus our final solution is

$$x = 2 \text{ and } y = 0$$

Try the following examples.

EXAMPLE 4

Redo Example 3 above by eliminating the y's.

Answers:
Example 4: (2, 0)

Notes

EXAMPLE 5

Solve the following equations by Elimination.

$$3x + 5y = 7$$
$$x - 7y = 11$$

EXAMPLE 6

Solve the following equations by Elimination.

$$2x - 3y = -21$$
$$-5x + 4y = 35$$

Answers:
Example 5: $(4, -1)$
Example 6: $(-3, 5)$

Chapter 5 Exercise Set

1. *Cost of a Telephone Call.*   The following graph shows data from a recent AT&T phone call between Burlington, VT, and Austin, TX. At what rate was the customer being billed?

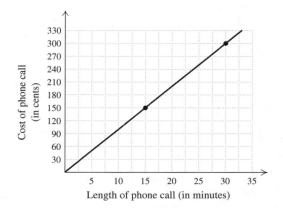

2. *Depreciation of an Office Machine.*   Data regarding the value of a particular color copier is represented in the following graph. At what rate is the value changing?

Notes

3. *Gas Mileage.*   The following graph shows data for a Honda Odyssey driven on interstate highways. At what rate was the vehicle consuming gas?

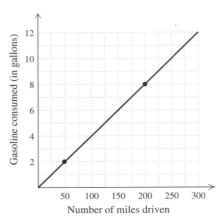

4. *Wages with Commissions.*   Each salesperson at Mike's Bikes is paid $140 a week plus 13% of all sales up to $2000, and then 20% on any sales in excess of $2000. Draw a graph in which sales are measured on the horizontal axis and wages on the vertical axis. Then use the graph to estimate the wages paid when a salesperson sells $2700 in merchandise in one week.

5. *Taxi Fares.*   The driver of a New York City Yellow Cab recently charged $2 plus 50¢ for each fifth of a mile traveled. Draw a graph that could be used to determine the cost of a fare.

Solve each system of equations by graphing. If there is no solution or an infinite number of solutions, state this.

6. $y = -2x + 5,$
$\quad y = -3x + 2$

7. $y = x - 2,$
$\quad y = x - 3$

8. $2x + y = 8,$
$\quad x - y = 7$

Solve each system using the substitution method. If a system has no solution or an infinite number of solutions, state this.

9. $y = x - 3,$
$\quad 3x + y = 5$

10. $y = 2x + 1,$
$\quad x + y = 4$

Solve using the elimination method. If a system has no solution or an infinite number of solutions, state this.

11. $x + y = 3,$
$\quad x - y = 7$

12. $\quad x + y = 6,$
$\quad -x + 2y = 15$

13. $-x - y = 8,$
$\quad 2x - y = -1$

14. $x + 3y = 19,$
$\quad x - y = -1$

15. $\quad 4x - 10y = 13,$
$\quad -2x + 5y = 8$

16. *Local Truck Rentals.*   Budget rents a 15-ft truck for $39.95 plus 79¢ per mile. Penske rents a 15-ft studio van for $49.95 plus 59¢ per mile (*Source*: Budget Truck Rental and Penske Truck Leasing, November 2003). For what mileage is the cost the same?

17. *Local Truck Rentals.* U-Haul rents a 17-ft truck for $29.95 plus 79¢ per mile. Penske rents a 15-ft studio van for $49.95 plus 59¢ per mile (*Source*: U-Haul International, Inc., and Penske Truck Leasing, November 2003). For what mileage is the cost the same?

18. *Phone Rates.* Recently, AT&T offered two long-distance calling plans. The One-Rate® 7¢ Plus Plan costs $4.95 per month plus 7¢ a minute. Another plan has no monthly fee, but costs 10¢ a minute (*Source*: www.consumer.att.com). For what number of minutes will the two plans cost the same?

In Exercises 19 and 20, find a linear cost function, using the given information.

19. With fixed costs of $4000, 20 items cost a total of $10,000.

20. With a slope of $25, 40 items cost a total of $4000.

In Exercise 21, use the given data to find a linear cost function that will give the total cost of producing x units of the item described.

21. Ten refrigerators cost $2000; 15 refrigerators cost $2700.

22. Enrollment Growth State University had an enrollment of 12,000 in 2000 and has experienced a growth of 600 students per year ever since.

(a) Find a linear function that gives the enrollment of State University for 2000 and beyond.

(b) Graph the function found in Exercise 22(a).

(c) State how the slope and y-intercept of your graph are related to enrollment.

(d) How many years will it take for State's enrollment to reach 20,000 at this rate?

23. Automobile Depreciation A new car initially costs $25,000 and loses value at the rate of $3000 each year.

(a) Write a linear function that gives the value of this car in terms of the years after its initial purchase.

(b) State how the slope and the y-intercept of the function found in Exercise 23(a) are related to the value of the car.

(c) How many years will it be before the value of the car will be $5000? $1500?

(d) Graph the function found in (a).

24. Sales Income Assume that you are offered a job paying $1500 per month plus 4% of gross sales.

(a) Find a linear function that will give your monthly income in terms of sales.

(b) Graph the function found in (a).

(c) If you make sales of $20,000 during a given month, what will your income be for that month?

(d) If you make sales of $10,000 at some point during the month, how much additional income will you gain if you make another sale for $1?

(e) What dollar amount in sales will yield a monthly income of $3000?

25. **Depreciating a Building** A building is purchased for $100,000 and is to be totally depreciated by the straight-line method over a 20-year period. (Assume no salvage value.)

(a) What is the amount to be depreciated each year?

(b) Find a linear function that expresses the book value of the building as a function of years from the date of purchase of the building.

(c) Graph the function found in (b).

26. **Depreciating a Machine** A particular machine costs $80,000 when purchased new and has a salvage value of $10,000 20 years later. Straight-line depreciation is applied to the net value of the machine over a 20-year period.

(a) How much is depreciated each year?

(b) Write a linear function that represents the book value of the machine during its lifetime.

(c) Graph the function found in (b).

27. **Depreciating a Building** An apartment building is bought for $550,000, of which $50,000 is estimated to be the cost of the land. The total cost minus the cost of the land is to be depreciated by the straight-line method over a period of 25 years.

(a) How much is depreciated each year?

(b) Write a linear function that represents the book value of the building during the 25-year period.

(c) Graph the function found in (b).

In each of Exercises 28 and 29, do the following:
(a) Find the break-even quantity.
(b) Find the break-even point.
(c) Graph R(x) and C(x) on the same set of axes.

28. $R(x) = 50x$ 29. $R(x) = 20x$
     $C(x) = 20x + 900$ $C(x) = 10x + 2500$

In each of Exercises 30 and 31, do the following:
(a) Find the break-even quantity.
(b) Find the break-even point.
(c) Find the profit function.
(d) Graph the revenue, cost, and profit functions on the same set of axes.

30. $R(x) = 3x$ 31. $R(x) = 20x$
     $C(x) = 2x + 12$ $C(x) = 12x + 490$

32. Revenue and Costs The Good CD Shop sells only CD's for stereo systems. The shop has a monthly overhead of $8000 (fixed costs) and an average direct cost of $8.36 per CD. Each CD sells for an average of $10.80. Let x be the number of CD's sold each month.

(a) If x CD's are sold during the month, find linear functions for the cost, revenue, and profit.

(b) Find the number of CD's that must be sold each month in order to break even.

(c) Graph $C(x)$, $R(x)$, and $P(x)$ on the same set of axes.

(d) If 800 CD's are sold during the month, will a profit or a loss be incurred? What if 2000 are sold?

33. Buying and Renting A car rental firm buys a new car for $20,000 and estimates the cost for maintenance, taxes, insurance, and depreciation at 40 cents per mile. The firm charges $50 per day plus 50 cents per mile to rent the car. Let x be the number of miles the car is rented during the first year, and assume that the car is rented for 160 days.

(a) What is the cost function for owning and renting the car, in terms of x?

(b) What is the revenue function in terms of x?

(c) How many miles must the car be driven in order for the company to break even during the first year?

(d) Graph the cost and revenue functions on the same set of axes for $0 \le x \le 150,000$ during the first year.

34. Printing Costs The High Point Printing Company has two methods of printing the orders it receives. One is a computer method, which costs $300 to set up and then costs $25 to print 1000 copies. The other is an offset process, which costs $500 to set up and then costs $20 to print 1000 copies.

(a) Let x be the number to be printed in thousands. Find the linear cost function for each of the two methods.

(b) Graph both functions on the same set of axes.

(c) Find the quantity for which the costs are the same.

(d) Assuming equal quality, which method would be most advantageous for the company to use to print an order of 30,000 copies? Of 70,000 copies?

For problems 35–37, we are given that x = the number of items produced and sold, $R(x)$ is the total revenue for sale of x items, $C(x)$ is the total cost for production of x items and $P(x)$ is the total profit from production and sale of x items.

35. If $R(x) = 40x$ and $C(x) = 25x + 6000$, then

(a) find $P(x)$

(b) determine how many items need to be produced and sold to obtain a profit of $28,500

36. If we sell items for $12 an item, while the total cost is $2400 plus $2 per item.

   (a) find $P(x)$

   (b) determine how many items need to be produced and sold to obtain a profit of $172,600

37. If we sell items for $43 an item, while the total cost is $12,000 plus $13 per item.

   (a) find $P(x)$

   (b) determine how many items need to be produced and sold to obtain a profit of $900,000.

Finance

6

6.1 Simple Interest

In section 2.2 we first encountered the formula for simple interest. In addition we also provide the formula for the simple amount.

$$I = \text{interest}$$
$$P = \text{principal (money invested or borrowed)}$$
$$R = \text{annual interest rate (decimal equivalent)}$$
$$T = \text{time (in years)}$$
$$A = \text{amount } (P + I)$$

$$I = P \cdot R \cdot T \qquad A = P(1 + R \cdot T)$$

We have four variables in each of these equations. Using our equation solving skills we can solve each equation for each of the variables thereby generating a total of four formulas for each of the equations.

$$I = P \cdot R \cdot T \qquad A = P(1 + R \cdot T)$$

$$P = \frac{I}{R \cdot T} \qquad P = \frac{A}{1 + R \cdot T}$$

$$R = \frac{I}{P \cdot T} \qquad R = \frac{A - P}{P \cdot T}$$

$$T = \frac{I}{P \cdot R} \qquad T = \frac{A - P}{P \cdot R}$$

EXAMPLE 1

You borrow $5,000 at 9% per year simple interest for 3 years. Find the interest and the amount due.

Note:

$$P = 5000 \qquad R = .09 \qquad T = 3$$

Substituting

$$I = PRT = 5000(.09)(3) = \$1,350$$
$$A = P + I = 5000 + 1350 = \$6,350$$

EXAMPLE 2

You borrow $5,000 at 9% per year simple interest for 10 months. Find the interest and the amount due.

$$P = 5000 \qquad R = .09 \qquad T = \frac{10}{12}$$

As compared to Example 1 the only difference is that the time is 10 months. Note that **does not mean T = 10** (that would we 10 years), rather T = 10/12 of a year.

$$I = PRT = 5000(.09)\left(\frac{10}{12}\right) = \$375$$
$$A = P + I = 5000 + 375 = \$5,375$$

EXAMPLE 3

How much would you need to invest at 8% simple interest for 4 years in order to obtain $20,000 in interest?

Note:

$$I = 20,000 \qquad P = ? \qquad R = .08 \qquad T = 4$$

We have two options for how to proceed. We may use the I = PRT formula and substitute the values of I, R, and T and solve for P. Or we may solve the equation for P first and then substitute and proceed with the calculation.

$$I = PRT \qquad\qquad P = \frac{I}{RT}$$

$$20,000 = P \cdot (.08)(4) \qquad P = \frac{20,000}{(.08) \cdot 4}$$

$$20,000 = P \cdot .32 \qquad\qquad P = \frac{20,000}{.32}$$

$$\frac{20,000}{.32} = \frac{P \cdot .32}{.32}$$

$$62,500 = P \qquad\qquad P = \$62,500$$

Which technique should you use? It is completely up to you and what you see as an easier approach.

EXAMPLE 4

What interest rate would be required to cause an investment of $25,000 to grow to an amount of $35,000 over 5 years?

Note:

$$A = 35,000 \quad P = 25,000 \quad R = ? \qquad T = 5$$

Substitute the values and solve for R:

$$A = P(1 + RT)$$
$$35,000 = 25,000(1 + R \cdot 5)$$
$$35,000 = 25,000 + 125,000R$$
$$-25,000 = -25,000$$
$$10,000 = 125,000R$$
$$\frac{10,000}{125,000} = \frac{125,000R}{125,000}$$
$$.08 = R$$

8% SIMPLE INTEREST RATE

Notes

Try the following examples.

EXAMPLE 5

How much would you need to invest at 4.25% simple interest for six years, in order to obtain $21,165 in interest.

EXAMPLE 6

If you invest $10,000 at 5% interest simple interest for 12 years, then find the interest and the amount.

EXAMPLE 7

Redo Example 4 by using the I = PRT formula. Hint: how are the amount, principal and interest related?

Answers:
Example 5: P = $83,000
Example 6: I = $6,000, A = $16,000
Example 7: R = .08

6.2 Compound Interest

Although simple interest is sometimes used in practice, the more prevalent method in financial calculations is compound interest. To illustrate how compound interest works, we will do an example with an investment of $P that is compounded quarterly at an annual rate **R**.

A_n = amount after n quarters (Future Value)

n = number of quarters

P = Principal (Present Value)

R = annual interest rate

$$i = \frac{R}{4}$$

We begin with an original amount of $A_0 = P$. For the first quarter (3 months) we simply apply simple interest. Thus at the end of the first quarter we have an amount $A_1 = P + PRT$. Since $T = 3/12 = 1/4$ we can simplify as

$$A_1 = P + PRT = P\left(1 + R \cdot \frac{1}{4}\right) = P(1 + i)$$

The amount after two quarters, A_2, is computed by applying simple interest to the new amount A_1, yielding $A_2 = P(1 + i)^2$. After three quarters the amount is after four quarters the amount is $A_4 = P(1 + i)^4$. The diagram below illustrates this pattern.

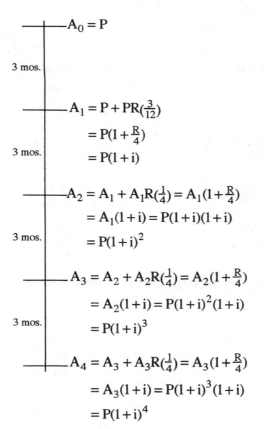

$A_0 = P$

3 mos.

$A_1 = P + PR(\frac{3}{12})$
$\quad = P(1 + \frac{R}{4})$
$\quad = P(1 + i)$

3 mos.

$A_2 = A_1 + A_1R(\frac{1}{4}) = A_1(1 + \frac{R}{4})$
$\quad = A_1(1 + i) = P(1 + i)(1 + i)$
$\quad = P(1 + i)^2$

3 mos.

$A_3 = A_2 + A_2R(\frac{1}{4}) = A_2(1 + \frac{R}{4})$
$\quad = A_2(1 + i) = P(1 + i)^2(1 + i)$
$\quad = P(1 + i)^3$

3 mos.

$A_4 = A_3 + A_3R(\frac{1}{4}) = A_3(1 + \frac{R}{4})$
$\quad = A_3(1 + i) = P(1 + i)^3(1 + i)$
$\quad = P(1 + i)^4$

In general, the **amount** after **n** quarters would be

$$A_n = P(1 + i)^n$$

where $i = {}^R/_4$.

What if the compounding was done monthly?

$$n = \text{number of months}$$
$$i = {}^R/_{12}$$
$$A_n = P(1 + i)^n$$

A_n is the amount after **n** months.

What if the compounding is done semiannually?

$$n = \text{number of semiannual periods}$$
$$i = {}^R/_2$$
$$A_n = P(1 + i)^n$$

A_n is the amount after **n** semiannual periods (6 month periods)

We summarize the simple and compound interest formulas below.

Simple Interest	**Compound Interest**
P = principal	P = Principal (Present Value)
R = annual interest rate (decimal equivalent)	R = annual interest rate (decimal equivalent)
T = time (years)	n = # of periods
	m = # of comp. periods per yr.
	$i = R/m$
I = interest	
A = amount (P + I)	A_n = amount after n periods (Future Value)
I = PRT	$A_n = P(1 + i)^n$
A = P(1 + RT)	

Let's apply the compound interest formula to several examples.

EXAMPLE 1

What is the future value of $25,000 invested at 8.6% compounded quarterly for 6 years?

The appropriate formula is:

$$A_n = P(1 + i)^n \quad \text{where} \quad i = {}^R/_m$$

Note:

$R = .086$

$m = 4$

$n = 24$

$i = {}^{.086}/_4 = .0215$

$P = 25000$

Using the formula and the TI-83 we find

$$A_{24} = 25000(1 + .0215)^{24} = 41,654.40$$

EXAMPLE 2

What is the amount of money required to generate a future value of $36,000 if the original amount is invested at 12% compounded semi-annually for 5 years?

The appropriate formula is:

$$P = \frac{A_n}{(1 + i)^n} \quad \text{where } i = {}^R/_m$$

Note:

$R = .12$

$m = 2$

$n = 10$

$i = {}^{.12}/_2 = .06$

$A_{10} = 36,000$

Substituting we get

$$P = \frac{A_n}{(1 + i)^n} = \frac{36,000}{(1 + .06)^{10}} = 20,102.21$$

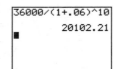

Notes

Using the FINANCE Features on the TI–83

We have used the calculator to do our computations for both simple and compound interest calculations, by implementing the appropriate formulas. However the TI-83 has a special set of financial features that we will begin to explore in this section. It is important to know that these features do not apply to simple interest calculations. Those need to be done by formula as in Section 6.1.

First set the calculator to two decimal places of accuracy by pressing **MODE** and making the the following choice.

Now press **APPS** and select **1:Finance** (for the TI-83 Plus) or **2nd** and x^{-1} (this is the **FINANCE** key) (for the TI-83). Select **CALC** and **1:TVM Solver.**

This gets us to the **T**ime **V**alue **M**oney Solver, which will be central to doing many different kinds of financial calculations.

Note:

$$\begin{aligned}
\mathbf{N} &= \text{total \# of payment periods} \\
\mathbf{I\%} &= \text{annual interest rate (as a \%)} \\
\mathbf{PV} &= \text{present value} \\
\mathbf{PMT} &= \text{payment amount} \\
\mathbf{FV} &= \text{future value} \\
\mathbf{P/Y} &= \text{\# of payment periods per year} \\
\mathbf{C/Y} &= \text{\# of compounding periods per year}
\end{aligned}$$

Let's try Example 1 and Example 2 with the aid of the TVM solver.

EXAMPLE 1

What is the future value of \$25,000 invested at 8.6% compounded quarterly for 6 years?

First we need to identify the values of the following variables:

N = 24	(6 years times 4 quarters per year)
I% = 8.6	(note this is entered as a %)
PV = −25000	(this is treated as a cash outflow)
PMT = 0	(there are no quarterly payments)
FV =	(this is our unknown)
P/Y = 4	(payments per year, note PMT = 0)
C/Y = 4	(compounding periods per year)

Now press **APPS** and select **1:Finance** (for the TI-83 Plus) or **2nd** and **x⁻¹** (this is the **FINANCE** key) (for the TI-83). Select **CALC** and **1:TVM Solver.** Enter the above information using the arrow keys.

Move the cursor to FV and solve for this value by pressing **ALPHA** (**GREEN** key) and **ENTER** (this is the **SOLVE** key).

Notice the small mark next to FV denoting that this is the quantity that we solved for. The other values were inputs.

Thus we have

$$FV = \$41,654.40$$

EXAMPLE 2

What is the amount of money required to generate a future value of $36,000 if the original amount is invested at 12% compounded semi-annually for 5 years?

First we need to identify the values of the following variables:

$N = 10$ (5 years times 2 periods per year)

$I\% = 12$ (note this is entered as a %)

$PV =$ (this is our unknown)

$PMT = 0$ (there are no payments)

$FV = 36000$ (this is treated as a cash inflow)

$P/Y = 2$ (payments per year, note PMT = 0)

$C/Y = 2$ (compounding periods per year)

Now press **APPS** and select **1:Finance** (for the TI-83 Plus) or **2nd** and **x⁻¹** (this is the **FINANCE** key) (for the TI-83). Select **CALC** and **1:TVM Solver.** Enter the above information using the arrow keys.

Move the cursor to PV and solve for this value by pressing **ALPHA** (**GREEN** key) and **ENTER** (this is the **SOLVE** key).

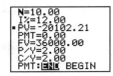

Thus our final result is:

$$PV = \$20,102.21$$

One of the significant advantages of using the TVM feature is that we may change inputs and solve again very quickly. For example in Example 2 if we changed the interest rate to 9.5%, then we would simply make that change and then solve for the present value.

The new present value is

$$PV = \$22,634.05$$

In Example 1 we solved for the Future Value, and in Example 2 we solved for the Present Value. Can we solve for other quantities like interest rate and time? We can, but this is more challenging if done by solving the formula

$$A_n = P\left(1 + \frac{R}{m}\right)^n$$

for R or for T (actually for n). Here are the three formulas that arise from the formula above.

$$P = \frac{A_n}{\left(1 + \dfrac{R}{m}\right)^n}$$

$$r = m\left[\left(\frac{A_n}{P}\right)^{1/n} - 1\right]$$

$$T = \frac{n}{m} = \frac{\left(\dfrac{\ln\left(A_n/P\right)}{\ln\left(1 + \frac{r}{m}\right)}\right)}{m}$$

While the top formula is not difficult to arrive at the second and third are beyond what would normally be expected of the average user of compound interest.

However, all of these problems (solving for Future Value, Present Value, Interest Rate, Time) on TVM solver are about the same degree of difficulty. Let's consider the interest rate problem.

Notes

EXAMPLE 3

At what annual interest rate, compounded quarterly, will an investment of $4,000 generate an amount of $10,000 in 10 years?

Using the TVM Solver we first note that

$N = 40$	(10 years times 4 periods per year)
$I\% =$	(this is our unknown)
$PV = -4000$	(this is treated as a cash outflow)
$PMT = 0$	(there are no payments)
$FV = 10000$	(this is treated as a cash inflow)
$P/Y = 4$	(payments per year, note $PMT = 0$)
$C/Y = 4$	(compounding periods per year)

Enter the inputs from above and move the cursor to I% and press **2nd** and **ENTER (SOLVE).**

 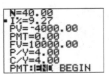

Thus our answer is

$$I\% = 9.27\%$$

Caution: In this kind of problem you must be careful with the signs for PV and FV. They can never have the same sign, one must be negative, denoting an outflow and one must be positive, denoting an inflow. Failure to do this will result in an error message

Consider the TVM screen below, where PV and FV have the same sign. When we move the cursor up I% and press ALPHA and ENTER, we get the error message. Select 2:Goto and that takes you back to the TVM screen.

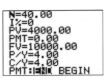 

We now make the correction by changing PV to −4000 and then moving the cursor to I% and pressing ALPHA and ENTER we get the correct result.

EXAMPLE 4

How long will it take for a present value of $10,000 to become a future value of 100,000 at 18% compounded monthly?

Using the TVM Solver, we determine the inputs and the unknown.

N =	(this is our unknown in terms of months)
I% = 18	(annual interest rate)
PV = −10000	(this is treated as a cash outflow)
PMT = 0	(there are no payments)
FV = 100000	(this is treated as a cash inflow)
P/Y = 12	(payments per year, note PMT = 0)
C/Y = 12	(compounding periods per year)

Notes

So the answer is N = 154.65. But what does that represent? It represents 154.65 periods. In this case, that is 154.65 months, since we are compounding monthly. To get the result in years we divide by 12 or we can use the TI-83 financial variables feature. First press 2nd and MODE (QUIT key) which gets us back to the home screen.

Now press **APPS** and select **1:Finance** (for the TI-83 Plus) or **2nd** and **x⁻¹** (for the TI-83) and select **VARS** and then select **1:N**.

 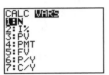

This pastes N onto the home screen. Divide this by 12 and you're done.

 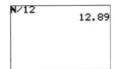

Thus our final result is

$$T = 12.89 \text{ years}$$

So, we can solve for the Future Value, the Present Value, the Rate, or the Time using the TVM Solver. Try the examples below using the TVM solver.

EXAMPLE 5

You invest $40,000 at 3.5% compounded semiannually for 3 years. Find the amount at the end of 3 years.

EXAMPLE 6

How long would it take an investment of $4,000 to double in value if the interest rate were 6% compounded quarterly?

EXAMPLE 7

What interest rate, compounded monthly, would be required to double a $4,000 investment in 8 years?

EXAMPLE 8

How much do you need to invest at 5% compounded daily (365 days = 1 year) so that you will have $35,000 in your account after 15 years?

Answers:
Example 5: $44,388.09
Example 6: 11.64 yrs.
Example 7: 8.70%
Example 8: $16,533.68

6.3 Effective Rate of Interest (ERI)

Suppose that $1000 is invested at 8% for 1 year. ($P = 1000$, $R = .08$, $T = 1$). The amount at the end of the year will depend upon how many times during the year compounding occurs.

| | **Compounded** | | |
Yearly	**Semi-Ann.**	**Quarterly**	**Daily**

$$\text{AMT}\begin{cases} A_1 = 1000\left(1 + \frac{.08}{1}\right)^1 \\ A_1 = 1080 \end{cases} \quad \begin{matrix} A_2 = 1000\left(1 + \frac{.08}{2}\right)^2 \\ A_2 = 1081.60 \end{matrix} \quad \begin{matrix} A_4 + 1000\left(1 + \frac{.08}{4}\right)^4 \\ A_4 = 1082.43 \end{matrix} \quad \begin{matrix} A_{365} = 1000(1 + \frac{.08}{365})^{365} \\ A_{365} = 1083.28 \end{matrix}$$

$$\text{ERI}\begin{cases} \dfrac{1080 - 1000}{1000} \\ .08 \\ 8\% \end{cases} \quad \begin{matrix} \dfrac{1081.60 - 1000}{1000} \\ .0816 \\ 8.16\% \end{matrix} \quad \begin{matrix} \dfrac{1082.43 - 1000}{1000} \\ .08243 \\ 8.243\% \end{matrix} \quad \begin{matrix} \dfrac{1083.28 - 1000}{1000} \\ .08328 \\ 8.328\% \end{matrix}$$

The Effective Rate of Interest (ERI) is the "equivalent simple interest rate." In other words, the ERI is the simple interest rate that will result in the same yield as the compound interest rate over one year. We compute the ERI using the following formula from simple interest with $T = 1$.

$$ERI = \frac{A - P}{PT} = \frac{A - P}{P}$$

$$ERI = R = \frac{A - P}{PT} = \frac{A - P}{P \cdot 1} = \frac{A - P}{P}$$

Using the formula for compound amount and splitting the fraction and simplifying

$$\begin{aligned} ERI &= \frac{A - P}{P} \\ &= \frac{P(1 + i)^n - P}{P} \\ &= \frac{P(1 + i)^n}{P} - \frac{P}{P} \\ &= (1 + i)^n - 1 \end{aligned}$$

Thus the formula for effective rate of interest is:

$$ERI = (1 + i)^n - 1 \qquad \text{where } i = \frac{R}{m}$$

Notice that this formula does not require a value for the principal. In fact the ERI is the same whether the principal was $1,000 or $100,000.

The Effective Rate of Interest is also called the Annual Percentage Rate or **APR**.

When computing the Effective Rate of Interest be sure to set your calculator to at least 4 decimal places of accuracy (press MODE and make your selection)

EXAMPLE 1
Find the ERI for 8% compounded quarterly for 1 year.

8% compounded quarterly means that R = .08 and m = n = 4.

$$\text{ERI} = \left(1 + \frac{.08}{4}\right)^4 - 1$$

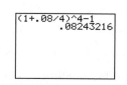

$$= (1.02)^4 - 1$$
$$= 1.0824322 - 1$$
$$= .0824322$$
$$= 8.243\%$$

EXAMPLE 2
Which gives a larger yield: 7.8% compounded monthly or 8% compounded semiannually

Comparing the Effective Rates of Interest for the two plans will give us the answer.

7.8% compounded monthly means that R = .078 and m = n = 12. Thus,

$$\text{ERI} = \left(1 + \frac{.078}{12}\right)^{12} - 1$$

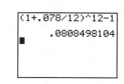

$$= (1.0065)^{12} - 1$$
$$= 1.0808498 - 1$$
$$= .0808498$$
$$= 8.08\%$$

8% compounded semiannually means that R = .08 and m = n = 2. Thus,

$$\text{ERI} = \left(1 + \frac{.08}{2}\right)^2 - 1$$

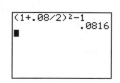

$$= (1.04)^2 - 1$$
$$= 1.0816 - 1$$
$$= .0816$$
$$= 8.16\%$$

Therefore, 8% compounded semiannually results in a larger yield (8.16%) than 7.8% compounded monthly (8.08%).

Notes

Notes

The TI-83 has the capability of computing effective rates of interest given nominal rates and the number of compounding periods. Similarly we can find nominal rates of interest given effective rates of interest and the number of compounding periods. This will be done from the **FINANCE CALC** menu by selecting **B:▶ Nom** and **C:▶ Eff.**

The general form for these features is as follows:

▶ Eff (*nominal rate, number of compounding periods*)

▶ Nom (*effective rate, number of compounding periods*)

Notes

EXAMPLE 1
Find the ERI for 8% compounded quarterly for 1 yr.

Starting at the Home Screen, press **APPS** and select **1:Finance** (for the TI-83 Plus) or **2nd** and **x⁻¹** (for the TI-83), and select **CALC** and **C:▶ Eff.** This pastes the Eff feature into your home screen. Type in the nominal rate and the number of compounding periods). Then press **ENTER.**

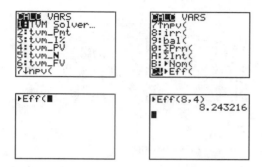

EXAMPLE 2
Which gives a larger yield: 7.8% compounded monthly or 8% compounded semiannually.

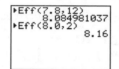

Recall how to call up the previous input line on the TI-83. Pressing 2nd and ENTER calls up the previous line which you can then edit and get your result.

EXAMPLE 3
Find the nominal rate for an effective rate of 6.25% compounded quarterly.

Notes

<table>
<tr><td>6.4</td><td>

Mortgage Calculations

</td></tr>
</table>

Recall that we access the TVM Solver by pressing **APPS** and select **1:Finance** (for the TI-83 Plus) or **2nd** and x^{-1} (for the TI-83). Select **CALC** and **1:TVM Solver.**

 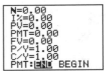

Note:

> **N** = total # of payment periods
> **I%** = annual interest rate
> **PV** = present value
> **PMT** = payment amount
> **FV** = future value
> **P/Y** = # of payment periods per year
> **C/Y** = # of compounding periods per year

In addition note that **PMT:END** specifies an ordinary annuity, where payments occur at the end of each payment period. Most loans are in this category. **PMT:BEGIN** specifies an annuity due, where payments occur at the beginning of each payment period. Most leases are in this category.

For mortgage loan calculations note:

1. PV is the amount of the mortgage loan
2. FV is always 0
3. Mortgage loans are typically paid monthly, so P/Y = C/Y = 12
4. PMT is the monthly mortgage loan payment
5. N is the total number of months for the mortgage loan
6. Set your calculator to two decimal places of accuracy

The formula to determine the monthly payment is given by

$$\text{PMT} = \frac{\text{PV}}{\left(\dfrac{1 - (1 + i)^{-n}}{i}\right)}$$

Once again, little is gained by using this formula when we can do the calculation using the TVM Solver. That is the way we will proceed to solve various mortgage loan problems.

EXAMPLE 1A

A home is priced at \$325,000. A down payment of \$25,000 is to be made, with the remainder financed at 5.75% for 30 years. **Find the monthly payment.**

Using the TVM solver we will need to enter the inputs and solve for the monthly payment.

$$N = 30*12 = 360$$

$$I\% = 5.75$$

$$PV = 300000$$

$$PMT = \text{this is our unknown}$$

$$FV = 0$$

$$P/Y = 12$$

$$C/Y = 12$$

After changing to 2 decimal places of accuracy (MODE), enter in the inputs as shown below.

Move the cursor to PMT and press **ALPHA** (**GREEN** key) and **ENTER** (**SOLVE** key). The result is **\$1750.72.** (Note the negative sign on the payment as this is an outflow.)

Suppose at the last second you were able to take advantage of a lowered interest rate (5.50%). To recompute the payment, all that is needed is to change the value of I% and move the cursor to PMT and press ALPHA and ENTER to solve.

EXAMPLE 1B

Find the Principal and Interest for the 1st, 10th, and 360th payment. Find the balance after the 1st, 10th, and 360th payment. Find the total principal and total interest paid over the 360 payments.

Notes

The three features we will need to access are found in the **FINANCE CALC** menu by scrolling down to 9:bal, 0:ΣPrn, A:ΣInt.

bal   bal (number of payment)
             computes the balance

ΣPrn   ΣPrn (payment 1,payment 2)
             computes the sum of the principal between payment 1
             and payment 2

ΣInt   ΣInt (payment 1,payment 2)
             computes the sum of the interest between payment 1
             and payment 2

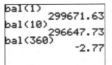

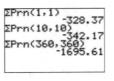 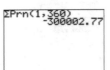

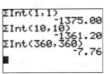 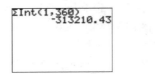

This tells us that the first payment will contain **$328.37** in **principal,** **$1375.00** in **interest,** and a remaining **balance** of **$299,671.63.**

This tells us that the 10th payment will contain **$342.17** in **principal,** **$1361.20** in **interest,** and a remaining **balance** of **$296,647.73.**

This tells us that the 360th payment will contain **$1695.61** in **principal,** **$7.76** in **interest,** and a remaining **balance** of −**$2.77.**

The monthly mortgage payment is $1,703.37. Suppose taxes and insurance are approximately another additional 30% above the mortgage payment. Thus

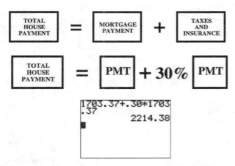

The total house payment is approximately **$2,214.38.**

EXAMPLE 1C

A loan company will finance a house if the potential total monthly house payment does not exceed 25% of a buyers monthly gross income. So in this case, the loan company would finance this house if 25% of the monthly gross is $2,214.38. Solving for monthly gross we find

$$\text{Monthly Gross} = \frac{\$2,214.38}{.25} = \$8,857.52$$

and thus the annual gross must be

$$\text{Annual Gross} = 12 \times \$8,857.52 = \$106,290.24$$

As is the case with any mathematical model, our mortgage model for the house price that a buyer can afford, depends on several assumptions. We assume that a buyer can reasonably afford to pay 25% of the buyer's monthly gross as the total house payment. We also assume that taxes and insurance are about 30% of the loan payment, and that the house payment equals the loan payment plus taxes and insurance. We also take into account the financial variables, and the percentage of down payment. This model is summarized as follows.

Mathematical Model
House Price a Buyer Can Afford

1. *25% of Monthly Gross Rule of Thumb
  Total House Payment (mortgage plus taxes and insurance cannot exceed this amount)

Notes

2. TAXES & INSURANCE
*30% of Mortgage Payment

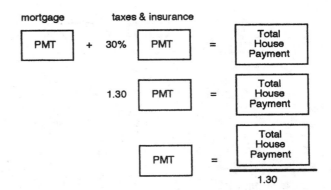

3. FINANCIAL CONDITIONS

*Length of Loan (# of months):	**N**
*Interest Rate:	**I%**
*# of compounding periods per year	**C/Y**
*# of payment periods per year	**P/Y**
*Monthly Mortgage Payment:	**PMT**
The maximum amount of loan:	**PV**

4. FINDING PRICE

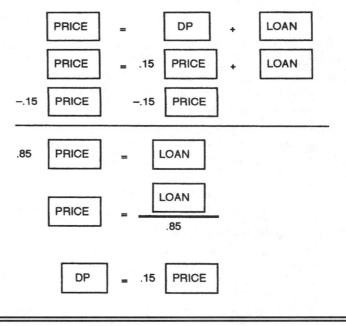

SUMMARY

MAXIMUM MONTHLY HOUSE PAYMENT . . . .

MAXIMUM MONTHLY MORTGAGE PAYMENT . . . .

ESTIMATED TAXES AND INSURANCE . . . .

LENGTH OF LOAN (# MONTHS) . . . .

INTEREST RATE (ANNUAL) . . . .

MAXIMUM LOAN . . . .

DOWN PAYMENT . . . .

MAXIMUM PRICE . . . .

EXAMPLE 2
Mortgage Model

A loan company will finance a house if the potential total monthly house payment does not exceed 25% of a buyers gross income. Assume a buyer has a gross income of $4000/month. What price house could the buyer afford to finance at 6% annual rate for 30 years, with a 15% down payment. Assume taxes and insurance are approximately 30% of the mortgage loan payment.

Use Mathematical Model for House Price a Buyer Can Afford:

1. $(.25)(4000) = 1,000$

2. $1.30 \cdot PMT = 1,000 \implies PMT = \dfrac{1000}{1.3} = 769.23$

3.

```
N=360.00
I%=6.00
▸PV=128301.11■
PMT=⁻769.23
FV=0.00
P/Y=12.00
C/Y=12.00
PMT:END BEGIN
```

4. $PRICE = \dfrac{128,301.11}{.85} = 150,942.48$

   $DOWNPAYMENT = .15 \cdot (150,942.48) = 22,641.37$

Notes

EXAMPLE 3

A family has annual gross income of $90,000. What price house could they afford to finance at an 5.85% annual rate for 30 years, with a 20% down payment? Use the 25% monthly gross rule of thumb and assume taxes and insurance equal approximately 30% of the mortgage payment.

1. $\dfrac{90,000}{12} = 7,500$

   $(.25)(7500) = 1,875$

2. $1.30 \cdot \text{PMT} = 1,875 \quad \Rightarrow \quad \text{PMT} = \dfrac{1,875}{1.3} = 1,442.31$

3.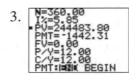

4. $\text{PRICE} = \dfrac{244483.80}{.80} = 305604.75$

   $\text{DOWNPAYMENT} = .20 \cdot (305604.75) = 61,120.95$

Try the following problems.

EXAMPLE 4

You are purchasing a house for $165,000 with a 20% down payment. You plan to finance the remainder at 7.85% for 30 years.

a. Excluding taxes and insurance, what will your monthly mortgage payment be?

b. If taxes and insurance are 30% of your monthly payment, how much will your total house payment be?

c. What must your annual gross income be so that this house is affordable (using the 25% monthly gross rule of thumb).

Answers:
Example 4: a. $954.80, 4b. $1,241.24, 4c. $59,579.52

EXAMPLE 5
Do Example 4a,b,c, with the financing being over 15 years.

EXAMPLE 6
Do Example 4a,b,c with a 10% down payment (financing over 30 years).

EXAMPLE 7
Do Example 4a,b,c with a 8.75% interest rate (over 30 years, with 20% down payment).

EXAMPLE 8
How expensive a house can you purchase if your annual income is $85,000, and you finance 80% of the purchase price at 7% over 25 years? Assume monthly taxes and insurance will be 30% of the loan payment. (Once again, use the 25% monthly gross rule of thumb.)

Answer:
Example 5: a. $1,250.06, 5b. $1,625.08, 5c. $78,003.84
Example 6: a. $1,074.15, 6b. $1,396.40, 6c. $67,027.20
Example 7: a. $1,038.44, 7b. $1,349.97, 7c. $64,798.56
Example 8: $240,913.29

6.5 Other Financial Computations

EXAMPLE 1

A 25 year old employee starts putting away $2,000 each year in an account that yields an interest rate of 10% per year. How much money will the individual have in the account when retirement looms at age 65?

Using the TVM Solver, with the present value, PV = 0 (since there was no money in the account originally) we are now solving for the future value FV.

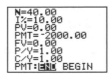

That's right, the amount will be $885,185, a tidy nest egg. But what if the goal was $1,000,000 by age 65. How much would the employee need to put aside.

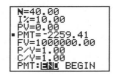

Suppose that the employee did decide to invest $2,000 each year for retirement (at 10% compounded annually). However, the employee decided to wait for 10 years (since this individual is only 25 and not thinking about retirement yet). So the employee will be investing $2,000 each year for only 30 years. What's the impact on the "nest egg" at age 65?

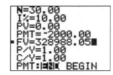

So waiting 10 years to start your retirement plan will cost this person over $550,000!

How much would this individual need to invest annually to make up for this loss?

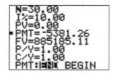

So the employee would need to invest almost $5400 annually to make up for the loss!

EXAMPLE 2

Suppose a long lost aunt left you $50,000 upon her passing. You were age 40 at that time, and you put those funds into a retirement account. You decide to put $5,000 each year into that same retirement account. If you get an annual return of 8% on your retirement fund, then how much money will you have in your account at age 68.

Once again, this is a relatively easy problem to do on the TI-83. We use PV = −50000 since we have that original amount in this account.

Just to check our answer, we can break up the calculation into two separate parts. First, we compute the future value of 28 years of annual payments of $5,000. Second we compute the future value of an investment of $50,000 for 28 years. And of course, these add up to $908,049.47.

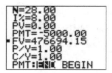 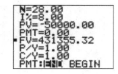

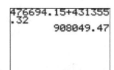

EXAMPLE 3

John James is 65 years of age and is trying to determine whether or not he will be financially able to retire. John has $850,000 in his retirement account which now earns a guaranteed interest rate of 5%, compounded annually. He expects to withdraw $60,000 each year of retirement. How old would John James be when his retirement fund is depleted ($0)?

We use the TVM Solver, with I% = 5.00, PV = −850,000 (since this the amount of money invested in the retirement account, thus an outflow), PMT = 60,000 (this is an inflow, as the annual withdrawal), and we solve for N.

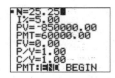

So John has sufficient funds to last approximately 25 years, to age 90.

Notes

Try the following examples.

EXAMPLE 4

Samantha Smith started putting $2,250 in her retirement account each year, at age 32. If she earns a 7.5% interest rate (compounded annually), then how much money will Samantha have at age 68?

EXAMPLE 5

If Samantha had a goal of $900,000 in this account by age 68, then how much money would would she need to place in this account each year?

EXAMPLE 6

Samantha Smith has reevaluated her priorities and has decided that she can afford to put $4,000 in this account each year. How old will she be when the account contains $900,000?

EXAMPLE 7

What interest rate would Samantha need to have so that her $4,000 annual contribution to her retirement fund will yield $900,000 by age 65?

EXAMPLE 8

Bob Bell has accumulated $1,000,000 in his retirement fund. He is currently 62 years of age and has retired. His annual withdrawal from his retirement fund is $80,000, and his retirement fund continues to earn 6% interest compounded annually. How old will Bob be when his retirement fund balance is $0.

Answers:
Example 4: $375,346.07
Example 5: $5,395.02
Example 6: approximately 72
Example 7: 10.06%
Example 8: approximately 86

Chapter 6 Exercise Set

In Exercises 1 through 4, find the amount that will be accumulated in each account under the conditions set forth.

1. A principal of $2000 is accumulated with 7.5% interest compounded monthly for 4 years.

2. A principal of $3000 is accumulated with 6% interest compounded quarterly for 12 years.

3. A principal of $6000 is accumulated with simple interest of 12% for 1 year.

4. A principal of $800 is accumulated for 12 years

   (a) At 7% simple interest

   (b) At 7% compounded quarterly

   (c) At 7% compounded monthly

In Exercises 5 through 7, find the rate of interest required to achieve the conditions set forth.

5. $A = \$20,000$; $P = \$8000$; $t = 10$ years; interest is compounded annually

6. $A = \$5000$; $P = \$1250$; $t = 12$ years; interest is compounded quarterly

7. $A = \$7500$; $P = \$2500$; $t = 6$ years; interest is compounded semiannually

In Exercises 8 through 10, find the number of interest periods required to achieve the conditions set forth. Also find years.

8. $A = \$3500$; $P = \$1200$; interest is 8% compounded semiannually

9. $A = \$6000$; $P = \$1000$; interest is 12% compounded quarterly

10. $A = \$50,000$; $P = \$6000$; interest is 10% compounded annually

In Exercises 11 through 13, find the principal P required to achieve the stated conditions.

11. $A = \$5000$; rate is 6% compounded annually for a period of 10 years

12. $A = \$30,000$; rate is 12% compounded quarterly for a period of 10 years

13. $A = \$3000$; rate is 7.5% compounded monthly for a period of 10 years

14. **Investing** If $5000 is invested at the rate of 7% compounded semiannually, what will be the value of the investment 10 years from now, assuming no withdrawals?

Notes

15. **Investing** Dr. Bishop is saving money to send his children to college. How much will he need to invest now at 8% compounded quarterly if he wants the accumulated value of the investment to be $20,000 in 12 years?

16. **Investing** The Tanners have received an $8000 gift from one of their parents to invest in their child's college education. They estimate that they will need $20,000 in 12 years to achieve their educational goals for their child. What interest rate compounded semiannually would the Tanners need to achieve this goal?

17. **Growth of Money** How many years will be required to turn $5000 into $8000 if the interest rate 7.5% compounded semiannually?

18. **Saving for the Future** Nanette plans on putting $500 in an account on her daughter's birthday, beginning with the first one and continuing through age 16. If the account pays 8% compounded annually, how much should be in the account on Nanette's daughter's 16th birthday?

19. **Investing for College** Elena's son will enter college 16 years from now. At that time, she would like to have $20,000 available for college expenses. For that purpose, her bank will set up an account that pays 7% compounded quarterly. If she makes payments into the account at the end of each quarter, what must Elena's payments be to achieve her goal?

20. **Investing for Retirement** Eduardo is a 40-year-old individual who plans to retire at age 65. Between now and then, $2000 is paid annually into his IRA account, which is anticipated to pay 5% compounded annually. How much will be in the account upon Eduardo's retirement?

21. **Planning for Retirement** Compare the accumulated value of IRA accounts into which $500 is invested at the end of each quarter at an interest rate of 6% compounded quarterly if

    (a) You start at age 25 and retire at age 60.

    (b) You start at age 30 and retire at age 60.

    (c) You start at age 35 and retire at age 60.

    (d) You start at age 40 and retire at age 60.

22. **Planning for Retirement** Katy wants to have enough in her retirement accounts so that, upon retirement, she can withdraw $500 each month for the next 20 years. Assuming that her accounts will earn an average of 7% compounded monthly, what sum of money should she have in her accounts upon retirement?

23. **Savings** The Meek brothers are planning a trip around the world. They hope to work some as they go, but believe that they should have accessible $800 per month so they can live in relative comfort for the eight months they plan to be gone. How much should they have in an account earning 6% compounded monthly when they leave so that they can withdraw the desired $800 each month for eight months?

24. Lottery Earnings If you won a lottery that paid $5000 each year for the next 10 years, and interest rates were 10% compounded annually, what would be the present value of your prize?

In Exercises 25 through 27, convert the given interest rate to the APR.

25. 6.5% compounded quarterly

26. 4% compounded semiannually

27. 16% compounded monthly

In Exercise 28, calculate the APR and determine which rate will result in the most interest per year.

28. **(a)** 5% compounded semiannually

(b) 4.8% compounded quarterly

(c) 4.6% compounded monthly

29. Borrowing Money Pat and Maxine decide to buy a lot on which they plan to build a new house. The lot cost $28,500, and the bank agrees to finance 80% of the cost at 9% compounded semiannually for a period of eight years. Payments on the loan are to be made in equal semiannual installments.

(a) Find the amount of each payment.

(b) Assuming timely payments of the amount found in Exercise 29(a), what is the unpaid balance after the 12th payment?

30. Borrowing Money Diane decides to buy a small farm near the edge of town for $95,000. The bank agrees to finance 70% of the cost at 10% compounded quarterly for a period of 10 years. Payments on the loan are to be made in equal quarterly installments.

(a) What is the amount of each payment?

(b) Assuming timely payments of the amount found in Exercise 30(a), what is the unpaid balance after the 20th payment?

In Exercises 31 through 33, a couple gets financing for 90% of the $130,000 purchase price of a house at the rate of 9.5% on the monthly unpaid balance.
(a) Find the amount of the monthly payments to repay the loan only (excluding taxes and insurance).
(b) Find the total amount paid to the finance company (the monthly payment multiplied by the number of payments) for each of the following repayment periods.

31. The loan is repaid in 20 years.

32. The loan is repaid in 25 years.

33. The loan is repaid in 30 years.

Notes

34. A family wishes to purchase a home worth $350,000, with a 10% down payment, while financing the rest at a 5.5% interest rate (compounded monthly) for 30 years.

  (a) Find the monthly mortgage payment.

  (b) Assuming taxes and insurance are an additional 30% added on to the mortgage payment, then find the monthly total house payment (mortgage payment plus taxes and insurance).

  (c) Using the 25% of monthly gross rule of thumb, how much annual income will this family need to have to be approved for this loan (round to the nearest dollar)?

35. A family with annual income of $120,000 wishes to buy home. How expensive a home can this family purchase if they plan to have a 20% down payment, and finance the rest at 5.15% annual rate compounded monthly for 25 years? Use the 25% monthly gross rule of thumb and use the assumption that taxes and insurance are 30% of the mortgage loan payment and round your final answer to the nearest dollar.

Find the simple interest and amount in problems 36–38.

36. Investing $20,000 at 6.5% simple interest for 12 years.

37. Investing $120,000 at 8% simple interest for 9 months.

38. Investing $60,000 at 3.5% simple interest for 2 years.

Introduction to Statistics

7.1 Organizing Data: Tables & Graphs

EXAMPLE 1

Consider the following data which is obtained by selecting a sample of 30 applicants for positions at your company and noting each person's pre-employment test results.

15	18	22	63	52	63	18	19	15	31
15	18	22	15	63	69	63	19	61	30
22	22	52	52	52	69	63	63	15	31

How might we best organize, summarize, and present this data?

Notes

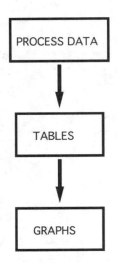

One technique that will aid in processing the data is called a **stem-leaf diagram.** First you draw a vertical line (called the stem) and then you draw a number of horizontal lines (called the leaves). In our first example we will use leaves of 6, 5, 4, 3, 2, 1, which represents the 60's, 50's, 40's, etc. It makes no difference whether you go from high to low or low to high in you ordering of the leaves.

6	
5	
4	
3	
2	
1	

We enter values in the diagram as follows: the number 15 is entered as a 5 in the leaf marked as 1.

6	
5	
4	
3	
2	
1	5

Proceeding to the rest of the data we obtain the following:

6	3,3,3,9,3,1,9,3,3
5	2,2,2,2
4	
3	1,0,1
2	2,2,2,2
1	5,8,8,9,5,5,8,5,9,5

EXAMPLE 2

You select a sample of 10 stocks and note their rate of return over the past year.

7.25%   7.42%   7.68%   6.93%   7.63%
7.53%   7.51%   7.18%   7.11%   7.36%

The stem leaf diagram is as follows:

6.9	3
7.0	
7.1	8,1
7.2	5
7.3	6
7.4	2
7.5	3,1
7.6	3,8

Notes

EXAMPLE 3

You select a sample of 12 boxes of 400 count nails. You proceed to count how many nails are in each box. The data is as follows:

435 411 428 423 399 416
396 400 398 401 391 411

The stem leaf diagram looks as follows:

39	6,9,1,8
40	1,0
41	1,6,1
42	3,8
43	5

In Example 2 and Example 3 we illustrate a tip with the stem leaf diagram. Namely the entries to the right of the stem should always be single digit numbers (as seen in Example 1, Example 2, and Example 3)

If we were to not pay attention to that tip the stem leaf displays for Example 2 and Example 3 would be as follows:

6	.93
7	.25,.53,.42,.51,.66,.18,.11,.63,.36

3	96, 98, 99, 91
4	35, 11, 00, 28, 23, 01, 16, 11

which would not be very effective in putting the data in numerical order.

Returning to our stem leaf diagram for Example 1.

6	3,3,3,9,3,1,9,3,3
5	2,2,2,2
4	
3	1,0,1
2	2,2,2,2
1	5,8,8,9,5,5,8,5,9,5

Our next step would be to arrange the data in numerical order, which is made easier because of the stem leaf diagram.

69 69 63 63 63 63 63 63 61 52
52 52 52 31 31 30 22 22 22 22
19 19 18 18 18 15 15 15 15 15

This ordered list of data is still an inefficient way of representing this data. We must have a better way to communicate the fact that 6 people scored a 63 on this exam, than looking at

63   63   63   63   63   63

We can present the information more efficiently using a **frequency table,** which pairs scores and frequencies. Frequency in this context means frequency of occurrence.

Frequency Table

Scores	Frequency
69	2
63	6
61	1
52	4
31	2
30	1
22	4
19	2
18	3
15	5
	30

What are the advantages of such a table?

If you need to see every individual value and how many times it occurs then that's exactly what this table shows.

What are the disadvantages of such a table?

There's a lot of detail here, possibly too much detail. The question here is, do you need to know that exactly 3 people scored 18 or that only 1 person scored a 30, or that 4 people scored 52? If the answer is yes, then you've got the table you need. If the answer is no, that you have too much detail here, then we need to summarize and simplify.

We can group our data into intervals, thereby simplifying and summarizing our data.

Group Frequency Table

Class	Interval	Freq.
1	10–19	10
2	20–29	4
3	30–39	3
4	40–49	0
5	50–59	4
6	60–69	9
		30

There are many possible interval formats that we might use. For example, if the data had one decimal place of accuracy the above table would be insufficient. For instance, where would 39.6 be counted? What about 59.2? This problem is remedied as follows.

Class	Interval	Freq.
1	10–19.9	10
2	20–29.9	4
3	30–39.9	3
4	40–49.9	0
5	50–59.9	4
6	60–69.9	9
		30

If the data were accurate to two decimal places then the following format would work (where the prior would not).

Class	Interval	Freq.
1	10–19.99	10
2	20–29.99	4
3	30–39.99	3
4	40–49.99	0
5	50–59.99	4
6	60–69.99	9
		30

If the data were accurate to three decimal places then the following format would work (where the prior would not).

Class	Interval	Freq.
1	10–19.999	10
2	20–29.999	4
3	30–39.999	3
4	40–49.999	0
5	50–59.999	4
6	60–69.999	9
		30

The following format would work regardless of the number of decimal places of accuracy in the data.

Class	Interval	Freq.
1	10–20	10
2	20–30	4
3	30–40	3
4	40–50	0
5	50–60	4
6	60–70	9
		30

There may be some ambiguity with the above set up. Where does a score of 30 go? What about 50? Actually the above interval format is shorthand for the following

Class	Interval	Freq.
1	$10 \leq$ score < 20	10
2	$20 \leq$ score < 30	4
3	$30 \leq$ score < 40	3
4	$40 \leq$ score < 50	0
5	$50 \leq$ score < 60	4
6	$60 \leq$ score < 70	9
		30

and clearly there are no ambiguities here.

Also note that all of these interval set ups have widths of **10,** where the width = difference in successive left endpoints.

Rules for Setting Up Group Frequency Tables

1. Classes do not overlap.
But understand that intervals like 10-20, 20-30, etc. do not overlap as per our understanding on the previous page.

2. No gaps between classes.
But understand that for whole number data, intervals like 10-19, 20-29, etc., do not have gaps.

3. All values accounted for.
Every value has one and only one place to go

4. Classes of equal width
(width = difference in successive left endpoints)

5. The number of classes is between 5 and 15.
You don't want to have too many or too few intervals.

+
KEEP IT SIMPLE!

**CORRECTNESS & SIMPLICITY
ARE BOTH VERY IMPORTANT!**

Notes

When do we decide whether to group the data or not?

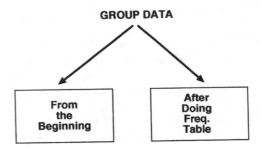

Once we have decided to do a group frequency table and have decided on a format, **how wide should the intervals be?**

The intervals need to be wide enough (or narrow enough) so that we have between 5 and 15 intervals.

How do we make that happen?

First you need to know that there are many correct ways of setting up your group frequency table. Just be sure that you follow the 5 rules and that you keep it simple. We also know that the wider you choose your intervals, the fewer you need to cover the data. The narrower you choose your intervals, the more you need to cover the data. We have some help here.

Relationship Between # of Classes and the Width of Classes

$$\frac{\text{Largest} - \text{Smallest}}{\#\text{classes}} \approx \text{Width}$$

$$\frac{\text{Largest} - \text{Smallest}}{\text{Width}} \approx \#\text{classes}$$

For our data:

69 69 63 63 63 63 63 63 61 52
52 52 52 31 31 30 22 22 22 22
19 19 18 18 18 15 15 15 15 **15**

If we choose to have 5 classes:

$$\frac{69 - 15}{5 \text{ classes}} = \frac{54}{5} = 10.8 \text{ and so we choose 10 for the width}$$

Note: this actually gives us 6 classes.

If we tried using a width of 3, we would find that to be a problem.

$$\frac{69 - 15}{3 \text{ width}} = \frac{54}{3} = 18 \text{ intervals} \quad \text{TOO MANY!}$$

If we tried a width of 10, we would find this to be OK.

$$\frac{69 - 15}{10 \text{ width}} = \frac{54}{10} = 5.4 \text{ intervals}$$

(turns out to be 6 intervals)

EXAMPLE 4

You collect data on 1000 invoices; with the largest invoice of $5,089 and the smallest invoice of $33.

$$\frac{5,089 - 33}{5 \text{ classes}} = \frac{5,056}{5} = 1,011.2$$

Choose width of **1000:**
(DO NOT USE 1,011.2!)
KEEP IT SIMPLE!

0– 999.99
1000–1999.99
2000–2999.99
3000–3999.99
4000–4999.99
5000–5999.99

What if we decide to choose an interval width of 250? Will this give us too many intervals?

$$\frac{5,089 - 33}{250 \text{ width}} = \frac{5,056}{250} = 20.224$$

Thus we would have about 20 or 21 intervals (classes). TOO MANY!

Suppose we select a width of 1000.

$$\frac{5,089 - 33}{1000 \text{ width}} = \frac{5,056}{1000} = 5.056 \text{ intervals}$$

Thus, we will probably have 5 or 6 intervals. This would be OK!

Notes

Graphical Techniques

We use our group frequency table

Class	Interval	Freq.
1	10–19	10
2	20–29	4
3	30–39	3
4	40–49	0
5	50–59	4
6	60–69	9
		30

to generate a graph called a **histogram.**

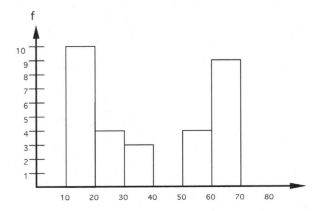

An alternative to the histogram is the frequency polygon. We first need to create a midpoint (MP) column in our group frequency table. The midpoint is one half the way between each successive left end point (the right end point is not relevant to this calculation).

Class	Interval	MP	Freq.
1	10–19	15	10
2	20–29	25	4
3	30–39	35	3
4	40–49	45	0
5	50–59	55	4
6	60–69	65	9
			30

We then plot the frequency versus the midpoint and connect the points with straight line segments.

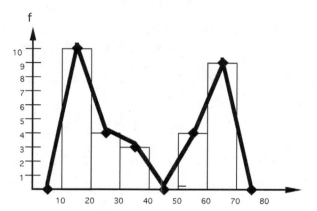

Notes

7.2 — Using the TI-83 to Organize Data

Press **STAT** and select **EDIT** and you will see the List Editor, where you can enter data into 6 lists named **L1, L2, L3, L4, L5,** and **L6.**

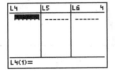

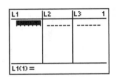

If you have values in these lists, you can clear these out as follows. Move the cursor on top of the list that has info that you need to erase. Next press CLEAR and ENTER, and your list is cleared.

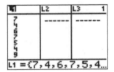

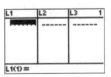

If you are missing one or more of the lists **L1, L2, L3, L4, L5, L6,** you can recover the list (or lists). In the example below we only see L1, and L6

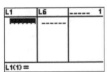

Press STAT and select 5:SetUpEditor and press enter twice.

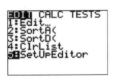

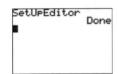

If you now press STAT and select 1:EDIT you should have the full complement of lists to work with: **L1, L2, L3, L4, L5, L6.**

We can enter the information on exam scores in **L1** by moving the cursor to the first row of **L1** and proceeding to type in the scores and pressing **ENTER,** until we have posted all 30 scores (see Example 1 in Section 7.1 for the original data set).

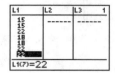 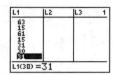

Another option for entering the data would be to use two lists, one for the individual values and one for the frequencies. This would be like entering the frequency table (from Section 7.1) into two lists (say **L2** and **L3**) in our list editor.

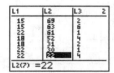 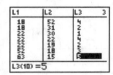

To generate a histogram and a group frequency table, press **2nd** and **Y =** (**STAT PLOT** key) and select **1:Plot1.**

Move the cursor to **On** and press **ENTER** (this turns on Plot1).

Select the histogram feature by moving the cursor to the third icon in the first row of Type, and pressing **ENTER.**

Move the cursor to Xlist and press **2nd** and **1** (this is the **L1** key), and then move the cursor to **Freq:** and enter **1.**

Before we proceed with the graph we need to turn off all **Y =** functions. All other STAT PLOTs should be off as well (Plot2 and Plot3 in our case). Press **ZOOM** and select **9:ZoomStat.**

Here's the histogram for our exam data.

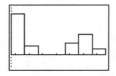

Pressing **TRACE** and pressing the right arrow key shows us the intervals and frequencies.

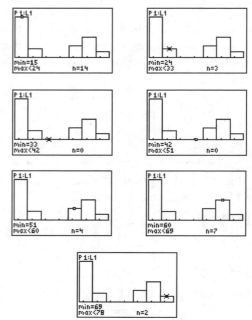

This gives us the following group frequency table

Class	Interval	Freq.
1	15–24	14
2	24–33	3
3	33–42	0
4	42–51	0
5	51–60	4
6	60–69	7
7	69–78	2
		30

Suppose we are not happy with this set up and we decide we want a different interval set up. Let's say we want the following

Class	Interval	Freq.
1	$10 \leq$ score < 20	10
2	$20 \leq$ score < 30	4
3	$30 \leq$ score < 40	3
4	$40 \leq$ score < 50	0
5	$50 \leq$ score < 60	4
6	$60 \leq$ score < 70	9
		30

Press **WINDOW** and you will see the default window that has been set up by the TI-83. Since we want to change this, move the cursor to **Xmin** and change the value to 10, **Xmax** to 70, **Xscl** to 10 (this specifies the interval width).

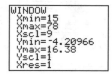

Here's the result (upon pressing **GRAPH**):

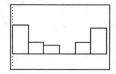

Pressing **TRACE** and the right arrow will give us the intervals and frequencies.

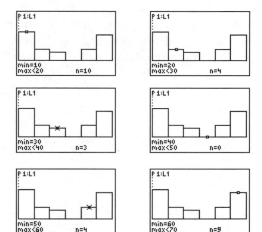

Here is another window that we might have used in this example.

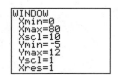 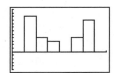

Now let's see how we can generate this sort of graph using frequency table information (as in **L2** and **L3** in our example).

Press **2nd** and **Y =** (**STAT PLOT** key) select **1:Plot1** and turn off that plot by moving the cursor to Off and pressing **ENTER.** Move the cursor to **Plot2** (at the very top of the screen) and press **ENTER.**

Notes

 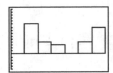

Turn **Plot2 On,** select the histogram feature, and choose **L2** for **Xlist** and **L3** for **Freq.** If we press **GRAPH** we get the identical graph from the bottom of page 25. If we pressed **ZOOM** and select **9:ZoomStat,** we would get the same graph as on the previous page.

Thus far we have processed data, created various tables and graphs in our attempt to summarize and present data. Next we want to consider numerical methods to summarize data.

Numerical Methods of Summary: Measures of Central Tendency

7.3

EXAMPLE 1

You sample seven people and determine their ages:

35   24   30   25   42   50   28

How would we compute the average age of these seven people?

What most people would say is "add the ages up and divide by the number of people." Implementing this we get

$$\text{Average} = \frac{35 + 24 + 30 + 25 + 42 + 50 + 28}{7} = 33.4$$

And of course they would be correct if they were thinking about the average as actually one of the three "averages" namely the mean. Statisticians refer to these averages as **measures of central tendency.**

In this section we will discuss how to compute these averages and what these three averages tell us about the data.

Measures of Central Tendency (Average)
MEAN, MEDIAN, MODE

MEAN

If $x_1, x_2, x_3, \ldots, x_n$ are **n** measurements or scores then the **mean** is

$$\text{Mean} = \frac{x_1 + x_2 + \cdots + x_n}{n} = \frac{\sum x_1}{n}$$

So in our first example

$$x_1 = 35$$
$$x_2 = 24$$
$$x_3 = 30$$
$$x_4 = 25$$
$$x_5 = 42$$
$$x_6 = 50$$
$$x_7 = 28$$

and

$$\text{Mean} = \frac{35 + 24 + 30 + 25 + 42 + 50 + 28}{7} = 33.4$$

One of the purposes of statistics is to draw conclusions about populations based upon information from a sample. In Example 1 we sampled 7 people from a larger group (or population). In some instances, to keep things

Notes

straight, we need to have different terminology and notation for information about samples and information about populations. So when looking at a set of data, you'll want to determine whether the data arises from a sample or from the entire population.

If the data arises from a **sample** of the population then the mean is called the **sample mean** and denoted by

$$\overline{X} = \frac{x_1 + x_2 + \cdots + x_n}{n} = \frac{\sum x_1}{n}$$

where **n = sample size.**

If the data arises from a **complete census of the population** then the mean is called the **population mean** and denoted by

$$\mu = \frac{x_1 + x_2 + \cdots + x_n}{n} = \frac{\sum x_1}{n}$$

where **n = population size.**

EXAMPLE 2
Population Data: 1, 12, 8

$$\mu = \frac{1 + 12 + 8}{3} = \frac{21}{3} = 7$$

EXAMPLE 3
Population Data: 3, 3, 3, 3, 3

$$\mu = \frac{3 + 3 + 3 + 3 + 3}{5} = \frac{15}{5} = 3$$

EXAMPLE 4
Sample Data: 3, 10, 17, 20

$$\overline{X} = \frac{3 + 10 + 17 + 20}{4} = \frac{50}{4} = 12.5$$

EXAMPLE 5
Sample Data: 3, 10, 17, 1000

$$\overline{X} = \frac{3 + 10 + 17 + 1000}{4} = \frac{1033}{4} = 257.50$$

EXAMPLE 6
Compute the mean for the following population data:

145, 162, 100, 162, 200

Answers:
Example 6: 153.8

EXAMPLE 7

Compute the mean for our sample data on pre employment exam score:

15	18	22	63	52	63	18	19	15	31
15	18	22	15	63	69	63	19	61	30
22	22	52	52	52	69	63	63	15	31

You should be able to do these calculations using the statistical features on your calculator!

Since we have the data from Example 7 entered into list **L1,** beginning at the Home Screen, we can press **STAT** choose **CALC** and **1:1–Var Stats.**

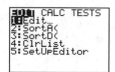 

Now press **2nd** and **1** (this is the **L1** key).

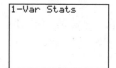 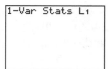

Pressing **ENTER** gives a number of quantities (we'll discuss these later) which can be seen by scrolling down. Note the value of the mean.

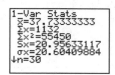 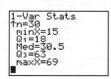

Before we proceed further, let's clear out some of the lists (specifically **L2** and **L3**). Press **STAT** and select **1:Edit.**

Move the cursor to **L2** and press **CLEAR** and **ENTER.** Move the cursor to **L3** and press **CLEAR** and **ENTER.**

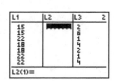

Answers:
Example 7: 37.73

Another way to clear lists **L2** and **L3** would be to select option **4:ClrList** from the **STAT** menu.

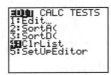 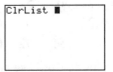

Press **2nd** and **2** (this is the **L2** key) then **,** then **2nd** and **3** (this is the **L3** key) and finally press **ENTER.** Checking the **STAT** editor you see that **L2** and **L3** have been cleared.

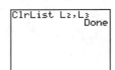 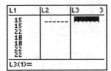

EXAMPLE 8

The following sample data represents the number of sales orders for 5 randomly selected days in June: 35, 46, 72, 87, 94.

Enter the data into a list (say **L2**) and then press **STAT** then select **CALC** and **1:1-Var Stats,** and press **2nd** and **2** (**L2** key).

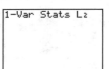 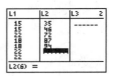

Press **ENTER** and scroll down.

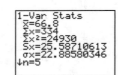 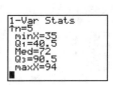

$$\overline{X} = 66.8 \text{ sales orders per day}$$

EXAMPLE 9

The following data represents the hours worked for your 20 employees. Find the mean number of hours worked per week per employee.

hrs. worked per week	# of employees
15	10
20	3
21	2
22	5
	————
	20

Enter the data into lists L3 (values) and L4 (frequencies) and then use the 1-Var Stats feature with those lists. When you call up the 1-Var Stats feature (**STAT, CALC,** and **1-Var Stats**) you then press **2nd** and **3** (for L3) followed by a comma **,** (one row up from the 7 key) and then press **2nd** and **4** (for L4) followed by **ENTER.**

Thus the population mean $\mu = 18.1$. Note that the TI-83 does not distinguish between population and sample mean in terms of notation.

Notes

EXAMPLE 10

A sample of 53 salespeople are selected. Find the mean number of sales per day.

# of sales per day	# of occurrences
0	15
1	17
2	12
3	9
	———
	53

Enter the data into two lists **L5** (values) and **L6** (frequencies) and then use the 1-Var Stats feature with those lists.

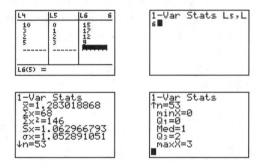

$$\overline{X} = 1.28 \text{ sales per day}$$

MEDIAN

As mentioned earlier, there are other "averages" to consider. The mean is the most often used. The median gives us a different approach, as it tells us about the middle of the data.

To determine the **median** of a set of data, you must first *put the data in rank order*. With the ordered list of data, the score in the middle is the median.

a. If the number of measurements is odd (n odd), then the **median is the middle measurement.**

  In this situation, the position of the middle score is

$$\frac{n + 1}{2}$$

b. If the number of measurements is even (n even), then the **median is the mean of the two middle measurements.**

  In this situation, the positions of the two middle scores are

$$\frac{n}{2} \text{ and } \frac{n}{2} + 1$$

This looks more complicated than it actually is. Let's say we have 5 people and there ages are listed in order:

$$A_1, A_2, A_3, A_4, A_5$$

The "middle" age here is A_3, and note that there were two people that were younger and two people that were older than the median age.

If there were 9 people and their ages are listed in order:

$A_1, A_2, A_3, A_4, A_5, A_6, A_7, A_8, A_9$

The middle age here is A_5, with four people that were younger and four people that were older than the median.

If there were 103 people then how would we find the median?

Since there are an odd number of people that means that there is one and only one age in the middle. This leaves 102 ages split equally with 51 below and 51 above the median age. Thus the median is the 52nd age in order (whatever that number is).

Let's suppose we only have four people:

A_1, A_2, A_3, A_4

There is no single middle score. So to determine the median, we "split the difference" between the two values closest to the middle or more simply we compute the mean of the two middle values. The median age would have two people that were younger and two people that were older.

If we had eight people:

$A_1, A_2, A_3, A_4, A_5, A_6, A_7, A_8$

then the median is the mean of A_4 and A_5 and one again we have an equal number of people younger than the median age and an equal number older than the median age.

So what if we wanted to determine the median age for 212 people. We divide this group in to the youngest 106 and the oldest 106, realizing there is no middle score in the data. To determine the median age we compute the mean of the 106th and 107th age in order.

Let's return to our earlier examples (for the mean) and find the median.

Notes

EXAMPLE 1
Find the median of: 35, 24, 30, 25, 42, 50, 28

Put the data in numerical order:

24   25   28   30   35   42   50

Thus the median M = 30.

EXAMPLE 2
Find the median of: 1, 12, 8

EXAMPLE 3
Find the median of: 3, 3, 3, 3, 3

EXAMPLE 4
Find the median of: 3, 10, 17, 20

$$M = \frac{10 + 17}{2} = 13.5$$

EXAMPLE 5
Find the median of: 3, 10, 17, 1000

EXAMPLE 6
Find the median of: 145, 162, 100, 126, 200

Answers:
Example 2: 8
Example 3: 3
Example 5: 13.5
Example 6: 145

EXAMPLE 7

Find the median of:

15	18	22	63	52	63	18	19	15	31
15	18	22	15	63	69	63	19	61	30
22	22	52	52	52	69	63	63	15	31

Put the data in numerical order:

69	69	63	63	63	63	63	63	61	52
52	52	52	31	**31**	**30**	22	22	22	22
19	19	18	18	18	15	15	15	15	15

$$M = \frac{15\text{th} + 16\text{th}}{2} = \frac{31 + 30}{2} = 30.5$$

Earlier we generated the following output using the TI-83.

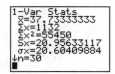 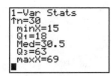

EXAMPLE 8

Find the median of : 35, 46, **72,** 87, 94

$$M = 72$$

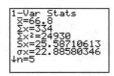 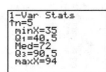

EXAMPLE 9

Find the median number of hrs. worked per week.

hrs. worked per week	# of employees
15	10
20	3
21	2
22	5
	──
	20

Since there are 20 scores we have the 10 lowest and the 10 highest, so the median will be the mean of the 10th and 11th scores. Note that the first 10 scores are all 15's and the next 3 are 20's, which tells us that the 10th score is 15 and the 11th score is 20. Therefore the median is

$$M = \frac{10\text{th} + 11\text{th}}{2} = \frac{15 + 20}{2} = 17.5$$

Notes

Notes

From earlier work on the TI-83

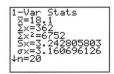 

EXAMPLE 10

Find the median number of sales per person

# of sales per day	# of occurrences
0	15
1	17
2	12
3	9
	———
	53

Since we have 53 scores (15-0's, 17-1's, 12-2's, and 9-3's) we have a middle score. There are 52 other scores divided equally below and above the middle score (26 below and 26 above). Thus the 27th score is the median. Since the first 15 scores are 0's and the next 17 are 1's, that tells us that the 16th through the 32nd scores are all 1. Thus

$$M = 27\text{th score} = 1$$

From earlier work on the TI-83

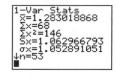 

MODE

The third average is called the mode which represents the **most frequent score or scores.** But if all scores occur *only* once then we say we have *no mode*. Depending on the data you can have 1 mode, 2 modes, or more.

Find the mode for the following examples.

EXAMPLE 1

    35   24   30   25   42   50   28

Since there were no repeated scores there is **no mode.**

EXAMPLE 2

    1, 12, 8

Answers:
Example 2: no mode

EXAMPLE 3

3, 3, 3, 3, 3

EXAMPLE 4

3, 10, 17, 20

EXAMPLE 5

12, 14, 14, 14, 16, 18, 18, 18, 27, 27

EXAMPLE 6

15	18	22	63	52	63	18	19	15	31
15	18	22	15	63	69	63	19	61	30
22	22	52	52	52	69	63	63	15	31

Put the data in numerical order:

69	69	**63**	**63**	**63**	**63**	**63**	**63**	61	52
52	52	52	31	31	30	22	22	22	22
19	19	18	18	18	15	15	15	15	15

The Mode is 63

EXAMPLE 7

hrs. worked per week	# of employees
15	10
20	3
21	2
22	5
	————
	20

The Mode is 15

Answers:
Example 3: 3
Example 4: no mode
Example 5: 14 and 18

EXAMPLE 8

# of sales per day	# of occurrences
0	15
1	17
2	12
3	9
	53

SUMMARY

MEAN
"Arithmetic Average"

MEDIAN
"Middle Value"

MODE
"Most Frequent"

Do these averages tell us the whole story about a data set? Consider the following example of performance of three salespeople and the number of sales made each week, for a ten week period. Please note that the data was ordered from low weekly performance to high weekly performance.

Week	SMITH	JONES	DAVIS
1	6	0	0
2	6	3	0
3	6	4	0
4	6	5	6
5	6	6	6
6	6	6	6
7	6	7	6
8	6	8	12
9	6	9	12
10	6	12	12
Mean	6	6	6
Median	6	6	6
Mode	6	6	6

Did these three salespeople perform equally?

The answer is yes if you are just looking at the average results, but there's a lot more going on here. The three salespeople performed quite differently in terms of consistency, predictability, and reliability. Smith's performance had the least amount of variability, the most consistent, predictable performance. Both Jones and Davis had a lot more variability in their performance and they were much less consistent. So how do we measure this? The next section will address this issue.

Answer:
Example 8: 1

Numerical Methods of Summary: Measures of Variability

We will look at three measures of variability: **range, variance,** and **standard deviation.**

Range: Largest Score–Smallest Score

Find the range of each of the following examples.

EXAMPLE 1

35   24   30   25   42   50   28

$$\text{Range} = 50 - 24 = 26$$

EXAMPLE 2

3, 3, 3, 3, 3

$$\text{Range} = 3 - 3 = 0$$

EXAMPLE 3

3, 10, 17, 20

EXAMPLE 4

3, 10, 17, 1000

EXAMPLE 5

15   18   22   63   52   63   18   19   15   31
15   18   22   15   63   69   63   19   61   30
22   22   52   52   52   69   63   63   15   31

Answers:
Example 3: 17
Example 4: 997
Example 5: 54

EXAMPLE 6

hrs. worked per week	# of employees
15	10
20	3
21	2
22	5
	20

$$\text{Range} = 22 - 15 = 7$$

EXAMPLE 7

# of sales per day	# of occurrences
0	15
1	17
2	12
3	9
	53

Returning to the three salesperson example, we can compute the range for each person:

Range for Smith $= 0$

Range for Jones $= 12$

Range for Davis $= 12$

The range for Smith being 0 tells us quite a bit about Smith's performance, namely that there was no variability at all. Smith was 100% consistent in performance. Notice also that Jones and Davis both had ranges of 12, which might lead one to believe that they were equally variable. However looking over the data suggests that Davis was less consistent than Jones. In fact Jones was at the extreme values of 12 and 0 exactly once, while Davis was at these extremes 6 out of 10 weeks.

This highlights one of the weaknesses of the range, in that it does not take into account how often you perform at the extremes. To rectify the situation we will need to use a more complicated measure of variability.

POPULATION VARIANCE σ^2

If the data $x_1, x_2, \ldots, x_n$ arises from a **complete census of the population** then the **population variance** is

$$\sigma^2 = \frac{(x_1 - \mu)^2 + (x_2 - \mu)^2 + \cdots + (x_n - \mu)^2}{n}$$

with

$$\mu = \frac{x_1 + x_2 + \cdots + x_n}{n}$$

Answers:
Example 7: 3

POPULATION STANDARD DEVIATION σ

$$\sigma = \sqrt{\sigma^2}$$

SAMPLE VARIANCE s^2

If the data $x_1, x_2, \ldots, x_n$ arises from a **sample** then the **sample variance** is

$$s^2 = \frac{(x_1 - \overline{X})^2 + (x_2 - \overline{X})^2 + \cdots + (x_n - \overline{X})^2}{n - 1}$$

with

$$\overline{X} = \frac{x_1 + x_2 + \cdots + x_n}{n}$$

SAMPLE STANDARD DEVIATION s

$$s = \sqrt{s^2}$$

Note again the different notation between sample and population mean and now also the different notation and different formulas for the population and sample variance and the population and sample standard deviation.

Let's look at data from some of our previous examples in this chapter, and compute the variance and standard deviation.

Notes

Notes

EXAMPLE 8

Population Data: 3, 3, 3, 3, 3

$$\mu = \frac{3 + 3 + 3 + 3 + 3}{5} = \frac{15}{5} = 3$$

$$\sigma^2 = \frac{(3 - 3)^2 + (3 - 3)^2 + (3 - 3)^2 + (3 - 3)^2 + (3 - 3)^2}{5}$$

$$= \frac{0}{5}$$

$$\sigma^2 = 0$$

$$\sigma = \sqrt{0} = 0$$

EXAMPLE 9

Sample Data: 35 46 72 87 94

$$\overline{X} = \frac{35 + 46 + 72 + 87 + 94}{5} = \frac{334}{5} = 66.8$$

$$s^2 = \frac{(35 - 66.8)^2 + (46 - 66.8)^2 + (72 - 66.8)^2 + (87 - 66.8)^2 + (94 - 66.8)^2}{5 - 1}$$

$$= \frac{2,618.8}{4}$$

$$s^2 = 654.7$$

$$s = \sqrt{654.7} = 25.58710613$$

This is already looking a bit tedious. Let's return to the 1-Var Stats feature in the TI-83.

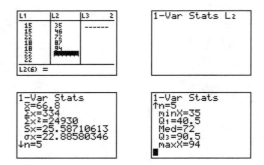

Note that **Sx** is the sample standard deviation.

EXAMPLE 10
Sample Data

15	18	22	63	52	63	18	19	15	31
15	18	22	15	63	69	63	19	61	30
22	22	52	52	52	69	63	63	15	31

You can see why we might not want to compute the mean and standard deviation for this data using the formulas. The 1-Var Stats feature comes into play here

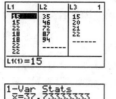
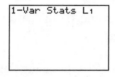
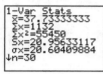
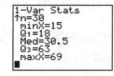

What do all of these quantities represent?

$\bar{x}$ = mean mean score 37.73

$\sum x$ = sum of the scores x 1132

$\sum x^2$ = sum of the squares of scores x not important

Sx = sample standard deviation for x 20.956

σx = population standard deviation for x not appropriate

n = number of data items 30

min X = smallest value of x lowest score was 15

Q_1 = 1st quartile or 25th percentile 25% score below 18

Med = median or 50th percentile 50% score below 30.5

Q_3 = 3rd quartile or 75th percentile 75% score below 63

max X = largest value of x highest score was 69

What about the sample variance?

As we'll see, the variance is not as important a measure of variability as the standard deviation. But if you do want to compute it simply square the standard deviation.

The following five quantities,

min X = smallest value of x

Q_1 = 1st quartile or 25th percentile

Med = median or 50th percentile

Q_3 = 3rd quartile or 75th percentile

max X = largest value of x

are called the five number summary, and are often used along with the mean and standard deviation to describe data.

We can show some of this numerical information graphically, using the Boxplot feature.

Turn off all plots by pressing **2nd** and **Y =** (STATPLOT) and then selecting option **4:PlotsOff.** Then press **ENTER.**

Press **2nd** and **Y =** (STATPLOT) and select **1:Plot1** and turn the Plot **ON** and select the **Boxplot** icon (middle graph 2nd row). Also use **L1** for **XList** and **1** for **Freq.**

Press **ZOOM** and select **9:ZoomStat.** The following graph is generated.

Press **WINDOW** and make the following selections

Press **TRACE** and use the left and right arrow keys to find the Median, Q1, Q3, minX, and maxX

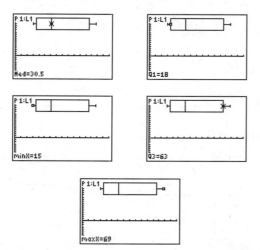

Notes

EXAMPLE 11
Population Data

hrs. worked per week	# of employees
15	10
20	3
21	2
22	5
	20

Using the TI-83 with

L3 = hours worked   and   **L4** = #of employees

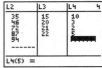 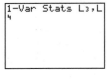

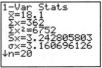

$\bar{x}$ = mean	mean hrs. 18.1
$\sum x$ = sum of the scores x	total hrs. 362
$\sum x^2$ = sum of the squares of scores x	not important
Sx = sample standard deviation for x	not appropriate
σx = population standard deviation for x	3.160696126
n = number of data items	20
min X = smallest value of x	lowest hrs. 15
Q_1 = 1st quartile or 25th percentile	25% hrs. below 15
Med = median or 50th percentile	50% hrs. below 17.5
Q_3 = 3rd quartile or 75th percentile	75% hrs. below 21.5
max X = largest value of x	highest hrs. 22

Let's return to where we started this section, namely with the data on performance of three salespeople

Week	SMITH	JONES	DAVIS
1	6	0	0
2	6	3	0
3	6	4	0
4	6	5	6
5	6	6	6
6	6	6	6
7	6	7	6
8	6	8	12
9	6	9	12
10	6	12	12
Mean	6	6	6
Median	6	6	6
Mode	6	6	6
Range	0	12	12
St. Dev.	0	3.16	4.65

How can we do this problem on the TI-83?

L1–L6 are all filled. Do we need to clear these or can we insert these three columns of data within our data editor?

We will insert this data and name the columns SMITH, JONES, DAVIS.

Enter the data editor by pressing **STAT** selecting **1:Edit** and then move the cursor to **L1.**

Press **2nd** and **DEL** (this is the **INS** key). Type in the name SMITH by using the green alphabetic keys (for example T is the 4 key). Then press **ENTER.**

Move the cursor to **L1** and press **2nd** and **DEL** (**INS** key). Type in the name JONES. Then press **ENTER.**

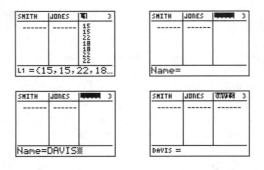

Move the cursor to **L1** and press **2nd** and **DEL** (**INS** key). Type in the name DAVIS. Then press **ENTER.**

Now enter the data into these three named lists.

Press **STAT** then select **CALC** and **1:1–Var Stats.**

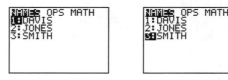

To paste in the name of the list you wish to analyze press **2nd** and **STAT** (this is the **LIST** key). Then select **NAMES** and **3:SMITH.**

Press **ENTER** and scroll down to see the results.

Notes

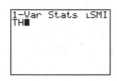

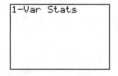

Repeat the steps to select JONES.

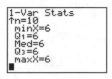

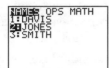

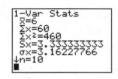

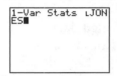

Repeat the steps for DAVIS.

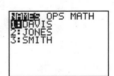

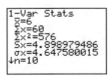

Interpretation

1. s, s^2, σ, σ^2 are all ≥ 0.
2. s, s^2, σ, σ^2 are equal to 0 if and only if all scores are identical (no variation). We saw this with Example 8 and with salesperson Smith.
3. In comparable situations, a lower standard deviation implies less variability. Looking at the salesperson example we see

   Smith $\sigma = 0$

   Jones $\sigma = 3.16$

   Davis $\sigma = 4.65$

   Smith is the most consistent (actually perfectly consistent), with Jones being more consistent than Davis, who was the least consistent (most variable in performance).
4. In general the standard deviation is a more important tool for measuring variability, than the variance because of the units.

Let's say that we have collected data on sale price of homes in a city. The data is units of dollars (\$). The mean sale price of homes is also in units of dollars (\$). The variance of sale price is in dollars-squared (\$^{2}), which is a nonsensical, meaningless unit. However the standard deviation for sale price is in dollars (\$). Note the data, the mean, and the standard deviation are all in the same units, while the variance is not and in fact has units that are inappropriate.

Statistics Worksheet

1. Do a stem-leaf display, frequency table, group frequency table, histogram, and frequency polygon for each of the data sets below. Also find the mean, median, mode, standard deviation, minimum, maximum, Q1 and Q3.

   A. Sample Data

   12 15 16 89 12 16 45 45 37 83 12 67 12 12
   45 67 67 57 55 50 90 08 70 70 16 12 45 83
   12 55 40 11 12

   B. Population Data

   123 134 123 134 123 120 134 111 110 100 100 109 134 123
   120 134 100 125 090 105 109 134 120 101 125 108 100

2. Find the mean, median, mode, standard deviation, minimum, maximum, Q1 and Q3 for each of the following data sets.

   A.   Sample Data

Score	Freq.
108	10
90	5
89	18
76	2
67	1
65	2
	38

   B.   Population Data

Score	Freq.
0	10
1	25
2	47
3	25
4	10
	117

Partial Answers:

1A. Mean = 40.55	Median = 45	Mode = 12	Min = 8	Max = 90
St. Dev. = 27.39	Q1 = 12	Q3 = 67		
1B. Mean = 116.63	Median = 120	Mode = 134	Min = 90	Max = 134
St. Dev. = 13.06	Q1 = 105	Q3 = 125		
2A. Mean = 91.61	Median = 89	Mode = 89	Min = 65	Max = 108
St. Dev. = 12.00	Q1 = 89	Q3 = 108		
2B. Mean = 2	Median = 2	Mode = 2	Min = 0	Max = 4
St. Dev. = 1.054	Q1 = 1	Q3 = 3		

Chapter 7 Exercise Set

1. **Bears** Refer to the data set in the Chapter 7 appendix and construct a frequency distribution and histogram of the weights of bears. Use 11 classes beginning with a lower class limit of 0 and use a class width of 50 lb.

2. **Marathon Runners** Refer to the data set in the Chapter 7 appendix and construct a frequency distribution and histogram for the ages of the females. Do the same with the males. In both cases start the first class with a lower class limit of 19 and a class width of 10. Compare the results and determine whether there appears to be any notable difference between the two groups.

3. **Speeding Tickets** The given frequency distribution describes the speeds of drivers ticketed by the Town of Poughkeepsie police. These drivers were traveling through a 30 mi/h speed zone on Creek Road, which passes the author's college. Construct a histogram corresponding to the given frequency distribution. What does the distribution suggest about the enforced speed limit compared to the posted speed limit?

Speed	Frequency
42–45	25
46–49	14
50–53	7
54–57	3
58–61	1

In Exercise 4, construct the stem-and-leaf plot for the given data sets found in the Chapter 7 Appendix.

4. **Bears** The lengths (in inches) of the bears. (*Hint:* First round the lengths to the nearest inch.)

In Exercises 5–6, find the (a) mean, (b) median, (c) mode for the given sample data.

5. **Drunk Driving** The blood alcohol concentrations of a sample of drivers involved in fatal crashes and then convicted with jail sentences are given below (based on data from the U.S. Department of Justice). Given that current state laws prohibit driving with levels above 0.08 or 0.10, does it appear that these levels are significantly above the maximum that is allowed?

0.27	0.17	0.17	0.16	0.13	0.24	0.29	0.24
0.14	0.16	0.12	0.16	0.21	0.17	0.18	

6. **Motorcycle Fatalities** Listed below are ages of motorcyclists when they were fatally injured in traffic crashes (based on data from the U.S. Department of Transportation). Do the results support the

common belief that such fatalities are incurred by a greater proportion of younger drivers?

17	38	27	14	18	34	16	42	28
24	40	20	23	31	37	21	30	25

***In Exercises 7 and 8, find the mean, median, mode, for each of the
two samples, then compare the two sets of results.***

7. Customer Waiting Times Waiting times (in minutes) of customers
at the Jefferson Valley Bank (where all customers enter a single
waiting line) and the Bank of Providence (where customers wait in
individual lines at three different teller windows):

Jefferson Valley: 6.5 6.6 6.7 6.8 7.1 7.3 7.4 7.7 7.7 7.7

Providence: 4.2 5.4 5.8 6.2 6.7 7.7 7.7 8.5 9.3 10.0

Interpret the results by determining whether there is a difference between the two data sets that is not apparent from a comparison of the
measures of center. If so, what is it?

8. Mickey D vs. Jack When investigating times required for drive-
through service, the following results (in seconds) are obtained
(based on data from QSR Drive-Thru Time Study).

McDonald's: 287 128 92 267 176 240 192 118 153 254 193 136

Jack in   190 229 74 377 300 481 428 255 328 270 109 109
the Box:

Which of the two fast-food giants appears to be faster? Does the difference appear to be significant?

***In Exercises 9 and 10 find the range and standard deviation for the
given sample data.***

9. Drunk Driving The blood alcohol concentrations of a sample of
drivers involved in fatal crashes and then convicted with jail sentences are given below (based on data from the U.S. Department of
Justice). When a state wages a campaign to "reduce drunk driving,"
is the campaign intended to lower the standard deviation?

0.27	0.17	0.17	0.16	0.13	0.24	0.29	0.24
0.14	0.16	0.12	0.16	0.21	0.17	0.18	

10. Motorcycle Fatalities Listed below are ages of motorcyclists when
they were fatally injured in traffic crashes (based on data from the
U.S. Department of Transportation). How does the variation of these
ages compare to the variation of ages of licensed drivers in the general population?

17	38	27	14	18	34	16	42	28
24	40	20	23	31	37	21	30	25

In Exercises 11–12, find the range and standard deviation for each of the two samples, then compare the two sets of results.

11. Customer Waiting Times Waiting times of customers at the Jefferson Valley Bank (where all customers enter a single waiting line) and the Bank of Providence (where customers wait in individual lines at three different teller windows):

    Jefferson Valley: 6.5 6.6   6.7 6.8   7.1   7.3   7.4   7.7   7.7   7.7
    Providence: 4.2 5.4   5.8 6.2   6.7   7.7   7.7   8.5   9.3 10.0

12. Mickey D vs. Jack When investigating times required for drive-through service, the following results (in seconds) are obtained (based on data from QSR Drive-Thru Time Study).

    McDonald's: 287 128 92 267 176 240 192 118 153 254 193 136

    Jack in
    the Box: 190 229 74 377 300 481 428 255 328 270 109 109

13. Consider the following sample data set:

25	30	30	26	60	62	48	78	75	89
12	89	75	75	85	40	85	89	85	82
30	26	45	45	45	50	52	50	50	52

    (a) Do a stem leaf display for the above data.
    (b) Group the data in a group frequency table with intervals and frequencies.
    (c) Draw a histogram
    (d) Compute the mean, median, mode, range, standard deviation for this data.

14. Consider the following population data:

Age of Employees	Number of Employees
30	52
31	42
32	29
33	19
34	14
35	11
36	10
Total	177

    Find the mean, median, mode, range, and standard deviation for this data.

Chapter 7 Appendix

Data Set 1: New York City Marathon Finishers

Sample is 150 runners randomly selected from the population of 29,373 runners who finished the New York City Marathon in a recent year.

Order	Age	Gender	Time (sec)	Order	Age	Gender	Time (sec)
130	32	M	9631	7082	38	M	13851
265	39	M	10209	7093	32	F	13854
314	39	M	10351	7933	50	M	14057
490	36	M	10641	7966	43	M	14066
547	34	M	10723	8011	25	M	14078
708	28	M	10905	8027	39	M	14082
834	42	M	11061	8042	31	M	14086
944	46	M	11188	8186	37	M	14121
1084	32	M	11337	8225	46	M	14128
1086	34	M	11338	8609	23	F	14216
1132	41	M	11382	8707	30	F	14235
1593	36	M	11738	8823	24	M	14256
1625	50	M	11761	9451	29	M	14375
1735	36	M	11830	9630	30	M	14402
1792	40	M	11874	10130	36	M	14512
1826	33	M	11897	10191	40	M	14528
2052	29	F	12047	10556	51	M	14617
2108	28	M	12077	10585	51	M	14623
2167	40	M	12115	10643	51	M	14632
2505	30	F	12289	10821	30	M	14677
2550	28	M	12312	10910	38	M	14698
3344	44	M	12639	10979	59	M	14720
3376	45	M	12652	10982	28	F	14721
4115	45	M	12940	11091	49	M	14752
4252	54	M	12986	11413	55	M	14836
4459	33	M	13063	11699	53	M	14919
4945	49	M	13217	11769	53	M	14935
5269	45	M	13315	11792	40	M	14942
5286	40	M	13322	11869	38	M	14964
5559	26	M	13408	11896	35	M	14971
6169	23	F	13593	11997	54	M	14996
6235	21	M	13615	12019	21	M	15002
6552	50	F	13704	12160	33	F	15036
6618	33	M	13722	12306	58	F	15077
6904	38	M	13802	12683	43	M	15167
6996	40	M	13829	12845	33	M	15210

(continued)

Notes

Notes

Data Set 1: New York City Marathon Finishers (*continued*)

Order	Age	Gender	Time (sec)	Order	Age	Gender	Time (sec)
12942	35	M	15232	21013	38	M	17396
13226	31	M	15309	21017	47	M	17397
13262	38	M	15318	21524	34	M	17563
13297	28	F	15326	21787	37	F	17636
13434	30	F	15357	22009	37	M	17711
13597	23	F	15402	22042	31	F	17726
14391	40	M	15608	22258	29	F	17799
14633	43	M	15671	22285	49	M	17807
14909	43	M	15741	22638	31	M	17918
15282	29	M	15825	22993	52	M	18041
16030	34	F	16013	23092	38	M	18080
16324	30	M	16090	24018	30	F	18469
16723	65	M	16194	24283	31	F	18580
16840	50	M	16229	24290	40	M	18583
17104	37	F	16297	24417	50	F	18647
17298	30	F	16352	24466	29	M	18677
17436	32	M	16389	24649	21	M	18784
17483	19	F	16401	24845	53	M	18906
17487	42	M	16402	25262	41	M	19164
17694	33	M	16461	25287	50	F	19177
18132	42	M	16582	25956	45	M	19669
18765	51	M	16752	26471	27	F	20084
18783	54	F	16758	26545	32	M	20164
18825	32	F	16771	26637	53	M	20269
18897	34	F	16792	27035	42	F	20675
19002	31	M	16812	27046	45	M	20698
19210	50	F	16871	27133	39	M	20808
19264	60	M	16886	27152	31	M	20841
19278	49	M	16889	27196	68	F	20891
19649	51	F	16991	27277	51	M	20970
19789	45	M	17034	27800	51	M	21649
20425	40	F	17211	27955	31	F	21911
20558	30	M	17245	27995	25	F	21983
20562	25	M	17246	28062	25	M	22087
20580	32	M	17252	28085	61	M	22146
20592	34	M	17257	28578	31	M	23545
20605	42	F	17260	28779	32	M	24384
20700	34	F	17286	28986	47	F	25399
20826	52	M	17327	29045	61	F	25898

Data Set 2: Bears (wild bears anesthetized)

AGE is in months, MONTH is the month of measurement (1 = January),
SEX is coded with 1 = male and 2 = female, HEADLEN is head length (inches),
HEADWTH is width of head (inches), NECK is distance around neck (in
inches), LENGTH is length of body (inches), CHEST is distance around chest
(inches), and WEIGHT is measured in pounds. Data are from Gary Alt and
Minitab, Inc.

Age	Month	Sex	Headlen	Headwth	Neck	Length	Chest	Weight
19	7	1	11.0	5.5	16.0	53.0	26.0	80
55	7	1	16.5	9.0	28.0	67.5	45.0	344
81	9	1	15.5	8.0	31.0	72.0	54.0	416
115	7	1	17.0	10.0	31.5	72.0	49.0	348
104	8	2	15.5	6.5	22.0	62.0	35.0	166
100	4	2	13.0	7.0	21.0	70.0	41.0	220
56	7	1	15.0	7.5	26.5	73.5	41.0	262
51	4	1	13.5	8.0	27.0	68.5	49.0	360
57	9	2	13.5	7.0	20.0	64.0	38.0	204
53	5	2	12.5	6.0	18.0	58.0	31.0	144
68	8	1	16.0	9.0	29.0	73.0	44.0	332
8	8	1	9.0	4.5	13.0	37.0	19.0	34
44	8	2	12.5	4.5	10.5	63.0	32.0	140
32	8	1	14.0	5.0	21.5	67.0	37.0	180
20	8	2	11.5	5.0	17.5	52.0	29.0	105
32	8	1	13.0	8.0	21.5	59.0	33.0	166
45	9	1	13.5	7.0	24.0	64.0	39.0	204
9	9	2	9.0	4.5	12.0	36.0	19.0	26
21	9	1	13.0	6.0	19.0	59.0	30.0	120
177	9	1	16.0	9.5	30.0	72.0	48.0	436
57	9	2	12.5	5.0	19.0	57.5	32.0	125
81	9	2	13.0	5.0	20.0	61.0	33.0	132
21	9	1	13.0	5.0	17.0	54.0	28.0	90
9	9	1	10.0	4.0	13.0	40.0	23.0	40
45	9	1	16.0	6.0	24.0	63.0	42.0	220
9	9	1	10.0	4.0	13.5	43.0	23.0	46
33	9	1	13.5	6.0	22.0	66.5	34.0	154
57	9	2	13.0	5.5	17.5	60.5	31.0	116
45	9	2	13.0	6.5	21.0	60.0	34.5	182
21	9	1	14.5	5.5	20.0	61.0	34.0	150
10	10	1	9.5	4.5	16.0	40.0	26.0	65
82	10	2	13.5	6.5	28.0	64.0	48.0	356

(continued)

Notes

Data Set 2: Bears (wild bears anesthetized) (*continued*)

Age	Month	Sex	Headlen	Headwth	Neck	Length	Chest	Weight
70	10	2	14.5	6.5	26.0	65.0	48.0	316
10	10	1	11.0	5.0	17.0	49.0	29.0	94
10	10	1	11.5	5.0	17.0	47.0	29.5	86
34	10	1	13.0	7.0	21.0	59.0	35.0	150
34	10	1	16.5	6.5	27.0	72.0	44.5	270
34	10	1	14.0	5.5	24.0	65.0	39.0	202
58	10	2	13.5	6.5	21.5	63.0	40.0	202
58	10	1	15.5	7.0	28.0	70.5	50.0	365
11	11	1	11.5	6.0	16.5	48.0	31.0	79
23	11	1	12.0	6.5	19.0	50.0	38.0	148
70	10	1	15.5	7.0	28.0	76.5	55.0	446
11	11	2	9.0	5.0	15.0	46.0	27.0	62
83	11	2	14.5	7.0	23.0	61.5	44.0	236
35	11	1	13.5	8.5	23.0	63.5	44.0	212
16	4	1	10.0	4.0	15.5	48.0	26.0	60
16	4	1	10.0	5.0	15.0	41.0	26.0	64
17	5	1	11.5	5.0	17.0	53.0	30.5	114
17	5	2	11.5	5.0	15.0	52.5	28.0	76
17	5	2	11.0	4.5	13.0	46.0	23.0	48
8	8	2	10.0	4.5	10.0	43.5	24.0	29
83	11	1	15.5	8.0	30.5	75.0	54.0	514
18	6	1	12.5	8.5	18.0	57.3	32.8	140

Probability

8

8.1 Introduction to Probability

So what is probability all about?

Probability—the assignment of a number to the likelihood of the occurrence of an event.

Probabilistic Statements Quantify Likelihood

EXAMPLE 1

The probability of precipitation for tomorrow is 40%.

EXAMPLE 2

The odds that the White Sox will win the World Series in the next season is 7 to 3

Notes

EXAMPLE 3

When tossing a fair coin, you would expect that heads would come up 1/2 of the time.

EXAMPLE 4

The probability that a meteor will strike the earth in the next year is .0000001.

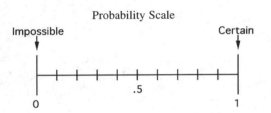

The probability of an event can be expressed as a number between 0 and 1 (inclusive) or equivalently as a percent.

Rules

The probability of an **impossible** event is **0.**

The probability of an **absolutely certain** event is **1.**

Events that are impossible or absolutely certain are so because of the structure of the situation. For example, in a standard 52 card deck, the cards are either red or black. Thus the probability of picking a card from this deck and getting a yellow card is 0, since that event is impossible, due to the structure of the situation. If you roll a fair die with numbers 1 through 6 on the six faces, then it is absolutely certain that you will get a number between 1 and 6 (inclusive) when you roll the die. Thus the probability of this event is 1. But again, notice this is due to the structure of the situation.

How are probabilities determined?

There are three approaches. We will focus on the first two.

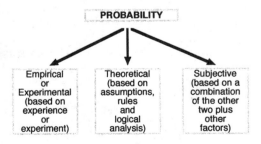

Experimental Probability

We perform the experiment of flipping a fair coin 100 times. We do this experiment a total of five times. The results are found below.

EXP.	Heads	Tails
1	52	48
2	46	54
3	51	49
4	57	43
5	45	55

Consider experiment 1, the relative frequency of heads is $52/100 = .52 = 52\%$.

Consider experiment 2, the relative frequency of heads is $46/100 = .46 = 46\%$.

The experimental probability is the relative frequency of occurrence.

More precisely, the experimental probability of an event A occurring is denoted by **P(A)** and is given by

$$P(A) = \frac{\text{number of times event A occurs}}{\text{total number of trials}}$$

So in experiment 5, P(Heads) $= 45/100 = .45$ or 45%.

What would you expect if a coin is flipped 100 times? What percentage of heads would you predict?

Most people would say 50%. Why didn't this happen in the 5 experiments performed? Is there something wrong with our coin or our experiments?

Even if the coin were truly fair, we are not guaranteed that in 100 flips we'll 50 heads. Random chance or luck is involved here. If you notice the cumulative statistics on the the five experiments you'll see that the results are very close to the predicted 50% heads.

EXP.	Heads	Tails	P(Heads)
1	52	48	0.520
2	46	54	0.460
3	51	49	0.510
4	57	43	0.570
5	45	55	0.450
Total	251	249	0.502

Theoretical Probability

Experiment   process of making an observation or taking a measurement.

Sample Space   set of all possible outcomes of an experiment.

Event   a subset of the sample space.

EXAMPLE 5
Toss Coin Once

H   T

Thus the sample space is **S** = {H, T}

EXAMPLE 6
Toss Coin Twice

HH   HT   TH   TT

Thus the sample space is **S** = {HH, HT, TH, TT}

Examples of events:

    E = at least one tail = {TH, HT, TT}
    F = exactly one tail = {HT, TH}
    G = two heads = {HH}

Note that you will need to be careful and precise with terms like "at least," "at most," "more than," "less than," etc.

EXAMPLE 7
Toss Coin Three Times

| HHH HHT HTH HTT |
| THH THT TTH TTT |

$$S = \{HHH, HHT, HTH, HTT, THH, THT, TTH, TTT\}$$

Examples of events:

Q = at least two tails = {HTT, THT, TTH, TTT}
R = at most two tails = {HHH, HHT, HTH, HTT, THH, THT, TTH}

Can we find another way to describe this sample space? It's already getting a little bit complicated. How would I find the sample space for tossing a coin four times?

To make this easier, we will use a tool called a **decision tree.**

Here is the decision tree for tossing a coin once (Example 5). Note that there are two possible outcomes.

Here is the decision tree for tossing a coin twice (Example 6). Note that there are four possible outcomes.

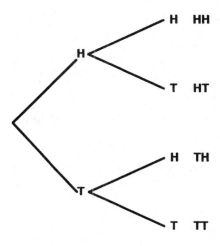

Notes

Here is the decision tree for tossing a coin three times (Example 7). Note that there are eight possible outcomes.

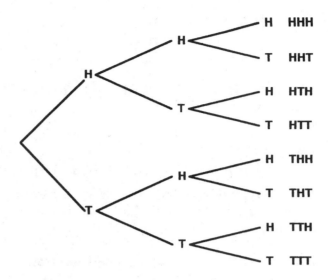

Can you see how to do the sample space for tossing a coin four times?

How many branches would that decision tree have?

Rules for Assigning Probabilities

Consider the sample space with outcomes O_1, O_2, O_3, $\cdots$, O_n and with probabilities p_1, p_2, p_3, $\cdots$, p_n.

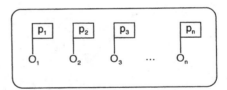

1. All probabilities must be between 0 and 1.

$$0 \le p_1 \le 1$$
$$0 \le p_2 \le 1$$
$$0 \le p_3 \le 1$$
$$\vdots$$
$$0 \le p_n \le 1$$

2. The probability of all outcomes within a sample space must sum to 1.

$$p_2 + p_2 + p_3 + \cdots + p_n = 1$$

Let's consider again Example 5, tossing a coin once.

Answer: 16

EXAMPLE 5
Toss Coin Once

Bill's Probability Model

Dave's Probability Model

Both of the probability models follow the two rules on the previous page. They differ in the underlying assumptions made by Bill versus Dave. Dave assumes equal probability, while Bill assumes that heads should come up nines time more often than tails.

Is one model "better" than the other? What does better mean?

When probability models are constructed, they are done with the purpose of modeling reality as well as possible, in this case, tossing coins. Without ever flipping a coin, Bill has decided to assign probabilities of .9 for head and .1 for tail, while Dave assigned equal probabilities of .5 to both head and tail. Which model is better depends on which model better predicts reality. If we collect some data (i.e., toss some coins) we can see which model does better in predicting reality.

If we toss a coin 100 times and we get 52 heads and 48 tails, then neither Bill nor Dave modeled reality perfectly. However, Dave can reasonably explain the difference between what he predicted (50% heads and 50% tails) and what actually happened by simply invoking random chance . That is, the reason we did not get 50 heads and 50 tails is just chance (luck). Bill will have a very difficult time in convincing anyone that he had an accurate model and that he was just unlucky with the actual results.

The assumption of equal probability that Dave made is a quite common one. Often we assume equal probabilities until proven otherwise.

EXAMPLE 6
Toss Coin Twice

We make the equal probability assumption once again. With four possible outcomes, each equally likely, then our probabilities are as shown below.

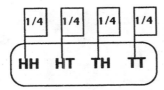

Notes

EXAMPLE 7
Tossing Coin Three Times

With eight equally likely possibilities, each has a 1/8 probability.

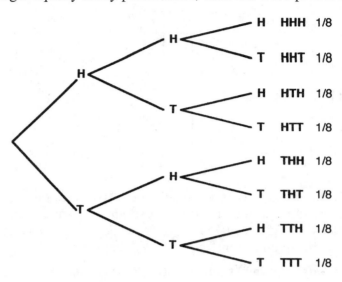

EXAMPLE 8
You roll one die (six sided). Assign the probabilities below.

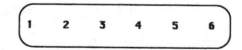

EXAMPLE 9
You roll 2 dice, one red and one green.

Red Die	1	2	3	4	5	6
Green Die	1	2	3	4	5	6

Although we could have used a decision tree here the table below is a better representation of this sample space.

	1	2	3	4	5	6
1	(1,1)	(1,2)	(1,3)	(1,4)	(1,5)	(1,6)
2	(2,1)	(2,2)	(2,3)	(2,4)	(2,5)	(2,6)
3	(3,1)	(3,2)	(3,3)	(3,4)	(3,5)	(3,6)
4	(4,1)	(4,2)	(4,3)	(4,4)	(4,5)	(4,6)
5	(5,1)	(5,2)	(5,3)	(5,4)	(5,5)	(5,6)
6	(6,1)	(6,2)	(6,3)	(6,4)	(6,5)	(6,6)

Answers:
Example 8: each is 1/6

If both dice are fair, then each outcome in this sample space will have probability of 1/36.

EXAMPLE 10

Pick one ball from a bag containing 2 red balls and 1 black. Set up the sample space and assign probabilities to all of the outcomes.

EXAMPLE 11

Select one card at random from a standard 52 card deck.

♥ **Hearts**	♦ **Diamonds**	♣ **Clubs**	♠ **Spades**
Ace	Ace	Ace	Ace
2	2	2	2
3	3	3	3
4	4	4	4
5	5	5	5
6	6	6	6
7	7	7	7
8	8	8	8
9	9	9	9
10	10	10	10
Jack	Jack	Jack	Jack
Queen	Queen	Queen	Queen
King	King	King	King

Set up the probabilities for each of the 52 outcomes.

So thus far we have defined our experiment, listed out all the possible outcomes and assigned probabilities using assumptions and rules. Recall earlier we defined an event as a subset of the sample space, meaning that events are made up of one or more outcomes. How do we find probabilities of events?

The **probability of an event A** is the sum of the probabilities of the outcomes corresponding to A.

Answers:
Example 10: P(Red) = 2/3 and P(Black) = 1/3
Example 11: each card has 1/52 prob.

EXAMPLE 6
Toss Coin Twice

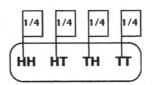

Recall the following events:

E = at least one tail = {TH, HT, TT}

F = exactly one tail = {HT, TH}

G = two heads = {HH}

Let's find the probabilities of each of these three events.

$$P(E) = P(TH) + P(HT) + P(TT) = \frac{1}{4} + \frac{1}{4} + \frac{1}{4} = \frac{3}{4} = .75$$

$$P(F) = P(HT) + P(TH) = \frac{1}{4} + \frac{1}{4} = \frac{1}{2} = .50$$

$$P(G) = P(HH) = \frac{1}{4} = .25$$

EXAMPLE 9
Roll 2 dice

Find the probability of getting a sum of 4

	1	2	3	4	5	6
1	(1,1)	(1,2)	(1,3)	(1,4)	(1,5)	(1,6)
2	(2,1)	(2,2)	(2,3)	(2,4)	(2,5)	(2,6)
3	(3,1)	(3,2)	(3,3)	(3,4)	(3,5)	(3,6)
4	(4,1)	(4,2)	(4,3)	(4,4)	(4,5)	(4,6)
5	(5,1)	(5,2)	(5,3)	(5,4)	(5,5)	(5,6)
6	(6,1)	(6,2)	(6,3)	(6,4)	(6,5)	(6,6)

$$P(\text{Sum} = 4) = P((3, 1)) + P((2, 2)) + P((1, 3))$$

$$= \frac{1}{36} + \frac{1}{36} + \frac{1}{36}$$

$$= \frac{3}{36}$$

$$= \frac{1}{12}$$

Find the probability of getting a sum of 7

	1	2	3	4	5	6
1	(1,1)	(1,2)	(1,3)	(1,4)	(1,5)	(1,6)
2	(2,1)	(2,2)	(2,3)	(2,4)	(2,5)	(2,6)
3	(3,1)	(3,2)	(3,3)	(3,4)	(3,5)	(3,6)
4	(4,1)	(4,2)	(4,3)	(4,4)	(4,5)	(4,6)
5	(5,1)	(5,2)	(5,3)	(5,4)	(5,5)	(5,6)
6	(6,1)	(6,2)	(6,3)	(6,4)	(6,5)	(6,6)

$$P(\text{Sum} = 7) = P((6, 1)) + P((5, 2)) + P((4, 3)) + P((3, 4)) + P((2, 5)) + P((1, 6))$$

$$= \frac{1}{36} + \frac{1}{36} + \frac{1}{36} + \frac{1}{36} + \frac{1}{36} + \frac{1}{36}$$

$$= \frac{6}{36}$$

$$= \frac{1}{6}$$

The Equal Probability Assumption

Using this assumption in a sample space having **N** outcomes, means that each outcome must have probability of **1/N.**

Furthermore, the process for computing probabilities of events is simplified.

The probability of an event **E** is given by

$$P(E) = \frac{\text{number of outcomes favorable to E}}{\text{total number of outcomes}}$$

$$= \frac{n(E)}{n(S)}$$

where S is the sample space.

Returning to Example 9, rolling two dice.

Find the probability of getting a sum of 7

	1	2	3	4	5	6
1	(1,1)	(1,2)	(1,3)	(1,4)	(1,5)	(1,6)
2	(2,1)	(2,2)	(2,3)	(2,4)	(2,5)	(2,6)
3	(3,1)	(3,2)	(3,3)	(3,4)	(3,5)	(3,6)
4	(4,1)	(4,2)	(4,3)	(4,4)	(4,5)	(4,6)
5	(5,1)	(5,2)	(5,3)	(5,4)	(5,5)	(5,6)
6	(6,1)	(6,2)	(6,3)	(6,4)	(6,5)	(6,6)

$$P(\text{Sum} = 7) = \frac{6}{36} = \frac{1}{6}$$

since there are six ways to get a sum of 7 out of a total of 36 possible outcomes.

EXAMPLE 11

Select 1 card from a 52 card deck

Find the probability that the card is

a. a spade,

b. an ace,

c. red.

♥ Hearts	♦ Diamonds	♣ Clubs	♠ Spades
Ace	Ace	Ace	Ace
2	2	2	2
3	3	3	3
4	4	4	4
5	5	5	5
6	6	6	6
7	7	7	7
8	8	8	8
9	9	9	9
10	10	10	10
Jack	Jack	Jack	Jack
Queen	Queen	Queen	Queen
King	King	King	King

Answers:
Example 11: a. .25, b. .0769, c. .5000

Odds and Probability

Odds provide another way of communicating the chance of an event occurring. Theoretically there are two kinds of odds: odds against and odds in favor. Practically, however, when you see odds mentioned in describing a situation they always refer to **odds against.** We want to be able to convert from odds against to probability in favor and against. But instead of memorizing a formula to do this it might be easier to model the situation.

Let's suppose that you read in the newspaper that the odds that the stock market drops by 20% or more next year is 10 to 1. In reality the odds are 10 to 1 against. Here's another situation where the odds are 10 to 1 against. Consider a box with 10 red balls and 1 white ball. The odds are 10 to 1 against you selecting the white ball. The probability of selecting the white ball would be 1/11. Thus the probability that the stock market drops by 20% or more next year is 1/11 (which is approximately 9%).

If the odds had been 5 to 2 then the situation is equivalent to a box with 5 red balls and 2 white balls. The probability of selecting the white ball is 2/7 which is then also the probability that the stock market drops by 20% or more next year.

Notes

Notes

If the odds had been 1 to 1 then that is equivalent to a box with 1 red ball and 1 white ball. The probability of selecting the white ball is 1/2.

The following tables gives some additional examples of converting odds against into probability for and probability against. The last entry shows the formula for conversion from odds to probability.

Odds (against)	Prob. For	Prob. Against
10 to 1	1/11	10/11
5 to 1	1/6	5/6
5 to 2	2/7	5/7
2 to 3	3/5	2/5
1 to 1	1/2	1/2
a to b	$\dfrac{b}{a+b}$	$\dfrac{a}{a+b}$

Notice that in every case the probability for the event and the probability against the event add up to 1.

EXAMPLE 12

Find the probability that the White Sox win the world series next year if the odds that are quoted in Las Vegas are 7 to 3. Do the same computation for the Cubs winning the world series next year given their odds as 9 to 1.

Answers:
Example 12: 3/10, 1/10

8.2 Properties of Compound Events

We first introduced the concepts of complement of a set, union of sets and intersection of sets in Chapter 3. We revisit them here in the context of sets of outcomes and probability. As you recall there were key words that linked into these concepts:

$$
\begin{array}{ll}
\text{Complement} \ \text{------} \ \text{NOT} \\
\text{Union} \ \text{------------} \ \text{OR} \\
\text{Intersection} \ \text{------} \ \text{AND}
\end{array}
$$

EXAMPLE 1

Select 1 card at random from a 52 card deck

$$P(\text{not an Ace}) = \frac{48}{52} \qquad P(\text{Ace}) = \frac{4}{52}$$

Note: $P(\text{Ace}) + P(\text{not an Ace}) = \dfrac{52}{52} = 1$

Complementary Events

The ***complement*** of any event **A** is the event **not A** (that is, the event that A does not occur).

Notation: A' (also A^c and $\overline{A}$)

Rule:

$$P(A) + P(A') = 1$$
$$\Downarrow$$
$$P(A') = 1 - P(A) \quad \text{and} \quad P(A) = 1 - P(A')$$

Venn Diagram for Complement

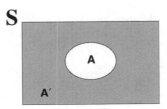

Notice that the Sample Space (set of all possible outcomes) is our Universal Set.

Notes

EXAMPLE 2
Toss 2 Dice

$$P(\text{sum not } 7) = 1 - P(\text{sum} = 7) = 1 - \frac{6}{36} = \frac{30}{36} = \frac{5}{6}$$

EXAMPLE 3
Flip a Coin Twice

$$P(\text{not getting 2 heads}) = 1 - P(\text{HH})$$
$$= 1 - \frac{1}{4}$$
$$= \frac{3}{4}$$

Intersection of Events

The *intersection* of two events **A** and **B** is the event that occurs if **both A *and* B** occur on a single performance of the experiment

Notation: $A \cap B$

Rule: Later

Venn Diagram for Intersection

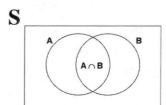

EXAMPLE 4
Select 1 card from a 52 card deck

Find the probability that the card is a red 10.

$$P(\text{Red } 10) = P(\text{Red} \cap 10) = \frac{2}{52} = \frac{1}{26} = .038$$

EXAMPLE 5

Select 1 card from a 52 card deck

Find P(Red or 10)

Since there are 26 red cards and 4 10's, and each card is equally likely of being selected one could argue that

$$P(\text{Red or } 10) = \frac{26 + 4}{52} = \frac{30}{52}$$

What's wrong with this argument?

Consider the Venn Diagram for this situation:

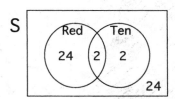

Thus, there are only 28 outcomes that belong to the event "Red or 10," so the probability should be 28/52.

$$P(\text{Red or } 10) = \frac{n(\text{Red} \cup 10)}{n(S)}$$
$$= \frac{n(\text{Red}) + n(10) - n(\text{Red} \cap 10)}{n(S)}$$
$$= \frac{26 + 4 - 2}{52}$$
$$= \frac{28}{52}$$
$$= \frac{7}{13}$$
$$= 0.5384615$$

Union of Events

The *union* of two events **A** and **B** is the event that occurs if **either A *or* B** or both occur on a single performance of the experiment

Notation: $A \cup B$

Rule: $P(A \cup B) = P(A) + P(B) - P(A \cap B)$

Venn Diagram for Union

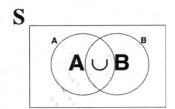

Notes

_____

_____

_____

_____

_____

_____

_____

_____

_____

_____

_____

_____

_____

_____

_____

_____

_____

_____

_____

_____

_____

_____

_____

_____

_____

_____

_____

_____

_____

_____

_____

EXAMPLE 6

Select 1 card from a 52 card deck

$$
\begin{aligned}
\text{P(Red or 10)} &= \text{P(Red} \cup 10) \\
&= \text{P(Red)} + \text{P(10)} - \text{P(Red} \cap 10) \\
&= \frac{26}{52} + \frac{4}{52} - \frac{2}{52} \\
&= \frac{28}{52} \\
&= \frac{7}{13} \\
&= 0.5384615
\end{aligned}
$$

EXAMPLE 7

Select 1 card from a standard 52 card deck

Find P(King or Club)

EXAMPLE 8

Select 1 card from a standard 52 card deck

Find P(Ace or King)

$$\begin{aligned}
\text{P(Ace or King)} &= \text{P(Ace} \cup \text{King)} \\
&= \text{P(Ace)} + \text{P(King)} - \text{P(Ace and King)} \\
&= \frac{4}{52} + \frac{4}{52} - 0 \\
&= \frac{8}{52} \\
&= \frac{2}{13} \\
&= 0.1538462
\end{aligned}$$

How does Example 8 differ from Example 6 or Example 7?

Mutually Exclusive Events

Events A and B are *mutually exclusive* if $A \cap B = \Phi$, that is, there is no intersection between A and B (A and B are disjoint sets).

Venn Diagram for Mutually Exclusive Events

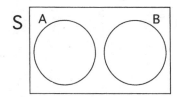

Note: When A and B are mutually exclusive, then we have

$$\mathbf{P(A \cap B) = 0}$$

and thus

$$\mathbf{P(A \cup B) = P(A) + P(B)}$$

Answers:
Example 7: 4/13 or .3077
Example 8: the two events have no intersection

Notes

Notes

In examples 6,7,8 Ace and King are **mutually exclusive,** while King and Club are not mutually exclusive, and Red and 10 are not mutually exclusive.

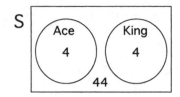

EXAMPLE 9
Roll 2 Dice

Find the probability that the sum of the two dice is either 4 or 7. Note that the events sum $= 4$ and sum $= 7$ are **mutually exclusive.**

$$\begin{aligned}
P(\text{Sum is 4 or Sum is 7}) &= P(\text{Sum} = 4 \cup \text{Sum} = 7)\\
&= P(\text{Sum} = 4) + P(\text{Sum} = 7)\\
&= \frac{3}{36} + \frac{6}{36}\\
&= \frac{9}{36}\\
&= \frac{1}{4}\\
&= 0.25
\end{aligned}$$

EXAMPLE 10

A survey of 100 middle level managers at your company reveals the following:

GENDER	MBA YES	MBA NO	Total
MALE	46	12	58
FEMALE	17	25	42
Total	63	37	100

Notice that there are only four different kinds of people in this survey, each represented by an intersection. Specifically we have Male and MBA, Male and not an MBA, Female and MBA, Female and not an MBA.

Let   A = MALE   B = MBA

	B	**B′**
A	**A ∩ B**	**A ∩ B′**
A′	**A′ ∩ B**	**A′ ∩ B′**

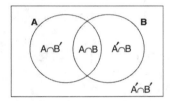

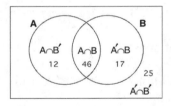

Notes

_____

_____

_____

_____

_____

_____

_____

_____

_____

_____

_____

_____

_____

_____

_____

_____

_____

_____

_____

_____

_____

_____

_____

_____

_____

_____

_____

_____

_____

_____

Find the probability that an individual chosen at random is:

a. male

$$P(\text{Male}) = P(A) = \frac{12 + 46}{100} = \frac{58}{100} = .58$$

b. male and an MBA

$$P(\text{Male and MBA}) = P(A \cap B) = \frac{46}{100} = .46$$

c. male or an MBA

$$P(\text{Male or MBA}) = P(A \cup B)$$
$$= P(A) + P(B) - P(A \cap B)$$
$$= \frac{58}{100} + \frac{63}{100} - \frac{46}{100}$$
$$= \frac{75}{100}$$
$$= .75$$

or

$$P(\text{Male or MBA}) = P(A \cup B) = \frac{12 + 46 + 17}{100} = \frac{75}{100} = .75$$

d. not an MBA

$$P(\text{not MBA}) = P(B') = 1 - P(B) = 1 - .63 = .37$$

or

$$P(\text{not MBA}) = P(B') = \frac{12 + 25}{100} = \frac{37}{100} = .37$$

e. not a male and not an MBA

$$P(\text{not Male and not MBA}) = P(A' \cap B') = \frac{25}{100} = .25$$

f. female and MBA

g. female or MBA

_____

Answers:
Example 10f .17
Example 10g .88

8.3 Conditional Probability and Independent Events

Sometimes, some information is already known that will effect the probability of an event A.

In situations like this we may want to find the probability of event A given that event B has occurred.

The **conditional probability** that an event **A** occurs, given that **B** has occurred is given by:

Notation: $P(A \text{ given } B) = P(A|B)$

Rule: $P(A|B) = \dfrac{P(A \cap B)}{P(B)}$

However, we will not use this rule to compute conditional probability. Rather, we will approach conditional probability via the concept of "reduced sample space."

EXAMPLE 1

Select one card at random from a 52 card deck. Find the probability that the card is the 7 of hearts.

$$P(7 \text{ of hearts}) = \frac{1}{52} = .019$$

Find the probability that the card is the 7 of hearts if it is known that the card is a heart.

$$P(7 \text{ of hearts}|\text{heart}) = \frac{1}{13} = .077$$

Find the probability that the card is the 7 of hearts if it is known that the card is a 7.

$$P(7 \text{ of hearts}|7) = \frac{1}{4} = .250$$

Note that in both of these examples, when doing the conditional probability we reduce the sample space to the given event.

EXAMPLE 2

Six firms bid on a contract; firms A, B, C, D, E and F. Firms A and B are Chicago based. If all firms have the same chance of winning the contract, then

P(A wins) =

P(A wins|Chi. based wins) =

P(C wins) =

P(C wins|non-Chi. based wins) =

P(C wins|Chi. based wins) =

EXAMPLE 3

A random sample of 1000 customers at a local pub is selected. The data is presented in the following table.

DRINK PREFERENCE

GENDER	Beer	Wine	Liquor	
Male	375	75	150	600
Female	75	225	100	400
	450	300	250	1000

If we focus on gender and whether the person is a beer drinker or not, we arrive at the following Venn Diagram.

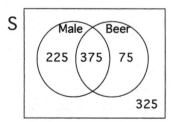

If one of these 1000 people is selected at random then find

a. $P(\text{Male}) = \dfrac{600}{1000} = .600$

b. $P(\text{Beer}) = \dfrac{450}{1000} = .450$

c. $P(\text{Male} \cap \text{Beer}) = \dfrac{375}{1000} = .375$

d. $P(\text{Male}|\text{Beer}) = \dfrac{375}{450} = .833$

Answers:
Example 2: 1/6, 1/2, 1/6, 1/4, 0

e. $P(\text{Beer}|\text{Male}) = \dfrac{375}{600} = .625$

f. $P(\text{Male} \cup \text{Beer}) = \dfrac{225 + 375 + 75}{1000} = \dfrac{675}{1000} = .675$

or

$$\begin{aligned} P(\text{Male} \cup \text{Beer}) &= P(\text{Male}) + P(\text{Beer}) - P(\text{Male} \cap \text{Beer}) \\ &= .600 + .450 - .375 \\ &= .675 \end{aligned}$$

Note that in c. we need to find the number of people in our survey that had both the properties listed, namely folks who were both male and preferred beer.

In d., the given condition is Beer, so we only consider the 450 Beer Drinkers, and of those how many were also Male (375).

In e., the given condition was Male, so we only consider the 600 males, and of those, how many were also Beer drinkers (375).

In f. we can either count up the members of the union from the Venn Diagram, or we can use the formula for the union of two events.

Now find the following probabilities

g. $P(\text{Wine}) =$

h. $P(\text{Female}) =$

i. $P(\text{Female} \cap \text{Wine}) =$

j. $P(\text{Female}|\text{Wine}) =$

k. $P(\text{Wine}|\text{Female})$

l. $P(\text{Female} \cup \text{Wine}) =$

Earlier we had introduced the following formula for conditional probability,

$$\mathbf{P(A|B)} = \frac{\mathbf{P(A \cap B)}}{\mathbf{P(B)}}$$

and then we proceeded to find conditional probabilities in another way, using the reducing of the sample space concept. So how are we going to use this formula? We will solve the formula for **P(A ∩ B)**, which gives us

$$\mathbf{P(A|B)} = \frac{\mathbf{P(A \cap B)}}{\mathbf{P(B)}}$$

$$\Downarrow$$

$$\mathbf{P(A \cap B)} = \mathbf{P(A|B)} \cdot \mathbf{P(B)}$$

which is called **The Multiplication Rule.**

Answers: Example 3g–l .30, .40, .225, .75, .5625, .475

EXAMPLE 4

Draw two cards from a standard 52 card deck, <u>without replacement</u>. Find the probability of drawing two red cards.

Let

$$R_1 = \text{1st card is red}$$
$$R_2 = \text{2nd card is red}$$

We need to recognize that the event of drawing two red cards is an intersection, that is, that the first card is red and the second card is also red.

Then we apply the Multiplication Rule as follows;

$$
\begin{aligned}
P(2 \text{ Reds}) &= P(R_1 \cap R_2) \\
&= P(R_2|R_1) \cdot P(R_1) \\
&= \frac{25}{51} \cdot \frac{26}{52} \\
&= \frac{650}{2652} \\
&= .245
\end{aligned}
$$

Note that

$$P(R_2|R_1) = \frac{25}{51}$$

since the first card was red and we did not replace it in the deck, then when picking the second card we have 51 cards to select from and 25 of those are red.

EXAMPLE 5

Draw two cards from a standard 52 card deck, <u>with replacement</u>. Find the probability of drawing two red cards.

Again let

$$R_1 = \text{1st card is red}$$
$$R_2 = \text{2nd card is red}$$

Proceeding as before, with the multiplication rule, we get the following.

$$
\begin{aligned}
P(2 \text{ Reds}) &= P(R_1 \cap R_2) \\
&= P(R_2 | R_1) \cdot P(R_1) \\
&= \frac{26}{52} \cdot \frac{26}{52} \\
&= \frac{676}{2704} \\
&= .250
\end{aligned}
$$

Notice that in this case,

$$P(R_2 | R_1) = \frac{26}{52}$$

since we replace the first card before selecting the second.

Let's consider a somewhat different approach to examples 4 and 5, namely using a decision tree. Why do we want to consider this? The multiplication rule is not impossible to implement, but it does require a bit of work. Using decision trees and implementing the multiplication rule gives a more visual approach.

Notes

EXAMPLE 4 REVISITED

Using a decision tree similar to the "tossing a coin twice" decision tee we arrive at a representation of the four possibilities in this situation.

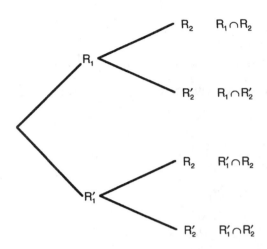

The thought process here is as follows. The first card could be red or not red. If the first card is red, then the second card could be red or not red. If the first card is not red, then the second card could be red or not red.

This gives us four possibilities: Red and Red, Red and not Red, not Red and Red, and not Red and not Red. Notice that each of the four possible outcomes is an intersection (an "and" situation).

Now label the probabilities along the branches in the decision tree. Notice the two first level probabilities are just ordinary probabilities, $P(R_1) = 26/52$, and $P(R_1') = 26/52$, whereas the four second level probabilities are conditional probabilities based on what happened with the first card. These are

$$P(R_2|R_1) = 25/51$$
$$P(R_2'|R_1) = 26/51$$
$$P(R_2|R_1') = 26/51$$
$$P(R_2'|R_1') = 25/51$$

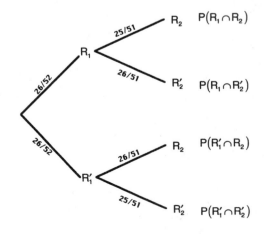

To find the probabilities of each of the four complete branches we implement the multiplication rule without the burden of the actual formula. All that we need to do is multiply the probabilities along the branches in the decision tree. The results are found below

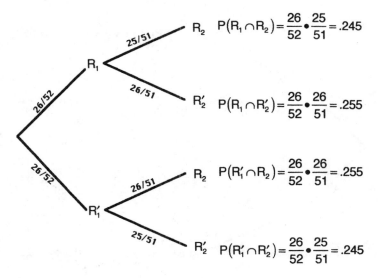

R_2 $P(R_1 \cap R_2) = \dfrac{26}{52} \cdot \dfrac{25}{51} = .245$

R_2' $P(R_1 \cap R_2') = \dfrac{26}{52} \cdot \dfrac{26}{51} = .255$

R_2 $P(R_1' \cap R_2) = \dfrac{26}{52} \cdot \dfrac{26}{51} = .255$

R_2' $P(R_1' \cap R_2') = \dfrac{26}{52} \cdot \dfrac{25}{51} = .245$

Now if we did this experiment with replacement (this would be Example 5) how would the decision tree change?

The second level probabilities will change due to putting the first card back and essentially reconstituting the original sample space.

Notes

Notes

EXAMPLE 5 REVISITED

With replacement, we obtain the following decision tree, with the following probabilities. Once again we used the multiplication rule by multiplying the probabilities along the branches in the decision tree.

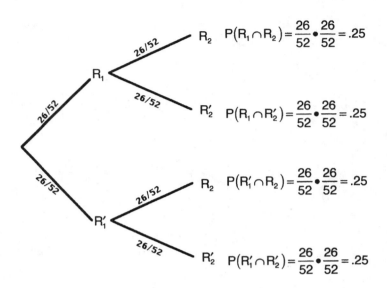

Note in this situation the given information made no difference in computing the second level conditional probability. That is,

$$P(R_2|R_1) = P(R_2) = .5$$

When this occurs we call events, like R_1 and R_2, **independent events.** We'll see another example of this concept next.

EXAMPLE 6

A random sample of 1000 customers at a local pub is selected. The data is presented in the following table.

DRINK PREFERENCE

GENDER	Beer	Wine	Liquor	
Male	375	75	150	600
Female	75	225	100	400
	450	300	250	1000

Sometimes the given information is of no help or influence. For example:

$$P(\text{Liquor}) = \frac{250}{1000} = .250$$

$$P(\text{Liquor}|\text{Male}) = \frac{150}{600} = .250$$

$$P(\text{Liquor}|\text{Female}) = \frac{100}{400} = .250$$

Thus, knowing the gender of an individual has no impact in predicting whether the individual prefers liquor. Gender and preferring liquor are independent. Are gender and preferring beer independent as well?

Independent Events

Events **A** and **B** are **independent** if the assumption that event **B** has occurred does not alter the probability of event **A** occurring. That is,

$$P(A|B) = P(A)$$

If the events A and B are independent and since

$$P(A \cap B) = P(A|B) \cdot P(B)$$

we have

$$P(A \cap B) = P(A) \cdot P(B)$$

So independence means that the events are unrelated. They may occur together but one event happening has no effect on the probability of the other event. (Independence $\Leftrightarrow P(A|B) = P(A)$).

Contrast this with the concept of mutually exclusive events which means that events are very strongly related, namely, the two events can not both occur. If one event happens, the other can not occur. (Mutually Exclusive $\Leftrightarrow P(A|B) = 0$).

Answer: Example 6: No

EXAMPLE 7

Let A = White Sox win the World Series next year.

Let B = Cubs win the World Series next year.

Let C = Bears win the Super Bowl next year.

Let D = Bulls win the NBA Championship next year.

Are events A and B mutually exclusive, independent or neither?

Events A and B are mutually exclusive, since both teams cannot win the World Series in the same year.

If $P(A) = .2$ and $P(B) = .1$, then $P(A \text{ or } B) = P(A) + P(B) = .2 + .1 = .3$. In other words, the chance that one or the other baseball team wins the World Series is .3

Are events C and D mutually exclusive, independent or neither?

Events C and D are independent, since it is doubtful that the Bears winning the Super Bowl would have any influence on the Bulls winning the NBA Championship. Both events could happen, it's just that one does not influence the other.

If $P(C) = .2$ and $P(D) = .1$, then $P(C \text{ and } D) = P(C) \cdot P(D) = .2 \cdot .1 = .02$. In other words, the chance that both the Bears and Bulls win their respective championships is .02.

On the next page you will see the Probability Summary which has all definitions, notation, formulas and Venn Diagrams that you'll need.

SUMMARY OF PROBABILITY

The **complement** of an event A is the event A does not occur.

Notation: $\overline{A}$

Formula:
$$P(\overline{A}) = 1 - P(A)$$

The **union** of two events A and B is the event that occurs if either A or B or both occur on a single performance of the experiment.

Notation: A∪B

Formula:
$$P(A \cup B) = P(A) + P(B) - P(A \cap B)$$

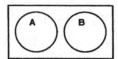

A and B are **mutually exclusive** if and only if $P(A \cap B) = 0$

Formula:
$$P(A \cup B) = P(A) + P(B)$$

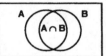

The **conditional probability** of A given B is the probability that A occurs given that B has already occurred.

Formula:
$$P(A \mid B) = \frac{P(A \cap B)}{P(B)}$$

The **intersection** of two events A and B is the event that occurs if both A and B occur on a single performance of the experiment.

Notation: A∩B

Formula:
$$P(A \cap B) = P(A \mid B) \bullet P(B)$$

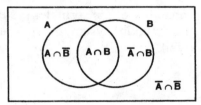

Events A and B are **independent** if the assumption that B has occurred does not alter the probability that A occurs. (That is, $P(A \mid B) = P(A)$)

Formula:
$$P(A \cap B) = P(A) \bullet P(B)$$

8.4   Applications

In this section we will investigate several applications of probability, in particular, situations involving independent events and decision trees

EXAMPLE 1A

Consider a sprinkler system that is 90% reliable

S_1 = sprinkler works $P(S_1) = .90$
$\overline{S}_1$ = sprinkler fails (does not work) $P(\overline{S}_1) = .10$

We can describe this situation with a simple decision tree.

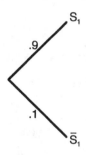

Clearly the probability of the sprinkler system working is .9. There is one way for the sprinkler system to work and one way for the sprinkler system to fail.

EXAMPLE 1B

Consider a sprinkler system that is 90% reliable and is backed up by another independent sprinkler system which is also 90% reliable. Find the probability that the system works (i.e., at least one of the sprinkler systems work).

S_1 = sprinkler 1 works $P(S_1) = .90$ $P(\overline{S}_1) = .10$
S_2 = sprinkler 2 works $P(S_2) = .90$ $P(\overline{S}_2) = .10$

We can describe this situation by a decision tree that is similar in nature to tossing a coin twice. Notice that we get a total of four branches and that we can compute the probabilities of each branch by multiplying the probabilities along the paths in the decision tree.

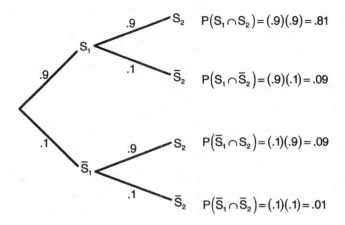

To find the probability that the system works we need to find the probability that at least one of the two sprinkler systems works. Which of the four branches corresponds to that event?

The top three branches do the trick! The top branch represents both sprinkler systems working and has probability of .81. The second branch represents the first sprinkler system working and the second sprinkler system not working and has probability of .09. The third branch represents the first sprinkler system not working and the second sprinkler system working and also has probability of .09. The fourth branch represents both sprinkler systems not working and has a probability of .01

Since the first three branches represent the three mutually exclusive ways that at least one of the sprinkler systems work, we add the probabilities to find our answer.

$$P(\text{at least one sprinkler system works}) = .81 + .09 + .09 = .99$$

Another, more efficient approach would have been to use the complement rule. Note that the complement of at least one system working is both systems not working, which is the bottom branch in our decision tree. Applying the complement rule we get the same result as above.

$$
\begin{aligned}
P(\text{at least one system works}) &= 1 - P(\text{neither system works}) \\
&= 1 - P(\overline{S}_1 \cap \overline{S}_2) \\
&= 1 - .01 \\
&= .99
\end{aligned}
$$

EXAMPLE 1C

Consider a sprinkler system that consists of 3 parallel independent systems, each of which is 90% reliable. Find the overall system reliability (i.e., probability that the system works, which means that at least one of the three sprinkler systems works).

S_1 = sprinkler 1 works	$P(S_1) = .90$	$P(\overline{S}_1) = .10$
S_2 = sprinkler 2 works	$P(S_2) = .90$	$P(\overline{S}_2) = .10$
S_3 = sprinkler 3 works	$P(S_3) = .90$	$P(\overline{S}_3) = .10$

Once again we use a decision tree to describe this situation, building off the prior two decision trees. The tree below is similar to the one representing the "tossing a coin three times" experiment.

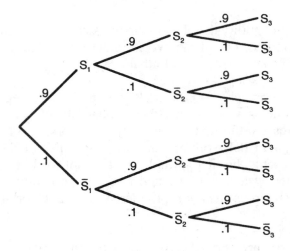

We multiply along the decision tree and find each of our 8 branch probabilities.

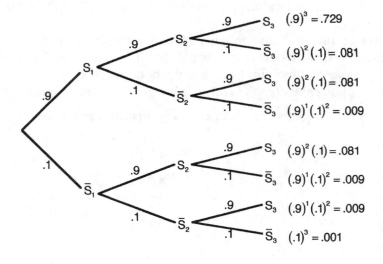

To find the probability that the system works we need to find the probability that at least one of the three sprinkler systems works. Which of the 8 branches corresponds to that event?

The top seven branches do the trick!

Since the top seven branches represent the seven mutually exclusive ways that at least one of the sprinkler systems work, we could add the probabilities to find our answer. However, having seen Example 1b we know there is a more efficient way to proceed.

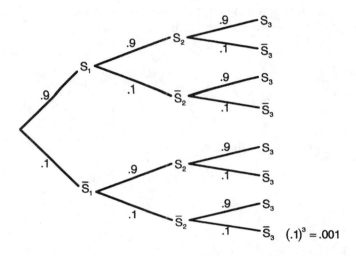

Note that the complement of at least one system working is all three systems not working, which is the bottom branch in our decision tree. Applying the complement rule we get the same result as if we has added the top seven branch probabilities.

$$P(\text{at least one system works}) = 1 - P(\text{none of the three systems work})$$
$$= 1 - P(\overline{S}_1 \cap \overline{S}_2 \cap \overline{S}_3)$$
$$= 1 - .001$$
$$= .999$$

Notice that the more back up systems we have the higher our overall reliability. That is precisely the purpose of having back up systems.

EXAMPLE 2A

A **quality characteristic** may defined as a component or feature of a product or service that if it is not right, the customer would deem the product or service as defective.

We produce a product that has 1 quality characteristic. Our production process is 90% reliable (that is, a defective rate of 10%).

C_1 = quality char. 1 works $P(C_1) = .90$

$\overline{C}_1$ = quality char. 1 defective $P(\overline{C}_1) = .10$

This simple situation can be represented by the following decision tree (note the similarity to Example 1a).

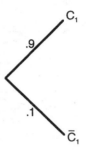

Thus,

$$P(\text{defect free product}) = .90$$

EXAMPLE 2B

Our product has two independent quality characteristics, each 90% reliable. Find the probability of a defect-free product.

C_1 = quality char. 1 works $P(C_1) = .90$ $P(\overline{C}_1) = .10$
C_2 = quality char. 2 works $P(C_2) = .90$ $P(\overline{C}_2) = .10$

Much like Example 1b, we can represent this situation with a decision tree.

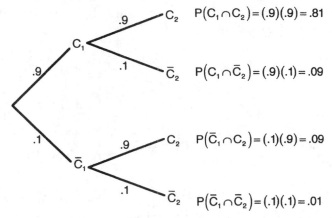

Which branch or branches correspond to a defect free product?

If we do a walk through the decision tree we find the following.

Branch 1 has both quality characteristics working and thus our product is defect free.

Branch 2 has characteristic one working and characteristic two not working and thus our product is defective.

Branch 3 has characteristic one not working and characteristic two working and thus our product is defective.

Branch 4 has both quality characteristics not working and thus our product is defective.

We get a defect free product in the top branch only.

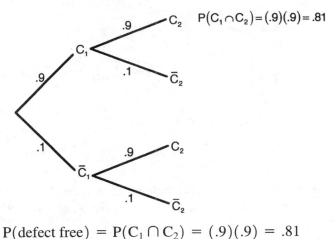

$P(\text{defect free}) = P(C_1 \cap C_2) = (.9)(.9) = .81$

EXAMPLE 2C

Our product has 3 independent quality characteristics, each 90% reliable. Find the probability of a defect-free product.

C_1 = quality char. 1 works $P(C_1) = .90$ $P(\overline{C}_1) = .10$
C_2 = quality char. 2 works $P(C_2) = .90$ $P(\overline{C}_2) = .10$
C_3 = quality char. 3 works $P(C_3) = .90$ $P(\overline{C}_3) = .10$

Much like Example 1c, we can represent this situation with a decision tree. And again, we need to determine which branch or branches correspond to a defect free product.

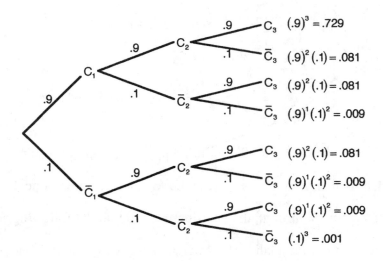

The only branch that gives a defect free product is the very top one. And thus

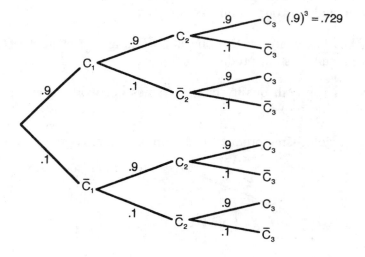

$$P(\text{defect free}) = P(C_1 \cap C_2 \cap C_3)$$
$$= (.9)^3$$
$$= .729$$

What happens if we have 100 independent quality characteristics (each 90% reliable)? **What would be the probability of no defects?**

Clearly we can't proceed with the decision tree approach as the trees become unmanageable. However, we can identify a pattern that we have seen. If we did have a product with 5 quality characteristics, then the only way the product is defect free is when all 5 quality characteristics work. That suggests we need to multiply probabilities to get our result as shown in the table below.

# of Quality Characteristics	P(product is not defective)
5	$(.9)^5 = .590$
10	$(.9)^{10} = .349$
20	$(.9)^{20} = .122$
30	$(.9)^{30} = .042$
50	$(.9)^{50} = .005$
100	$(.9)^{100} = .0000266$

So if we have a product with 100 independent quality characteristics, each with 90% reliability, then the probability of a defect free product is .0000266 or roughly 3 in 100,000. So virtually every item we produce has something wrong with it, thereby making it a "defective."

So what do we do? We need to improve the reliability of each characteristic. How good do we need to get?

Consider the product that has 100 independent quality characteristics. Let's do some "what if" with the reliability of each quality characteristic and see what happens to the probability that the product is not defective

Reliability of each Quality Characteristic	P(product is not defective)
.900	$(.900)^{100} = .0000266$
.950	$(.950)^{100} = .0059205$
.990	$(.990)^{100} = .3660323$
.995	$(.995)^{100} = .6057704$
.999	$(.999)^{100} = .9047922$

If we get the individual quality characteristics up to a .999 reliability, then we are able to produce over 90% of our items without defect.

Let's summarize what we have seen through this example.

So in general, if

  n = number   of quality characteristics

  r = reliability   of each quality characteristic

  P = probability of a defect free product

Then $P = r^n$ or $r = P^{1/n}$

We have come a long way from our decision trees!

Notes

EXAMPLE 3

If your product has 400 independent quality characteristics and you desire to have 99% of your production defect free, then how high must the reliability be for each of the 400 quality characteristics?

If n = 400 and P = .99 then

$$r = (.99)^{1/400}$$
$$= (.99)^{.0025}$$
$$= .999975$$

Which means a defective rate of $\frac{25}{1,000,000}$, or 25 parts per million (ppm).

Try the next example.

EXAMPLE 4

Your product has 35 quality characteristics.

If the reliability of each characteristic is .925, then find the probability of a defect free product.

If your goal is to produce 99.5% of your products defect free, then find the reliability for each quality characteristic that will make that happen.

Answers:
Example 4: .065, .9998567948

EXAMPLE 5

Your company buys cars from GM and Ford. 75% of these cars are from GM and 25% are from Ford. 3% of the GM cars have defects, while 5% of the Fords have defects. If you select one car at random, then find

a. P(Defective)

b. P(not Defective)

c. P(GM and not Defective)

d. P(Ford and Defective)

e. P(Ford or Defective)

First let define some basic events:

GM = car made by General Motors

F = car made by Ford

D = car defective

$\overline{D}$ = car not defective

with the given probabilities

$$P(GM) = .75 \qquad P(F) = .25$$
$$P(D|GM) = .03 \quad P(D|F) = .05$$
$$P(\overline{D}|GM) = .97 \quad P(\overline{D}|F) = .95$$

There are four kinds of cars here (corresponding to the four outcomes of this experiment), GM and Defective, GM and not Defective, Ford and Defective, Ford and not Defective. These are best illustrated by the following decision tree

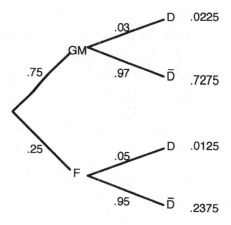

a. P(Defective)

To find this probability we need to identify which branches correspond to this event. The first and third branches yield defective cars. To find P(Defective) we add the probabilities of the two mutually exclusive ways this can happen, namely GM and Defective, and Ford and Defective.

$$P(\text{Defective}) = .0225 + .0125 = .035$$

b. P(not Defective)

We can use the complement rule to compute this probability.

P(not Defective) = 1 − .035 = .965

c. P(GM and not Defective)

This is the second branch on the decision tree and thus

P(GM and not Defective) = .7275

Another approach to this question would be to use the multiplication rule.

$$P(\text{GM and not Defective}) = P(\text{not Defective}|\text{GM}) \cdot P(\text{GM})$$
$$= (.97) \cdot (.75)$$
$$= .7275$$

d. P(Ford and Defective)

This is the third branch in the decision tree and thus

P(Ford and Defective) = .0125

Again we could have done this with the multiplication rule.

$$P(\text{Ford and Defective}) = P(\text{Defective}|\text{Ford}) \cdot P(\text{Ford})$$
$$= (.05) \cdot (.25)$$
$$= .0125$$

e. P(Ford or Defective)

We can look through the decision tree and find the branches that correspond to this event. In this case that would be the 1st, 3rd and 4th branches. Thus the result is

P(Ford or Defective) = .0225 + .0125 + .2375 = .2725

Another approach would be to use the formula for the union of two events (since this is an "or" situation).

$$P(\text{Ford or Defective}) = P(F) + P(D) - P(F \text{ and } D)$$
$$= .2500 + .0350 - .0125$$
$$= .2725$$

EXAMPLE 6

Bill, Sally, and Jennifer are the three mortgage closers for ABC Mortgages. Bill handles 30% of the closings, Sally handles 50% of the closings and Jennifer handles the remaining 20% of the closings. Bill makes an error in 4% of his closings, Sally makes an error in 3% of her closings, and Jennifer makes an error in 6% of her closings. If you select one closing at random, then find

    a. P(Bill and No Error)

    b. P(Sally or Jennifer)

    c. P(Error)

    d. P(No Error)

    e. P(Sally or Error)

Answers:
Example 6: .288,.7, .039, .961, .524

Chapter 8 Exercise Set

A single fair die is rolled. Find the probabilities of each event.

1. Getting a 2   **2.** Getting a number less than 5

3. Getting a 3 or a 4

A card is drawn from a well-shuffled deck of 52 cards. Find the probability of drawing the following.

4. A 9   **5.** A black 9

6. The 9 of hearts   **7.** A 2 or a queen

8. A red face card

A jar contains 2 white, 3 orange, 5 yellow, and 8 black marbles. If a marble is drawn at random, find the probability that it is the following.

9. White   **10.** Yellow

11. Not black

12. *Survey of Workers* The management of a firm wishes to check on the opinions of its assembly line workers. Before the workers are interviewed, they are divided into various categories. Define events *E*, *F*, and *G* as follows.

E: worker is female
F: worker has worked less than 5 years
G: worker contributes to a voluntary retirement plan

Describe each event in words.

  a. E' **b.** $E \cap F$ **c.** $E \cap G'$

  d. F' **e.** $F \cap G$ **f.** $F' \cap G'$

13. *Investment* As of September 2003, the Janus Mercury fund invested in equities throughout the world, as shown below.[†]

Region	% of Equities
Europe	5.29
Pacific Rim	3.42
United States	87.74
Other	3.55

Find the probability that a randomly selected equity would be from each region.

  a. The Pacific Rim   **b.** Europe

  c. The United States

[†]www.janus.com.

Decide whether the events in Exercises 14–16 are mutually exclusive.

14. Wearing glasses and wearing sandals

15. Being a teenager and being over 30 years old

16. Being a male and being a postal worker

Two dice are rolled. Find the probabilities of rolling the given sums.

17. a. 2   **b.** 4   **c.** 5   **d.** 6

18. a. 8   **b.** 9   **c.** 10   **d.** 13

19. a. 9 or more   **b.** Less than 7   **c.** Between 5 and 8 (exclusive)

One card is drawn from an ordinary deck of 52 cards. Find the probabilities of drawing the following cards.

20. a. A 9 or 10

   b. A red card or a 3

   c. A 9 or a black 10

   d. A heart or a black card

   e. A face card or a diamond

21. *Defective Merchandise* Suppose that 8% of a certain batch of calculators have a defective case, and that 11% have defective batteries. Also, 3% have both a defective case and defective batteries. A calculator is selected from the batch at random. Find the probability that the calculator has a good case and good batteries.

If two cards are drawn without replacement from an ordinary deck, find the probabilities of the following results.

22. The second is a heart, given that the first is a heart.

23. The second is a face card, given that the first is a jack.

24. A jack and a 10 are drawn.

25. Two black cards are drawn.

Banking The Midtown Bank has found that most customers at the tellers' windows either cash a check or make a deposit. The following table indicates the transactions for one teller for one day.

	Cash Check	No Check	Totals
Make Deposit	50	20	70
No Deposit	30	10	40
Totals	80	30	110

Letting C represent "cashing a check" and D represent "making a deposit," express each probability in words and find its value.

26. $P(C)$ **27.** $P(D)$ **28.** $P(C \cap D)$

29. $P(C \cup D)$ **30.** $P(C' \cap D')$ **31.** $P(C|D)$

32. $P(D'|C)$ **33.** $P(C'|D')$ **34.** $P(C'|D)$

35. $P[(C \cap D)']$

36. *Backup Computers* Corporations where a computer is essential to day-to-day operations, such as banks, often have a second backup computer in case the main computer fails. Suppose there is a .003 chance that the main computer will fail in a given time period, and a .005 chance that the backup computer will fail while the main computer is being repaired. Assume these failures represent independent events, and find the fraction of the time that the corporation can assume it will have computer service. How realistic is our assumption of independence?

Quality Control A bicycle factory runs two assembly lines, A and B. If 95% of line A's products pass inspection, while only 90% of line B's products pass inspection, and 60% of the factory's bikes come off assembly line B (the rest off A), find the probabilities that one of the factory's bikes did not pass inspection and came off the following.

37. Assembly line A   **38.** Assembly line B

39. Find the probability that one of the factory's bikes did not pass inspection.

40. Find the probability that one of the factory's bikes did pass inspection.

More Probability

9.1 Expected Value

We introduce the concept of expected value or mathematical expectation by way of the concept of a payoff table. For a probabilistic situation, we list all possible outcomes, the payoffs for each outcome and the probabilities for each outcome.

Payoff Table

Outcomes	O_1	O_2	$O_3...O_n$
Payoffs	x_1	x_2	$x_3...x_n$
Probabilities	p_1	p_2	$p_3...p_n$

To compute the **expected value** or **mean of X** by the following formula:

$$E = x_1p_1 + x_2p_2 + \cdots + x_np_n = \sum x_ip_i$$

Note this calculation is a sum of all of the products of payoffs with their associated probabilities.

EXAMPLE 1
Game of Chance

Flip one coin, you win $2 for Heads, lose $1 for Tails.

Outcomes	H	T
Payoffs	+2	−1
Probabilities	1/2	1/2

$$E = (2) \cdot \left(\frac{1}{2}\right) + (-1) \cdot \left(\frac{1}{2}\right) = +\$.50$$

This is easy enough to compute, but what does it mean?

You would *expect* to make an *average* of $.50 per play of this game. We could never make exactly $.50 on any one play of this game but we certainly could average $.50 over many plays of the game. In fact that will happen if over many plays of this game the probabilities that we expect to occur actually do. In other words, if our predicted theoretical probabilities work out experimentally then the expected value and the average result for your experimental results will be identical.

So in Example 1, the expected value was $.50. Thus if we played 100 times we would *expect* to win $50.

In 100 plays we **expect:** to get 50 heads and 50 tails, thus

$$50 \text{ Heads} \Rightarrow (50)(2) = 100$$
$$50 \text{ Tails} \Rightarrow (50)(-1) = -50$$
$$\text{Total} = 50 \quad \text{in 100 plays}$$

Since we have won a total of $50 in 100 plays of the game, then we have **an average of $.50/play.** But again, this is predicated on our theoretical probabilities being totally accurate.

Clearly the player of this game has the advantage and would win money playing this game, if the player plays enough times. One way to make this game fair would be to charge the player a certain amount to play this game each time.

How much should a player of this game pay to play this game in order to make it fair (fair means that E = 0)?

There are several approaches to solving this question. I prefer the more conceptual approach. Since the player is currently paying nothing to play and making an average of $.50 per play, then the player should be charged $.50 to play. If we compute the expected value while including the charge we get the following.

Outcomes	H	T
Payoffs	$+2 - .50$	$-1 - .50$
Probabilities	1/2	1/2

$$E = (1.50) \cdot \left(\frac{1}{2}\right) + (-1.50) \cdot \left(\frac{1}{2}\right) = 0$$

So charging the player $.50 per play does indeed make the game fair in that over the long haul, the player should average $0.

The other approach to determine what the player should be charged to make this a fair game depends on some algebra. Let x be the amount to be charged to play. Set up the payoff table, compute the expected value and set it equal to 0 and solve for x.

Outcomes	H	T
Payoffs	$+2 - x$	$-1 - x$
Probabilities	1/2	1/2

$$E = (2 - x) \cdot \left(\frac{1}{2}\right) + (-1 - x) \cdot \left(\frac{1}{2}\right) = 0$$

$$(2 - x) \cdot \left(\frac{1}{2}\right) + (-1 - x) \cdot \left(\frac{1}{2}\right) = 0$$

$$2 \cdot (2 - x) \cdot \left(\frac{1}{2}\right) + (-1 - x) \cdot \left(\frac{1}{2}\right) \cdot 2 = 0 \cdot 2$$

$$2 - x - 1 - x = 0$$

$$1 - 2x = 0$$

$$-2x = -1$$

$$x = \frac{-1}{-2}$$

$$x = .50$$

Notes

EXAMPLE 2
Friendly (or not so friendly) Game of Chance

The Game: flip a fair coin twice

player wins $4 for 2 heads

wins $4 for 2 tails

loses $8 for 1 head and 1 tail

Outcomes	TT	HH	TH or HT
Payoffs	+4	+4	−8
Probability	1/4	1/4	1/2

$$E = (4) \cdot \left(\frac{1}{4}\right) + (4) \cdot \left(\frac{1}{4}\right) + (-8) \cdot \left(\frac{1}{2}\right) = -\$2.00/\text{play}$$

In 100 plays, we would expect

TT 25 times	$25 \cdot 4$	$= +100$
HH 25 times	$25 \cdot 4$	$= +100$
HT or TH 50 times	$50 \cdot (-8)$	$= -400$
	Total	$= -200$ in 100 plays or an average of −$2/play

Las Vegas, Atlantic City, and other casino gambling institutions are not really gambling from the proprietors perspective. It's a business! Every casino game has a negative expected value for the player and a positive expected value for the house.

Important Considerations:
Significant Number of Repetitions

Accurate Theoretical Probabilities

EXAMPLE 3
Life Insurance

For a 25 year, $100,000 life insurance policy, what should the insurance company charge a 40 year old individual?

Let's take the approach assuming that there is no premium and see what the expected value will be.

Using a mortality table we find:

P(live to 65|now age 40) = .736

(Don't worry about how this is arrived at, this probability has to be provided to you to do the calculation)

Outcome	Alive at 65	Died Prior to 65
Payoff (no premium)	0	$-100,000$
Probability	.736	.264

$$E = (0)(.736) + (-100,000)(.264)$$
$$= -\$26,400/\text{policy}$$
$$\approx 1056/\text{yr.}$$

The insurance company then makes adjustments (actuarial and financial) to determine the actual premium. Note that if the insurance company used an annual premium of $1056, then the insurance company will have a lot more than $26,400 at the end of 25 years.

EXAMPLE 4
Life Insurance

An insurance company charges a 40 year old individual $500 for 1 year of life insurance with face value of $100,000. Find the expected value for the insurance company.

P(live to 41|now age 40) = .9965

Outcome	Customer Lives	Customer Dies
Payoff	500	$500 - 100,000$
Probability	.9965	.0035

$$E = (500)(.9965) + (500 - 100,000)(.0035)$$
$$= 498.25 + (-348.25)$$
$$= \$150 \text{ per policy}$$

If 10,000 such policies are in force, then the total expected net gain is:

$$(150)(10,000) = \$1,500,000 \text{ per year}$$

This will be the actual net gain if 9,965 policy holders live and 35 die in 1 year.

$$\text{Actual Net Gain} = 9,965 \cdot (500) + 35 \cdot (-99,500)$$
$$= 4,982,500 + (-3,482,500)$$
$$= \$1,500,000$$

Notes

EXAMPLE 5
"Oh What a Deal!"

You have a once in a lifetime real estate deal which gives a 60% chance of netting $5,000,000 in the deal, while you have a 40% chance of losing $400,000 in this deal. What should you do?

If you compute the expected value you get the following.

Outcome	Success	Failure
Payoff	5,000,000	−400,000
Probability	.60	.40

$$E = (5,000,000)(.60) + (-40,000)(.40)$$
$$= 3,000,000 - 160,000$$
$$= \$2,840,000$$

So does that mean that we should ***GO FOR IT?*** Are we expecting to make $2,840,000 on average in this deal?

What's wrong with this analysis?

Our computations are correct here but they are meaningless since we don't have a large number of repetitions of this situation. It's true that if we were in this situation many times we would average $2,840,000 per situation if we had 60% successes and 40% failures. However since this is a one shot deal one of two things will happen: we make $5,000,000 or we lose $400,000. The decision making here depends on our comfort level with a 40% chance of losing $400,000. The expected value calculation is useless in this situation.

9.2 Combinatorics

A factorial is a calculation denoted by the symbol ! and is described below.

$$0! = 1$$
$$1! = 1$$
$$2! = 2 \cdot 1 = 2$$
$$3! = 3 \cdot 2 \cdot 1 = 6$$
$$4! = 4 \cdot 3 \cdot 2 \cdot 1 = 24$$
$$5! = 5 \cdot 4 \cdot 3 \cdot 2 \cdot 1 = 120$$
$$\vdots$$
$$\vdots$$
$$10! = 10 \cdot 9 \cdot 8 \cdot 7 \cdot 6 \cdot 5 \cdot 4 \cdot 3 \cdot 2 \cdot 1 = 3{,}628{,}800$$

We can use the TI-83 to compute factorials. For example to compute 10!, first start from the home screen and type in **10** and then press **MATH** and select **PRB** and select **4: !** which pastes ! back to the home screen. Press ENTER and you get the result.

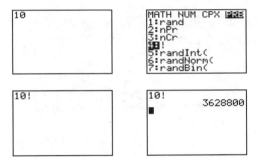

EXAMPLE 1
Compute:

$$\frac{6!}{4!\,2!} = \frac{6 \cdot 5 \cdot 4 \cdot 3 \cdot 2 \cdot 1}{4 \cdot 3 \cdot 2 \cdot 1 \cdot 2 \cdot 1}$$

$$= \frac{6 \cdot 5 \cdot \cancel{4} \cdot \cancel{3} \cdot \cancel{2} \cdot \cancel{1}}{\cancel{4} \cdot \cancel{3} \cdot \cancel{2} \cdot \cancel{1} \cdot 2 \cdot 1}$$

$$= \frac{30}{2}$$

$$= 15$$

Note:

$$\frac{6!}{4!\,2!} = \frac{6 \cdot 5 \cdot 4!}{4! \cdot 2 \cdot 1} = \frac{6 \cdot 5 \cdot \cancel{4!}}{\cancel{4!} \cdot 2 \cdot 1} = \frac{30}{2} = 15$$

Notes

EXAMPLE 2

$$\frac{50!}{2!\,48!} = \frac{50 \cdot 49 \cdot 48!}{2 \cdot 1 \cdot 48!}$$

$$= \frac{50 \cdot 49 \cdot \cancel{48!}}{\cancel{48!} \cdot 2 \cdot 1}$$

$$= 25 \cdot 49$$

$$= 1225$$

EXAMPLE 3

$$\frac{8!}{4!\,4!} = \frac{8 \cdot 7 \cdot 6 \cdot 5 \cdot 4!}{4 \cdot 3 \cdot 2 \cdot 1 \cdot 4!}$$

$$= \frac{8 \cdot 7 \cdot 6 \cdot 5 \cdot \cancel{4!}}{\cancel{4} \cdot 3 \cdot \cancel{2} \cdot 1 \cdot \cancel{4!}}$$

$$= 7 \cdot 2 \cdot 5$$

$$= 70$$

Combinations

EXAMPLE 4
Tennis Matches

Bob, Ted, Sam, Dave play tennis. How many different singles matches are possible among the four individuals?

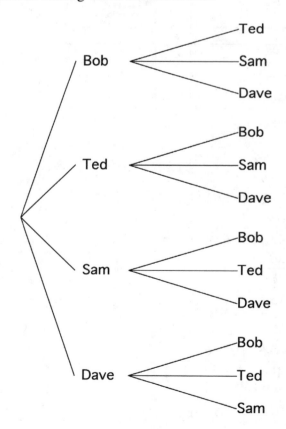

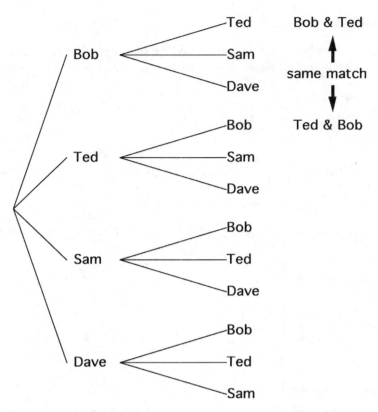

Bob & Ted

↑
same match
↓

Ted & Bob

There are lots of duplicate matches!

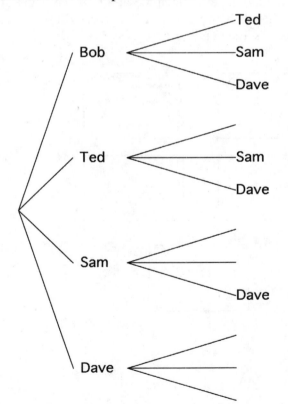

Thus there are 6 different matches.

Notes

Definition

The number of possible combinations of **n** things chosen **r** at a time, where *order is unimportant* and *repetition is not allowed* is denoted by:

$$C(n, r) \quad \text{or} \quad \binom{n}{r} \quad \text{or} \quad nCr$$

and can be found by

$$C(n, r) = \frac{n!}{r! \, (n - r)!}$$

In our tennis example $n = 4$, $r = 2$,

$$
\begin{aligned}
C(4, 2) &= \frac{4!}{2! \cdot 2!} \\
&= \frac{4 \cdot 3 \cdot 2!}{2 \cdot 1 \cdot 2!} \\
&= \frac{4 \cdot 3 \cdot 2!}{2 \cdot 1 \cdot 2!} \\
&= \frac{12}{2} \\
&= 6
\end{aligned}
$$

We can compute combinations using the TI-83. To compute the number of combinations of 4 tennis players selected 2 at a time we begin at the home screen and type in **4.** Then press **MATH**, select **PRB** and select **3:nCr.** Back at the home screen enter **2** and press **ENTER.**

```
4
```

```
MATH NUM CPX PRB
1:rand
2:nPr
3:nCr
4:!
5:randInt(
6:randNorm(
7:randBin(
```

```
4 nCr
```

```
4 nCr 2
```

```
4 nCr 2
                6
```

EXAMPLE 5
Lotto Game

Choose 6 numbers from the integers 1–48. How many ways can this be done?

$$\binom{48}{6} = \frac{48!}{6!\,(48-6)!}$$

$$= \frac{48!}{6!\,42!}$$

$$= \frac{48 \cdot 47 \cdot 46 \cdot 45 \cdot 44 \cdot 43 \cdot 42!}{6 \cdot 5 \cdot 4 \cdot 3 \cdot 2 \cdot 1 \cdot 42!}$$

$$= 8 \cdot 47 \cdot 23 \cdot 3 \cdot 11 \cdot 43$$

$$= 12{,}271{,}512$$

```
48 nCr 6
          12271512
```

Thus, there are 12,271,512 different ways of making this selection.

Assuming equal probabilities, each selection of 6 numbers has the probability of winning of

$$\frac{1}{12{,}271{,}512} = .00000008149$$

Since each Lotto ticket requires two selections of 6 numbers each and assuming the two selections are different, the probability that a Lotto ticket will be the winner is:

$$\frac{2}{12{,}271{,}512} = .0000002$$

9.3 Binomial Probability

Consider the following example.

EXAMPLE 1
Spinner

Consider a spinner that has 5 differently colored equal areas. One of the five colors is red. You spin the spinner 3 times and are interested in the number of reds that result.

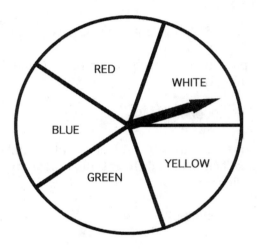

Let

R_1 = 1st spin is Red

R_2 = 2nd spin is Red

R_3 = 3rd spin is Red

	Probability	# of reds
R_3	$(.2)^3 = .008$	3
$\overline{R}_3$	$(.2)^2(.8) = .032$	2
R_3	$(.2)^2(.8) = .032$	2
$\overline{R}_3$	$(.2)(.8)^2 = .128$	1
R_3	$(.2)^2(.8) = .032$	2
$\overline{R}_3$	$(.2)(.8)^2 = .128$	1
R_3	$(.2)(.8)^2 = .128$	1
$\overline{R}_3$	$(.8)^3 = .512$	0

$P(3 \text{ Reds}) = 1 \cdot (.2)^3 = .008$

$P(2 \text{ Reds}) = 3 \cdot (.2)^2(.8)^1 = 3 \cdot .032 = .096$

$P(1 \text{ Reds}) = 3 \cdot (.2)^1(.8)^2 = 3 \cdot .128 = .384$

$P(0 \text{ Reds}) = 1 \cdot (.8)^3 = .512$

Binomial Probability

1. A sequence of trials **n = # of trials**
2. Each trial has two possible outcomes: success **S** and failure **F.**
3. The probability of S is the same from trial to trial (**independence**).

    $P(S) = p \qquad P(F) = q$

    with $p + q = 1$ (or $q = 1 - p$)

4. # of successes is of interest **X = # of successes**

    X = the number of successes in n trials is called
    the **Binomial Random Variable.** Note:
    X = 0, 1, 2, 3, . . . , n

Notes

Probability Function:

$$P(X = k = \binom{n}{k} \cdot p^k(1 - p)^{n-k} = \underbrace{\frac{n!}{k!\,(n - k)!} \cdot p^k(1 - p)^{n-k}}_{b(n,\,p,\,k)}$$

where b(n, p, k) represents the binomial probability with **n** trials, probability of success **p,** and **k** successes

EXAMPLE 1

X = # of reds in 3 spins

n = 3

p = .2

$$P(X = 0) = \binom{3}{0}(.2)^0(.8)^3 = \frac{3!}{0!\,3!}(.8)^3 = 1 \cdot .512 = .512$$

n = 3   p = .2
k = 0   1 − p = .8
n − k = 3

$$P(X = 1) = \binom{3}{1}(.2)^1(.8)^2 = \frac{3!}{1!\,2!}(.2)^1(.8)^2 = 3 \cdot (.128) = .384$$

n = 3   p = .2
k = 1   1 − p = .8
n − k = 2

$$P(X = 2) = \binom{3}{2}(.2)^2(.8)^1 = \frac{3!}{2!\,1!}(.2)^2(.8)^1 = 3 \cdot .032 = .096$$

n = 3   p = .2
k = 2   1 − p = .8
n − k = 1

$$P(X = 3) = \binom{3}{3}(.2)^3(.8)^0 = \frac{3!}{3!\,0!}(.2)^3 = 1 \cdot .008 = .008$$

n = 3   p = .2
k = 3   1 − p = .8
n − k = 0

Using the TI-83 and the combination feature we can generate the results as follows.

```
(3 nCr 0)*(.2^0)
*(.8^3)
            .512
```

```
(3 nCr 0)*(.2^0)
*(.8^3)
            .512
(3 nCr 1)*(.2^1)
*(.8^2)
            .384
```

```
            .512
(3 nCr 1)*(.2^1)
*(.8^2)
            .384
(3 nCr 2)*(.2^2)
*(.8^1)
            .096
```

```
            .384
(3 nCr 2)*(.2^2)
*(.8^1)
            .096
(3 nCr 3)*(.2^3)
*(.8^0)
            .008
```

Better yet, the TI-83 allows us to compute the binomial probability in a more direct fashion. Clear the home screen and press **2nd** and **VARS** (**DISTR** key). Scroll down and select 0:binompdf(.

binompdf stands for binomial probability distribution function and has the following form:

binompdf(number of trials, prob. of success, number of successes)

or

binompdf(n, p, k)

 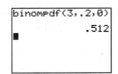

Pressing **2nd** and **ENTER** and editing the binompdf expression gives us the other results.

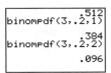

EXAMPLE 2

Suppose this same spinner is spun 15 times. Find the probability of getting exactly 2 reds.

X = # of reds in 15 spins

n = 15   k = 2   n − k = 13

p = .2   1 − p = .8

$$P(X = 2) = \binom{15}{2}(.2)^2(.8)^{13}$$

$$= \frac{15!}{2! \, 13!}(.2)^2(.8)^{13}$$

$$= \frac{15 \cdot 14 \cdot 13!}{2 \cdot 1 \cdot 13!}(.2)^2(.8)^{13}$$

$$= 15 \cdot 7 \cdot (.2)^2(.8)^{13}$$

$$= 105 \cdot (.002199)$$

$$= \mathbf{.2308974}$$

Notes

Notes

EXAMPLE 3

Consider spinning the spinner 15 times. Find the probability of getting at most 5 reds.

$$n = 15 \qquad p = .2 \qquad \text{Find } P(X \leq 5)$$

We can use the binomcdf feature (binomial cumulative distribution function). Press 2nd VARS (DISTR), scroll down and select A:binomcdf(.

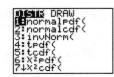 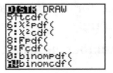

Note : $P(X \leq k) = \textbf{binomcdf}(\textbf{n, p, k})$

At this point you have pasted binomcdf(into the home screen and now type in the values for n, p, and k, and then press **ENTER.**

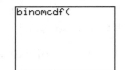 

EXAMPLE 4

Consider spinning the spinner 15 times. Find the probability of getting at least 5 reds.

$$n = 15 \qquad p = .2 \qquad \text{Find } P(X \geq 5)$$

Note: $P(X \geq 5) = 1 - P(X \leq 4)$

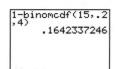

EXAMPLE 5

Consider spinning the spinner 15 times. Find the probability of getting less than 5 reds.

$$n = 15 \qquad p = .2 \qquad \text{Find } P(X < 5)$$

Note: $P(X < 5) = P(X \leq 4)$

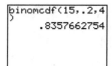

EXAMPLE 6

Consider spinning the spinner 15 times. Find the probability of getting more than 5 reds.

$$n = 15 \qquad p = .2 \qquad \text{Find } P(X > 5)$$

Note: $P(X > 5) = 1 - P(X \le 5)$

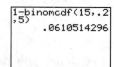

```
1-binomcdf(15,.2
,5)
          .0610514296
```

EXAMPLE 7
Passing a Multiple Choice Exam

A multiple choice test with 20 questions (4 choices for each question). If 70% correct is passing, find the probability of passing the test by sheer guessing.

$$X = \text{\# of correct answers} \qquad \text{(Binomial)}$$
$$n = 20 \qquad p = .25$$
$$70\% \text{ of } 20 = 14 \qquad \text{Find } P(X \ge 14)$$

Note: $P(X \ge 14) = 1 - P(X \le 13)$

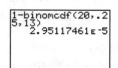

```
1-binomcdf(20,.2
5,13)
       2.95117461ᴇ-5
```

Thus our answer is $P(\text{passing}) = .0000295117461$

What if we could narrow our guesses to 2 answers? Find the probability of passing.

$$n = 20 \quad p = .5$$

```
1-binomcdf(20,.5
0,13)
          .0576591492
```

There is probably a moral to this story, especially when it comes to taking exams in certain subjects.

Notes

Chapter 9 Exercise Set

1. **Finding Expected Value in Craps** When you give a casino $5 for a bet on the "pass line" in the game of craps, there is a 244/495 probability that you will win $5 and a 251/495 probability that you will lose $5. What is your expected value? In the long run, how much do you lose for each dollar bet?

2. **Finding Expected Value in Roulette** When you give a casino $5 for a bet on the number 7 in roulette, you have a 1/38 probability of winning $175 and a 37/38 probability of losing $5. If you bet $5 that the outcome is an odd number, the probability of winning $5 is 18/38, and the probability of losing $5 is 20/38.
   a. If you bet $5 on the number 7, what is your expected value?
   b. If you bet $5 that the outcome is an odd number, what is your expected value?
   c. Which of these options is best: bet on 7, bet on odd, or don't bet? Why?

3. **Finding Expected Value for a Life Insurance Policy** The CNA Insurance Company charges Mike $250 for a one-year $100,000 life insurance policy. Because Mike is a 21-year-old male, there is a 0.9985 probability that he will live for a year (based on data from U.S. National Center for Health Statistics).
   a. From Mike's perspective, what are the values of the two different outcomes?
   b. If Mike purchases the policy, what is his expected value?
   c. What would be the cost of the insurance policy if the company just breaks even (in the long run with many such policies), instead of making a profit?
   d. Given that Mike's expected value is negative (so the insurance company can make a profit), why should Mike or anyone else purchase life insurance?

4. **Finding Expected Value for the Illinois Pick 3 Game** In Illinois' Pick 3 game, you pay 50¢ to select a sequence of three digits, such as 911. If you win by selecting the same sequence of three digits that are drawn, you collect $250.
   a. How many different selections are possible?
   b. What is the probability of winning?
   c. If you win, what is your net profit?
   d. Find the expected value.

5. **IRS Audits** The Hemingway Financial Company prepares tax returns for individuals. (Motto: "We also write great fiction.") According to the Internal Revenue Service, individuals making $25,000–$50,000 are audited at a rate of 1%. The Hemingway Company prepares five tax returns for individuals in that tax bracket, and three of them are audited.

a. Find the probability that when five people making $25,000–$50,000 are randomly selected, exactly three of them are audited.

b. Find the probability that at least three are audited.

c. Based on the preceding results, what can you conclude about the Hemingway customers? Are they just unlucky, or are they being targeted for audits?

6. Overbooking Flights Air America has a policy of booking as many as 15 persons on an airplane that can seat only 14. (Past studies have revealed that only 85% of the booked passengers actually arrive for the flight.) Find the probability that if Air America books 15 persons, not enough seats will be available. Is this probability low enough so that overbooking is not a real concern for passengers?

7. TV Viewer Surveys The CBS television show *60 Minutes* has been successful for many years. That show recently had a share of 20, meaning that among the TV sets in use, 20% were tuned to *60 Minutes* (based on data from Nielsen Media Research). Assume that an advertiser wants to verify that 20% share value by conducting its own survey, and a pilot survey begins with 10 households having TV sets in use at the time of a *60 Minutes* broadcast.

a. Find the probability that none of the households are tuned to *60 Minutes.*

b. Find the probability that at least one household is tuned to *60 Minutes.*

c. Find the probability that at most one household is tuned to *60 Minutes.*

d. If at most one household is tuned to *60 Minutes,* does it appear that the 20% share value is wrong? Why or why not?

For Exercises 8, 9, 10 find the expected winnings.

8. *Raffle* A raffle offers a first prize of $100 and 2 second prizes of $40 each. One ticket costs $1, and 500 tickets are sold. Find the expected winnings for a person who buys 1 ticket. Is this a fair game?

9. *Roulette* In one form of roulette, you bet $1 on "even." If 1 of the 18 even numbers comes up, you get your dollar back, plus another one. If 1 of the 20 noneven (18 odd, 0, and 00) numbers comes up, you lose your dollar.

10. *Numbers Numbers* is a game in which you bet $1 on any three-digit number from 000 to 999. If your number comes up, you get $500.

11. *Contests* A magazine distributor offers a first prize of $100,000, two second prizes of $40,000 each, and two third prizes of $10,000 each. A total of 2,000,000 entries are received in the contest. Find the expected winnings if you submit one entry to the contest. If it would cost you 50¢ in time, paper, and stamps to enter, would it be worth it?

Homework Answers for End of Chapter Exercises

Chapter 1

1.	5/7	2.	2/7	3.	1/4	4.	15/16	5.	3/14
6.	27/8	7.	7/6	8.	5/6	9.	5/18	10.	35/18
11.	10/3	12.	-3	13.	4	14.	0	15.	-8
16.	-15	17.	0	18.	7	19.	11	20.	-33
21.	-2	22.	-6	23.	0	24.	-5	25.	11
26.	17	27.	-36	28.	-24	29.	45	30.	-4
31.	-2	32.	4	33.	16	34.	9	35.	-9
36.	625	37.	86	38.	5	39.	9	40.	-7

41.	1	42.	-2	43.	6	44.	-17	45.	15
46.	.82	47.	.09	48.	.437	49.	.0046	50.	29%
51.	99.8%	52.	192%	53.	28%				

Chapter 2

1.	x=15	2.	y=-10	3.	x=15	4.	y=19	5.	x=16
6.	x=-23	7.	a=52	8.	x=36	9.	x=6/7	10.	r=9/2
11.	x=7	12.	t=5	13.	z=-7	14.	x=-7	15.	x=-5
16.	t=-11	17.	x=6	18.	y=7	19.	x=3	20.	x=4
21.	t=64/3	22.	m=6	23.	r=8	24.	x=-8	25.	t=8
26.	d=2Q-c	27.	A=Ms						

28. $y > 7$ $(7, \infty)$

7

29. $x \geq 5$ $[5, \infty)$

5

30. $x < 0$ $(-\infty, 0)$

0

31. $y \leq 9$ $(-\infty, 9]$

9

32. $x > -13/7$ $(-\infty \, 13/7,)$

-13/7

33. $x < 9$ $(-\infty, 9)$

9

34.   t ≤ 7   (−∞, 7]

35.   x ≤ 15 (−∞, 15]

36.	$428.57	37.	37.5 gal.	38.	36.67 km	39.	7.2 miles
40.	25%	41.	24%	42.	140/3 or 46.7	43.	5/2 or 2.5
44.	84	45.	75	46.	90	47.	85
48.	95	49.	350				

Chapter 3

1.	{3,5}	2.	{7,9}	3.	∅	4.	F={TBS, Discover Channel, ESPN}
5.	G={TBS, ESPN}			6.	M={TBS, USA}	7.	F ∩ G = {TBS, ESPN}
8.	M ∪ G = {TBS, ESPN, USA}			9.	F′ = {USA, C-SPAN}		

10.

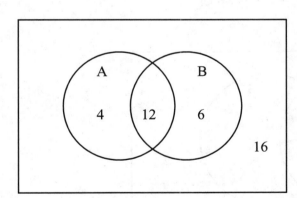

11.   E=early   L=late   X=extra late

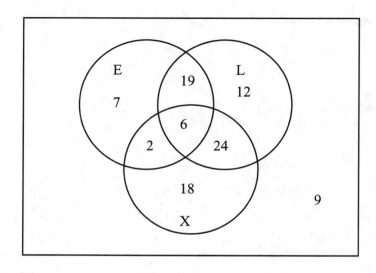

a.   12   b.   18   c.   37   d.   97

12.   131

13.
a.   A-negative   b.   AB-negative   c.   B-negative   d.   A-positive
e.   AB-positive   f.   B-positive   g.   O-positive   h.   O-negative

14.

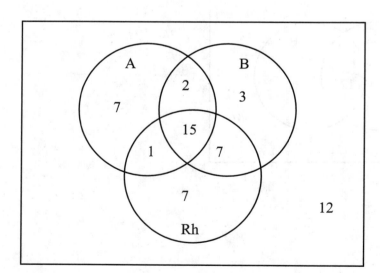

a.   54   b.   17   c.   10   d.   7
e.   15   f.   3   g.   12   h.   1

15. 1,359,000

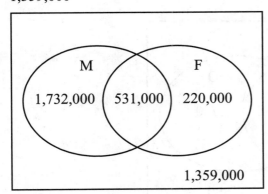

16. a. 342   b. 192   c. 72   d. 86

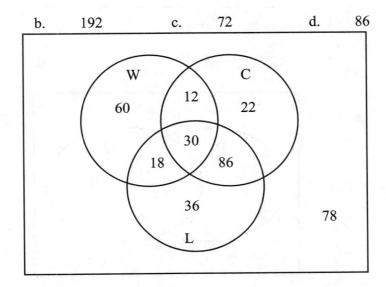

17. a. 20   b. 160   c. 35   d. 80

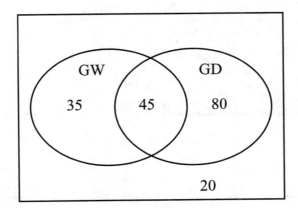

18.   a.   2500   b.   1300   c.   950   d.   1950

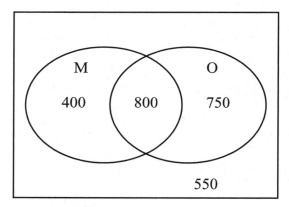

19.   a.   35   b.   45   c.   60   d.   65

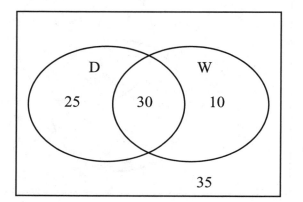

Chapter 4

1.

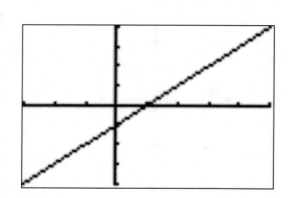

2.

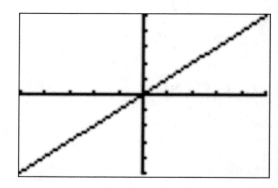

3.

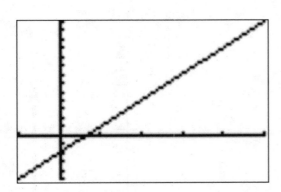

4.

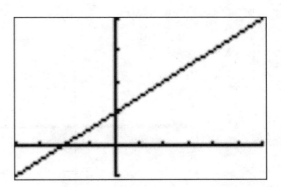

5.

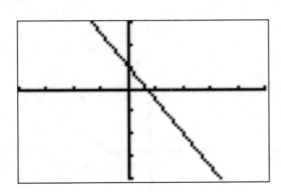

6.

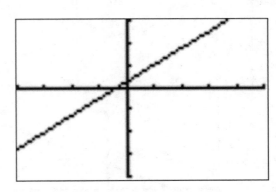

7.

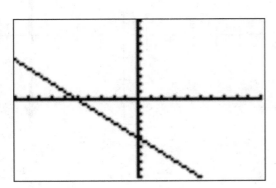

8.

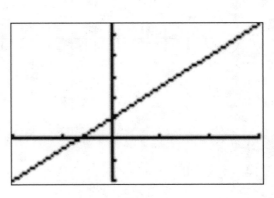

9a.

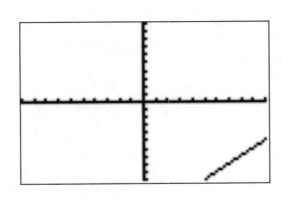

9b.

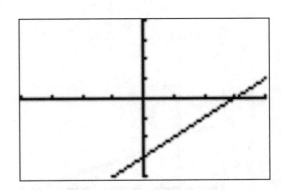

10. (0,5) and (2,0)

11. (0,-4) and (3,0)

12.

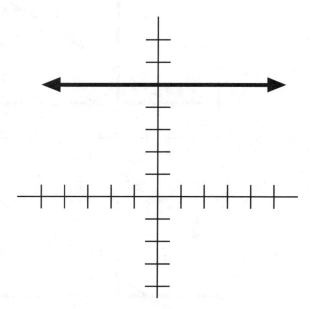

13.

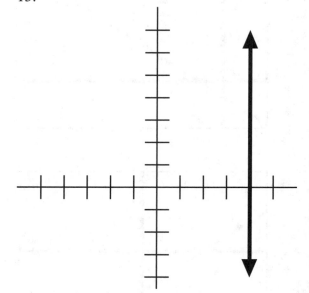

14. x=-1

15. y=-1

16. 3/4

17. 3/2

18. -1

19. 0

20. undefined

21. 3/2

22. -4/5

23. 7/9

24. 0

25. undefined

26. 0

27.

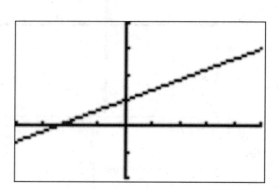

28.

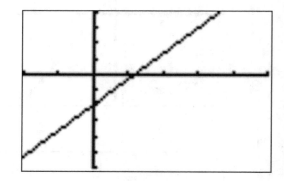

29.

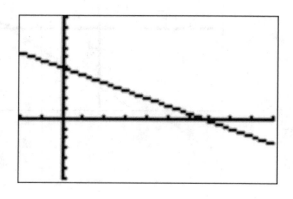

30.   slope=3/7   y-intercept=5

31.   slope=-5/6   y-intercept=2

32.   slope=9/4   y-intercept=-7

33.   slope=-2/5   y-intercept=0

34.   slope=0   y-intercept=4

35.   y=(7/8)x–1

36.   slope=3/5   y-intercept=2

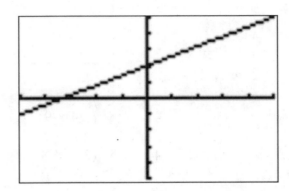

37.   slope=-3/5   y-intercept=1

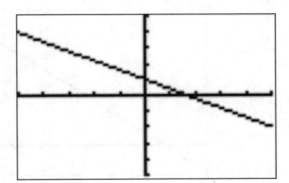

38.   slope=5/3   y-intercept=3

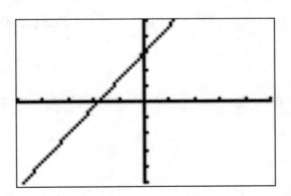

39.   slope=-3/2   y-intercept=-2

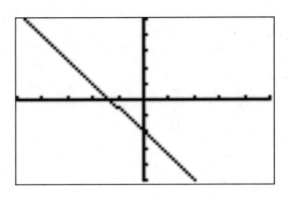

40.   y=2x-3

41.   y=(7/4)x-9

42.   y=-3x-2

43.   y=-x+6

44.   y=(2/3)x+3

45.   y=(2/5)x-2

46.   y=(4/3)x+2/3

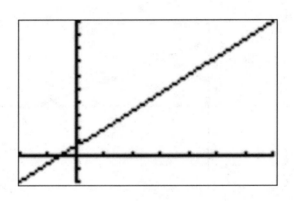

47.   y=2x-9

48.   y=(-4/3)x+(23/3)

Chapter 5

1.   10 cents/1 minute

2.   -$500/ 1 year or -$1000/ 2 years

3.   2 gal/50 miles or 1 gal/25 miles

4. $W(x) = \begin{cases} 140 + .13x & 0 \le x < 2000 \\ .20x & x \ge 2000 \end{cases}$ $W(2700) = .20 * 2700 = 540$

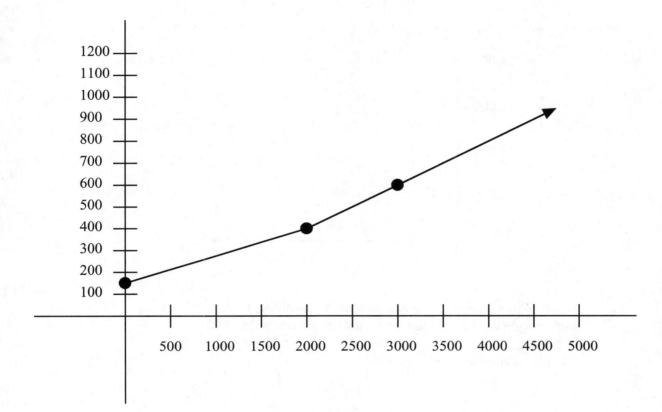

5.

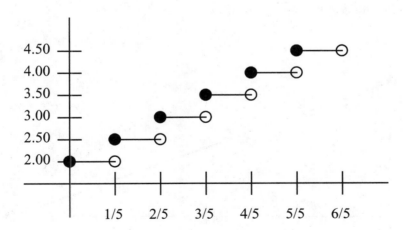

6. (-3,11)   7. No Solution   8. (5,-2)   9. (2,-1)   10. (1,3)

11. (5,-2)   12. (-1,7)   13. (-3,-5)   14. (4,5)

15. No Solution   16. 50 miles   17. 100 miles   18. 165 minutes

19. C(x)=300x+4000   20. C(x)=25x+3000   21. C(x)=140x+600

22. a. E(x)=600x+12,000   where x=# of years since 2000

     b.

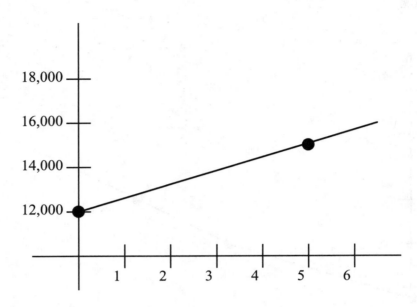

     c. slope=600, which is the annual increase in enrollment
         y-intercept=12,000 which is the number of students in 2000

     d. 14 years (actually 13 1/3 years)

23. a. $V(x) = -3000x + 25,000$ $0 \leq x \leq 8\frac{1}{3}$
     b. m=-3000 which is the annual depreciation and b=25,000 which is the original value
     c. 6.67 years and 7.8 years
     d.

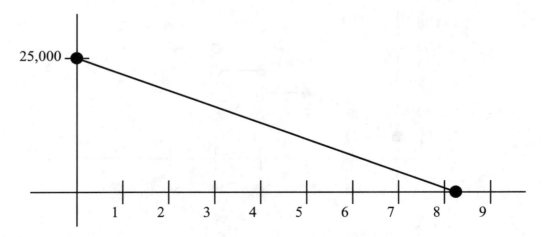

24. a. S(x)=1500+.04x

b.

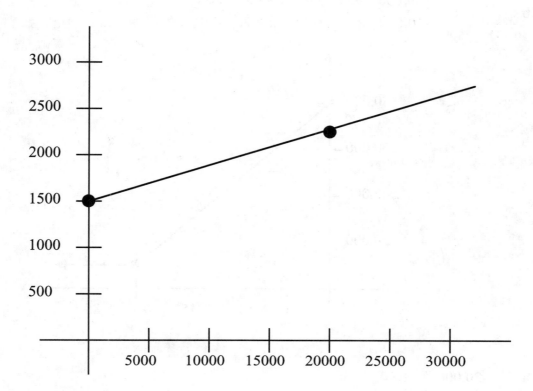

c. S(20,000)=$2,300
d. $0.04
e. 37,500

25. a. 5000
b. $V(x) = -5000x + 100,000 \qquad 0 \le x \le 20$
c.

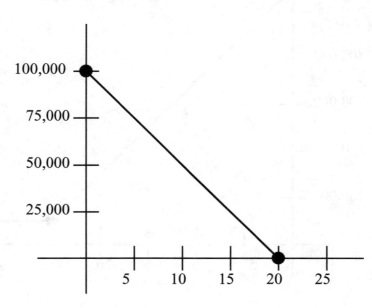

26.   a.   3500

b. $V(x) = \begin{cases} 80,000 - 3500x & 0 \le x \le 20 \\ 10,000 & x \ge 20 \end{cases}$

c.

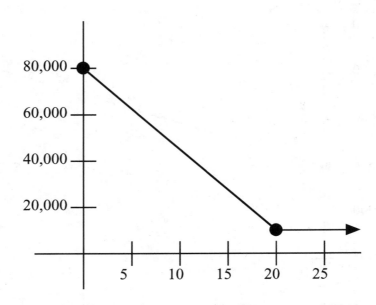

27.   a.   20,000

b. $V(x) = \begin{cases} 550,000 - 20,000x & 0 \le x \le 25 \\ 50,000 & x \ge 25 \end{cases}$

c.

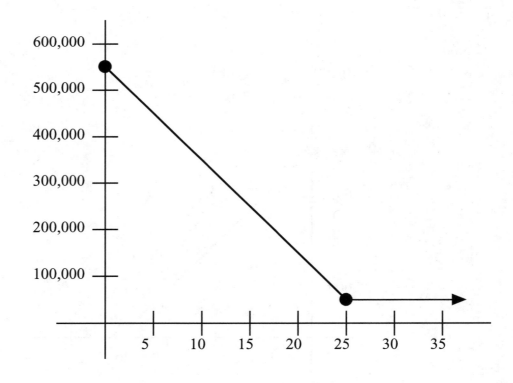

28. a. 30
     b. 1500
     c.

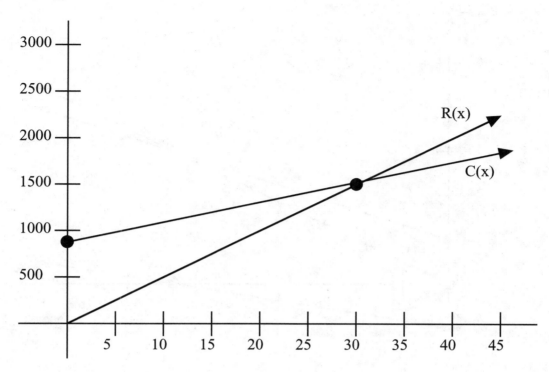

29. a. 250
     b. 5000
     c.

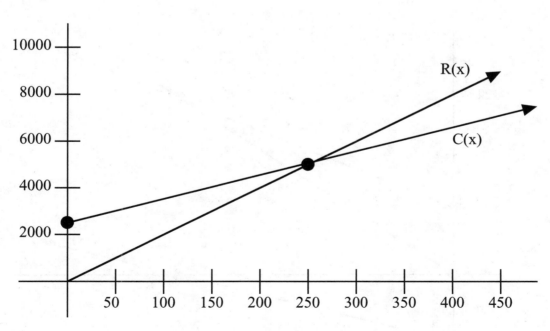

30.   a.   12
      b.   (12,36)
      c. $P(x) = x - 12$
      d.

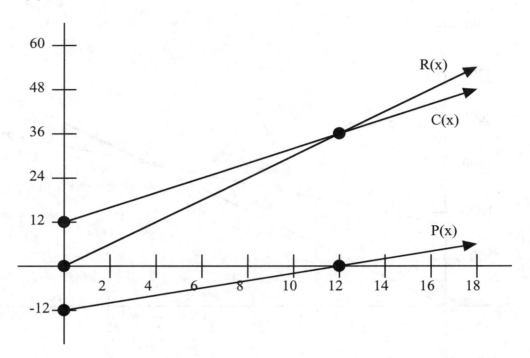

31.   a.   61.25
      b.   (61.25, 1225)
      c. $P(x) = 8x - 490$
      d.

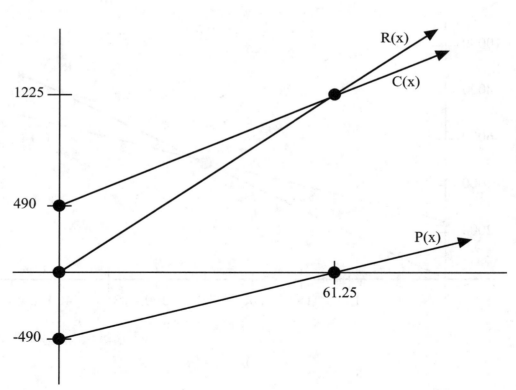

32.   a. $C(x) = 8000 + 8.36x$ $R(x) = 10.80x$ $P(x) = 2.44x - 8000$
      b.   approximately 3279
      c.

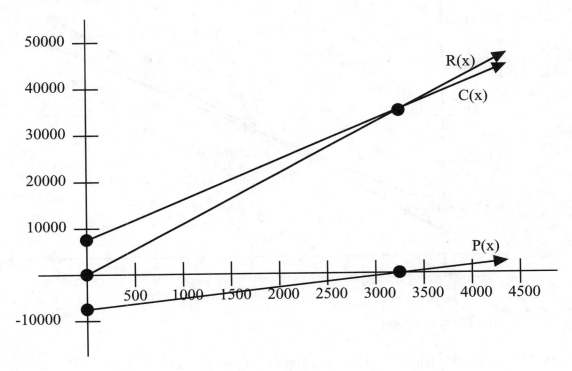

      d. $P(800) = $loss, $P(2000) = $loss

33.   a. $C(x) = .40x + 20000$
      b. $R(x) = .50x + 8000$
      c.   120,000 miles
      d.

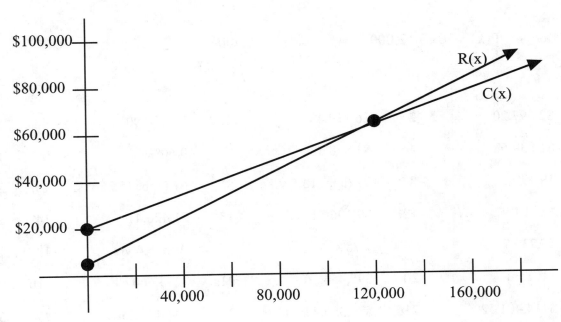

34.   a. $C_C(x) = 300 + 25x$ $C_O(x) = 500 + 20x$ $x = 1,000$'s of copies

b.

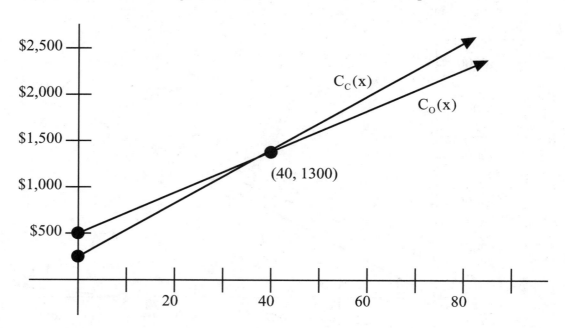

c.   40 (40,000 copies)

d.   for 30,000 copies $C_C(x)$,   for 70,000 copies $C_O(x)$

35.   a. $P(x) = 15x - 6000$ b.   2,300

36.   a. $P(x) = 10x - 2400$ b.   17,500

37.   a. $P(x) = 30x - 12,000$ b.   30,400

Chapter 6

1.	$2,697.20	2.	$6,130.43	3.	$6,720.00	4a.	$1,472
4b.	$1,839.68	4c.	$1,848.58	5.	9.60%	6.	11.72%
7.	19.17%	8.	27 (app. 13.5 yrs.)	9.	61 (app. 15.25 yrs.)	10.	22.25 years
11.	$2,791.97	12.	$9,196.71	13.	$1,420.41	14.	$9,948.94
15.	$7,730.75	16.	7.78%	17.	App. 6.4 yrs.	18.	$15,162.14
19.	$171.96	20.	$95,454.20	21a.	$234,660.41	21b.	$165,644.10
21c.	$114,401.52	21d.	$76,355.43	22.	$64,491.25	23.	$6,258.36

24. $30,722.84	25. 6.66%	26. 4.04%	27. 17.23%
28a. 5.06%	28b. 4.89%	28c. 4.70%	29a. $2,029.55
29b. $7,281.08	30a. $2,649.11	30b. $41,297.40	31. $1090.59
32. 1022.23	33. $983.80	34a. $1,788.54	34b. $2,325.10
34c. $111,605	35. $405,123		
36. $15,600 & $35,600	37. $7200 & $127,200	38. $4200 & $64,200	

Chapter 7

1.

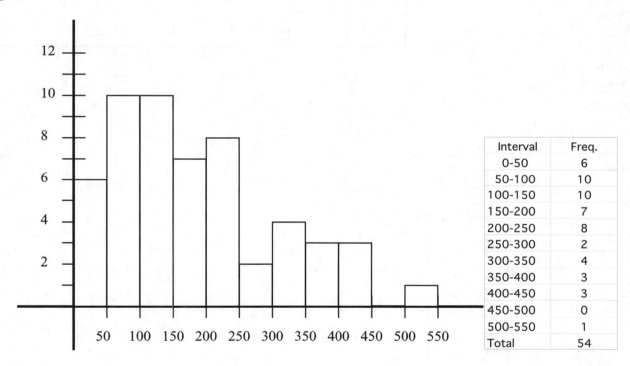

Interval	Freq.
0-50	6
50-100	10
100-150	10
150-200	7
200-250	8
250-300	2
300-350	4
350-400	3
400-450	3
450-500	0
500-550	1
Total	54

2.

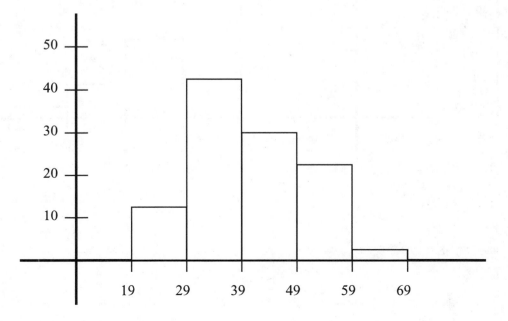

MALE	
Interval	Freq.
19-29	11
29-39	43
39-49	31
49-59	22
59-69	4
Total	111

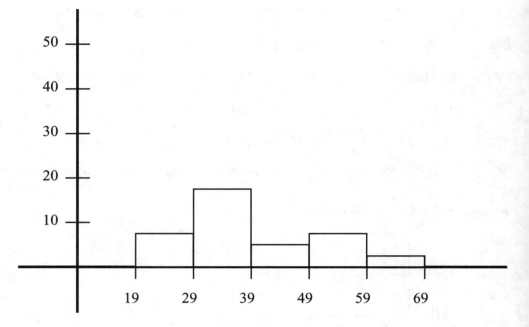

FEMALE	
Interval	Freq.
19-29	8
29-39	18
39-49	4
49-59	7
59-69	2
Total	39

3.

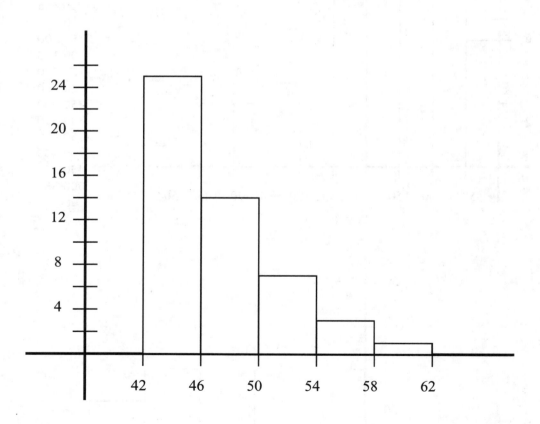

4.

3	7,6
4	0,3,0,9,7,8,6,8,1,6,4
5	3,8,2,9,9,8,4,9,0,3,3,7
6	8,2,9,4,3,7,4,1,3,7,1,0,1,4,5,5,3,2,4
7	2,2,0,4,3,2,2,1,7,5

5. $\overline{X} = .1873$ M = .17   Mode = .16 and .17   Seems significantly above levels

6. $\overline{X} = 26.9$ M = 26   Mode = none

7.   For Jefferson Valley: $\overline{X} = 7.15$ M = 7.2   Mode = 7.7
      For Providence: $\overline{X} = 7.15$ M = 7.2   Mode = 7.7
      No difference based on central tendency

8.   McDonald's: $\overline{X} = 186.33$ M = 184   Mode = none
      Jack in the Box: $\overline{X} = 262.5$ M = 262.5   Mode = 109
      McDonald's is faster

9.   Range = .17   s = .0511952379
10.   Range = 28   s = 8.660065359

11.   For Jefferson Valley: Range = 1.2   s = .4767
      For Providence: Range = 5.8   s = 1.8216
      Jefferson Valley is more consistent

12.   McDonald's: Range = 195   s = 63.89
      Jack in the Box: Range = 407   s = 129.01
      McDonald's is more consistent

13.

a.

1	2
2	5,6,6
3	0,0,0
4	5,5,5,0,8
5	0,2,0,0,2
6	0,2
7	5,5,8,5
8	9,5,5,9,5,9,2

b.

Interval	Freq.
10-19	1
20-29	3
30-39	3
40-49	5
50-59	5
60-69	2
70-79	4
80-89	7
Total	30

c.

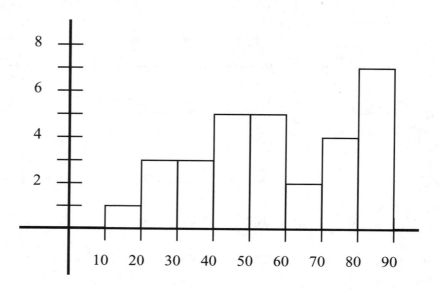

d.

$\overline{X} = 56.17$ $M = 51$ Modes $= 30, 45, 50, 75, 85, 89$

Range $= 77$ $s = 23.22$

14.

$\mu = 31.85$ $M = 31$ Mode $= 30$

Range $= 6$ $\sigma = 1.810485453$

Chapter 8

1.	1/6	2.	4/6=2/3	3.	2/6=1/3	4.	4/52=1/13
5.	2/52=1/26	6.	1/52	7.	8/52=2/13	8.	6/52=3/26
9.	2/18=1/9	10.	5/18	11.	10/18=5/9		

12a.   Male

12b.   Female who has worked less than 5 years.

12c.   Female and does not contribute to the voluntary retirement plan.

12d.   Worker has worked 5 years or more.

12e.   Worker has worked less than 5 years and contributes to the voluntary retirement plan.

12f.   Worker has worked 5 or more years and does not contribute to the voluntary retirement plan.

13a.	.0342	13b.	.0529	13c.	.8774		
14.	NO	15.	YES	16.	NO		
17a.	1/36	17b.	3/36=1/12	17c.	4/36=1/9	17d.	5/36
18a.	5/36	18b.	4/36=1/9	18c.	3/36=1/12	18d.	0
19a.	10/36=5/18	19b.	15/36=5/12	19c.	11/36	20a.	8/52=2/13
20b.	28/52=7/13	20c.	6/52=3/26	20d.	39/52=3/4	20e.	22/52=11/26
21.	.84	22.	12/51	23.	11/51	24.	.012
25.	.245	26.	80/110=8/11	27.	70/110=7/11	28.	50/110=5/11
29.	100/110=10/11	30.	10/110=1/11	31.	50/70=5/7	32.	30/80
33.	10/40=1/4	34.	20/70=2/7	35.	60/110=6/11	36.	.999985
37.	.02	38.	.06	39.	.08	40.	.92

Chapter 9

1. Lose 7.07 cents per $5 bet and 1.4 cent per $1 bet.

2a. -$.26
2b. -$.26
2c. Don't Bet!

3a. Lives: -$250, Dies: $99,750
3b. -$100
3c. $150

4a. 1000
4b 1/1000
4c. 249.50
4d. -$.25

5a. .000009801
5b. .0000098506
5c. Probably being targeted.

6. .0874

7a. .1074
7b. .8926
7c. .3758

8. No, since the expected value is -$.64

9. E=-$.053

10. E=-$.50

11. E=$.10, and no it would not be worth the $.50 expense.